Beyond Terror

Beyond Terror

Strategy in a Changing World

Ralph Peters

STACKPOLE
BOOKS

Published by
STACKPOLE BOOKS
5067 Ritter Road
Mechanicsburg, PA 17055
www.stackpolebooks.com

Printed in the United States

10 9 8 7 6 5 4 3 2

Library of Congress Cataloging-in-Publication Data

CIP data on file with Library of Congress

ISBN 0-8117-0024-0

To Our American Indian Veterans

There are more things in heaven and earth, Horatio,
Than are dreamt of in your philosophy.
—Shakespeare, *Hamlet,* I:5

Contents

Introduction   xi

Part I   At the Walls of Jericho
Our Place in History   3
When Devils Walk the Earth   22
The New Strategic Trinity   66
The Hourglass Wars   77
Heavy Peace   90
The American Mission   103
Killers and Constables   115
The Plague of Ideas   139
Stability, America's Enemy   167
The Black Art of Intelligence   193
The Rejection of the West   209

Part II   And Rumors of War
The Seeker and the Sage   261
The Casualty Myth   286
Hard Target   292
The Human Terrain of Urban Operations   299
Hucksters in Uniform   312
The Future of War   323

Coda
Dogma and the Dead   337

Introduction

A Small Matter of Honesty

A common practice in collecting past work for a book is to snip a bit here, add a line there, delete an embarrassingly wrong judgment, and correct one's prophecies to match intervening developments. I find that dishonest. If a writer presumes to publish a book of works that originally appeared in journals or magazines, he or she should live with the words as they first appeared. Facing one's errors in cold print is a due form of penance for past sins.

Further, I believe it to be far more useful to the reader to track the development of the writer's thoughts, and to be able to weigh that which had been gotten wrong against that which stands the test of time. Writing, if we are at all serious about it, is very different from lecturing. A lecture is meant to instruct, but the sort of writing that interests me is exploratory, a sort of fistfight with ideas. I do not write to impress my thoughts on others, but to challenge myself to discover what I truly think, to test propositions, and, to provoke independent thought in readers. I *learn* by writing. The act of writing forces us to think more deeply and more clearly than we otherwise would do. I offer no view from a mountaintop. I'm just trying to climb up the lower slopes and sweating a good bit in the process.

Most of the essays gathered here were written between 1998 and the close of 2001. I learned as I lived and wrote and saw things a bit more clearly as time passed. One thought leads to another; an insight submerges for a time then bobs back up with a startling companion; events underscore or destroy a supposition. And all of it happens in fits and starts, belied by the apparent steadiness of publication. If I have any gift at all, it is a simple willingness to see what others wish to ignore. Thus, a previously unpublished piece that appears here, "The Rejection of the West," written in 1994 and deemed too dark for publication and too impolitic for the Pentagon at the time, describes the world post–9-11-01 as well as I could describe it now. Yet, that essay had nothing to do with clever predictions— merely with observation of the world around us all. That world simply looked different from Azerbaijan than it did from Ann Arbor, and *very* different from Burma or Bolivia than from Boston (reality trumps theory in the end). The same piece includes some misjudgments, as well. I am content to live with them as the price of trying to get to the heart of the matter.

I have made a single exception in this volume to my belief that newspaper work should not be republished—I certainly stand behind every commentary to which I have signed my name, but newspaper subjects usually are specific to the day's headlines or the week's issues. Whenever I see a collection that includes a great deal of newspaper journalism, I suspect the writer of padding out the page count. I have inserted the piece in the second portion of this book, which ranges widely, to make the point that many of us took terrorism and Osama bin Laden seriously well before the attacks on the World Trade Center Towers and the Pentagon. The problem was not lack of awareness, but the most cowardly American administration in history, one that cared little for its uniformed dead—except as political liabilities—and wanted only to ignore what it lacked the courage to resolve. History will declare that a significant portion of the blame for the suffering and loss of September 11, 2001, lies with former President Clinton, who, despite his personal revisionism, disgraced himself and failed our nation. As terrorists successively bombed a U.S. barracks in Saudi Arabia, two of our embassies in Africa, and one of our warships, the Clinton administration barely pretended to retaliate, encouraging gloating murderers to ever more daring attacks. Cowardice is never a good strategy, and one's enemies do not simply disappear. We must stand up to foreign threats wherever they arise, promptly and with ferocious resolve. We have learned that now, and let us hope the knowledge will not fade too swiftly.

Ultimately, understanding our world has precious little to do with the ivory-tower genius. It is largely a matter of being an honest witness. I have done my best to look, to see, and to tell.

—Ralph Peters
December, 2001

PART I

At the Walls of Jericho

Our Place in History

September 11, 2001, marked the beginning of an American renaissance. In love with an apocalyptic vision, men from a failing civilization attacked America, and embarrassed her, and angered her people by killing thousands of her citizens. But history loves unintended consequences. In striking as wantonly as they did, America's enemies unified her people as they had not been unified in two generations. The attacks on the World Trade Center Towers and the Pentagon and the loss of a civilian aircraft in a Pennsylvania field involved thousands of personal tragedies and economic loss, but, rather than paralyzing America with fear, her enemies aroused a dormant fury, awakening deep reserves of courage and resolve. The attacks also sobered those citizens who, in their own comfortable safety, had imagined the world beyond our shores to be as benign as it seemed distant. In a day, a nation straightened from a prosperous slouch to a determined march.

In their moment of seeming triumph, the terrorists who attacked America overreached and began to fail. Had the attackers of 9-11-01 struck only the Pentagon, much of the world would have cheered and even our allies would have snickered behind our backs. (Those millions throughout the Muslim world who did cheer the attacks will have little or nothing to cheer in the years to come.) But the planes that struck the towers in New York struck the world—not so much in the sense of exciting sympathy for New Yorkers, but by alarming the citizens of other developed countries who saw, with irrefutable clarity, how easily they might become the next target of men whose hatred of the West is exceeded only by their fear of the future. When a European statesman said, "We are all New Yorkers," it had little to do with affection for the Big Apple and a great deal to do with a quickened sense of reality. Suddenly, the devil was at the door. The terrorists aroused an unexpected unanimity against themselves, breaking the golden rule of strategic judo: Divide and conquer.

Inevitably, allies will bicker over matters of detail and the present fervor will diminish with success and time, but the West's new resolve is unlikely to disappear entirely. The attacks of 9-11-01 destroyed the credibility of apologists for Islamic terror and irresponsibility in, literally, a flash, disillusioning even those most gullible of human beings, university undergraduates. Convinced that our civilizations are irreconcilably hostile to one another, the terrorists intended to strike a mortal blow against the West; instead, they sent the Islamic world reeling onto the defensive, unveiling its delusions and decay, and that world is unlikely to regain its footing again in our lifetimes. Those terror attacks in New York and Washington will prove to have caused far fewer changes in the West than they will have triggered in the Muslim world, where decrepit regimes have long been waiting to tumble and broken societies have been patched together with lies. The reverberations of that September morning are rolling east, not west.

Although they will be hunted, broken, and killed without remorse, some terrorists will manage to commit future atrocities against us. Our actions will dramatically reduce the frequency and effectiveness of such attacks, yet we cannot expect to escape all crimes of hatred in this jealous, hate-filled world. But our existence will not be threatened, nor even our general well-being, despite the frantic warnings of alarmists. (The surest way to deter attacks with weapons of mass destruction is to post a price list for such deeds, making it clear that such atrocities will be avenged at a devastating cost to *all* the perpetrators hold dear.) We are almost immeasurably powerful, and resilient, and robust. Those terrorist strikes that do succeed will serve, above all, to renew the bonds between those states governed by the rule of modern law and to rejuvenate our own anger and determination. Terrorists will keep on reminding us that we need to kill them and punish their hosts, sponsors, and supporters. Despite the cautious language of our public officials, we will do so with a potent mixture of grimness and glee. It may be impolitic to admit it, but the destruction of one's enemies is a very satisfying thing—especially when the enemy has broken the rules. The curious shame we felt at our own power and wealth fell away with the twin towers. We still do not know our own strength, but we are learning it. We have the might to do all that is necessary, and we shall learn to wield it to ever greater effect. And if we dare not speak publicly of the superiority of our civilization—even those who disavow it sense it—that which men say is often an attempt to evade what they cannot help but feel.

September 11, 2001, was, indeed, a moment of truth, but not for the United States or the West. Rather, it was a moment of truth for the Islamic world, with its various cultures and its consistent impulse to blame others for all its failures, personal or collective. Islam's leaders, holy men and intellectuals, its practices and cherished tenets, have failed that faith's believers. Bigoted, hopelessly corrupt, close-minded, uneducated, psychologically infantile, self-important, and incapable of dealing not only with the twenty-first century, but even with the demands and developments of the twentieth, Muslim states and societies are rotting while their ancient competitors flourish. Because it cannot progress without fundamental and pervasive changes in virtually every public and private sphere, the Islamic world will continue to be a source of trouble for every other civilization. The stasis of Islamic civilization is the most colossal failure of our time, a situation without precedent even in the early days of European imperialism. A billion people, as proud as they are ill-governed and ill-prepared for modern life, have found they cannot compete with other civilizations on a single front—not even in terror, for the West will, out of demonstrated need, learn to terrorize the terrorists. (Democracies, while poor at preemption, are very good at retribution.)

The world of Islam must now decide whether to wallow in a comforting, medieval form of religion that warms the heart with hatred of others and whose greatest strength lies in its ability to shift blame, or to make the far more difficult choice of attempting to build tolerant, more equitable, open, and honest societies. Most Islamic states will make the wrong choice, and they will pay for it by continuing to crumble into irrelevance. Nor can we do much to help. Americans and other foreign parties can only play at the margins, and to believe otherwise is both arrogant and naive. The followers of Islam must decide for themselves whether to cling to a mythologized past or to embrace a challenging future. If we may be honest, the likeliest future role for the Islamic world is that of an irrelevant annoyance, which intermittently wounds others, while building nothing of worth. Enmeshed within a religion frozen in time, and betrayed by their own viciously corrupt leaders and greedy elites, men, women, and children throughout most of the Muslim world will continue to slide deeper into poverty and bitterness. And it is not our fault. A civilization that is anti-meritocratic, that oppresses and torments women, that mocks the rule of law, that neglects education and lacks a work ethic simply cannot prosper under modern conditions. Flawlessly intolerant and blithely cruel, the Islamic world does far more harm to its own people than it has done—or will ever be able to do—to the West. Occasionally, we will have to punish unruly bits of Islamic civilization for excesses that affect us; but, between our interventions, Muslims will continue to do far more damage to each other than we are apt or able to inflict.

But what of the *American* renaissance heralded above? It might be argued that the United States long has been a land of per-petual renascence, constantly evolving, growing, and learning. But I believe we are at the beginning of something qualitatively new, although its social components have been maturing for decades. As the long autumn of 2001 stretches into the winter of 2002, it may be difficult to see past the surface effects—the terrorist attacks, a war abroad (with marked early successes, but a lengthy proposition, nonetheless), a stub-toed economy, and a nervous stock market—but this is simply one of those inter-vals when the economy has paused to catch its breath after sprinting ahead of the pack yet again. In military terms, we are regrouping on the objective, dealing with casualties, and refit-ting for the next phase in the campaign.

While we may not see hyperinflated prices for technology stocks again in the near future, that should not obscure the fact that the "high-tech" era has barely begun, and that networked computers, the icon of the 1990s, are only one part of a revolution in human capabilities that, barring cataclysms, will lead to richer lives in manifold senses for Americans and similarly empowered individuals elsewhere. We are so rich in discoveries that we can discard anything that appears to underperform, and the "thickness" of technological innovation, coupled with increases in productivity, has shattered old economic laws as dramatically improved capabilities become cheaper, rather than more expensive.

Yet, our emphasis on the technological aspects of change has clouded the even more profound alterations to our society—changes that are the true source of American power in our time. For the last fifty years, Americans have been reinventing collective and individual human relationships, and the next half-century is primed to produce even more rewarding changes in cooperative human organization. Already, our population's center of gravity has made the greatest leap in societal development in human history, from definition by gender, race, ethnicity, or religion, to definition by capability and contribution. While the process remains incomplete, the distance traveled in a matter of decades is phenomenal—utterly without historical precedent. With this "identity liberation" wed to the torrent of productive technologies that will continue to become available to us, America's future dynamism will be beyond challenge (especially in relation to those uncreative societies where status at birth determines status for life).

By altering social rules that have prevailed since the beginnings of civilization, we have been reinventing civilization itself, replacing the hierarchical, immobile, and predetermined with astonishing levels of freedom, mobility—in multiple senses—and unprecedented forms of opportunity. We have, to a stunning degree, replaced the coercive society—

virtually the only kind that mankind has known through the millennia—with the voluntary society. While inequities remain, they are now the result of individual, not institutional, prejudice, and of self-destructive behavior among the self-segregating. Ever more inequities will disappear as generations change, although, given humanity's complexity, diversity, and sheer contrariness, not every individual will be redeemed for society even in the distant future. We must open the doors to all of our brothers and sisters, but we cannot force everyone to cross the threshold.

If, as a mischievous scholar has put it, Shakespeare invented our conception of the human, the United States has invented new human possibilities. Conditioned to criticize yesteryear's America, Europe staggers under the burden of racism and persistent bigotry today, doubly cursed with aging populations and a fear of immigration. The laboratory of American society may be sloppy, but our experiments have been vigorous, relentless, and successful—while our nearest peers have been most concerned with keeping their lab shelves tidy. The transformation from a society that defined human beings to a society in which humans have the opportunity to define themselves is more than a revolution—it is a break with all previous social history. And while not all men and women will define themselves to their own satisfaction or to the fullest benefit of society, it is remarkable how well, and how swiftly, we have learned to match ourselves to changing opportunities and needs, with the possibility of multiple social and economic reincarnations within a single American lifetime. On the surface, the degree of freedom we enjoy may seem nearly chaotic and even threatening to some (as it does to Europeans, who still prefer security to opportunity), but underneath it throbs the most efficient system in history for maximizing human potential.

When this book appears, I will have turned fifty years old. Within my span of five decades, I have seen America's internal walls come down. In the anthracite coal fields of my childhood, work, ethnicity, and religion determined social standing, higher education was for the upper strata, workers believed themselves immobile and fixed in their skills, and women were housewives (except for schoolteachers and a few nurses or clerks). In fact, women of the upper classes were expected *not* to work, since labor of any sort would have suggested a lack of solidity in the family finances. Even working-class wives took jobs at the risk of implying that their husbands were insufficient providers (and, thus, inadequate men). Admittedly, the coal towns were particularly backward—but much of America resembled us: We were a museum model of social organization for the industrial revolution, designed to maximize brute strength with little regard for individual talent. Social lines were clear, and the masses were organized to support the male muscle-power required for mines, collieries, and factories. By the time I was a teenager, the great change had begun. Today, everything—*everything*—has changed. And fifty years is the historical blink of an eye.

Over the past half-century, the United States hosted the most powerful shift in human relationships in human history. With the transition to a society in which women are accorded equal status, America accomplished a peaceful revolution whose reverberations will be felt far longer than those of any violent change. The introduction of the vast pool of female talent and energy into the workplace supercharged economic development even as it altered traditional roles (horrifying traditional societies, such as those in the Islamic world). When today's American women complain of continuing inequities in individual cases, they may well be justified, but they fail to note that the modification of gender roles has happened with light-ning speed in historical terms. Enabled by developments as diverse as the advent of reliable, easy-to-use birth control (a revolution in its own right, giving women control of their bio-logical destiny) and enlightened family law, American women dismantled the fortress of male hegemony with a thoroughness appreciated only by terrified males on the order of Mohammed Atta, the hijacker whose testament demanded that women not be allowed to pollute his grave by their presence.

As a result of the equality revolution (not only as regards women, although that is the most profound development, but also in matters of race and religion), the United States econ-omy operates on a "wartime" basis every single day, coming as close to maximizing its human potential as current technolo-gies and business models allow. Meanwhile, another subrevolu-tion, the geriatric, not only keeps our citizens alive longer, but keeps them sufficiently healthy and alert to continue to con-tribute, upsetting the traditional role of the oldest members of society as resource consumers waiting to die (while also refus-ing to let the old continue to dictate society's rules, another critical break with the past and its cruelties). In the United States today, a man or woman in his or her seventies may be working productively or volunteering for the good of the com-munity—while, in other civilizations, hampered by corruption and rigid hierarchies, young males lack jobs. In fact, our taste for work is one of the least appealing—and most ineffable—American qualities to the tea-and-a-pillow cultures of the Middle East.

The oft-criticized American nuclear family itself is revolu-tionary, a ferocious economic tool. Highly mobile and uniquely flexible, nuclear families are the economic equivalent of shock troops. Nor has the breakdown of the old model of extended families, with their constraints upon merit and ambition, led to mass psychoses or moral collapse—the rates of illegitimate births and murders per capita are lower today than they were a hundred years ago. We are organized for success. And when we discover other traditions that do not work, we shall change them as well. In a nation of more than a quarter of a billion people, critics will always be able to find examples of failure and discord. But the real news is the phenomenal quality of most of our daily lives, from our much-criticized health care system to the choices we have for dinner. Thus far, at least, we have got it astonishingly right.

All this, wed to two centuries of accelerating technological development involving everything from the electric toaster to biotechnology, has created a society that transcends the notions of efficiency described by economists. We are the *transcendent society*, the breaker of fixed systems and fixed rules. And that is the source of unprecedented strategic power.

The much-vaunted internet is a model for the future, but by no means its defining feature. Historically, it will enjoy a niche similar to that of the telegraph. What is exemplary regarding the internet is the way so many seemingly diverse disciplines, technologies, visions, and individuals came together to create a genuinely new tool with broad applications. As powerful as we are today, our society remains less than the sum of its (remarkable) parts because we are only beginning to learn how to put them all together. (Traditional societies, in comparison, strive to keep people, disciplines, and knowledge separate and apart in order to preserve the power of existing hierarchies.) In the future, as stunning new technologies continue to cascade (and plenty of overtouted ones fall by the wayside—e-book, anyone?), the real gain will come from their nonlinear integration. One minor example appeared in the campaign in Afghanistan, when our military lashed strategic technologies together with individual special-operations soldiers on the ground, resulting in the most effective targeting in history. It was not the way military establishments are supposed to work, but it turned out to be how they *do* work, and we were able to figure it out almost overnight.

We cannot foretell what specifics the future will hold, but we may be assured that, in America and its free-market, rule-of-law, democratic companion states, that future is going to be dynamic beyond the reach of adjectives. Fortunately, our societies are synthetic and resilient—conditioned to change, that bugbear of all humanity. Even for us, change can be painful, of course, with worker dislocations and the erosion of cherished beliefs. But for traditional societies unwilling to relinquish the security of antique patterns, the news is almost all bad. We may be impressed that terrorists and criminals manage to use our technologies against us, but it is a parasitic use, imitative, not creative. A cell phone held to the ear does not mean a modern mind is at work on the other side of the eardrum. Societies cannot be measured by the scale of penetration of individual technologies, only by the uses to which integrated technologies are put. If technology does not assist a society in the generation of wealth and power, and in the improvement of the public welfare, it is meaningless except as a convenience. Ultimately, social organization determines the effectiveness of technologies, not the other way around.

Technology is only an enabler, if an often impressive one. What matters are a nation's human resources. But the measures employed by economists take you only so far. Education levels certainly do matter, as does public health. But another, deeply profound revolution is also under way in the United States, further enhancing our efficiency and broadening our potential: the social confluence of beliefs. The simultaneous resilience of religious feeling in America and the rejection of controlling, exclusive religious doctrine by the majority are tremendously unifying. As recent, disconcerted arrivals, American Muslims are not yet part of this trend, but what we have witnessed in our lifetimes is the collapse of religion as a social barrier, except among the least-successful, least-educated, and least-confident of our citizens. (As an aside, if Islam is to enjoy its overdue reformation, the break is likeliest to occur here, under exemplary pressures, and not in the sclerotic Muslim homelands.)

The growing frequency of interfaith and interdenominational marriage seems an obvious indicator of the socialization of our various religions, but such marriages are merely one signal of the generalization of belief. Some creeds worry about the pace of assimilation—a benign version of the Islamic fundamentalist's fear of religious pollution—but, over the long term, this is a trend that will not be arrested. Nor should it be.

I do not suggest that we are going to stop calling ourselves Catholics, or Jews, or Presbyterians—only that, for more and more Americans, a coworker's, or business partner's, or even a spouse's religious affiliation has collapsed from being a determining factor to being just one more bit of information among many. Among those tens of millions who drive our society forward, an American's identity as a Methodist increasingly has no more social weight than his or her identity as a Pennsylvanian or a Texan—and considerably less weight than his or her education, profession, and tastes. Quietly, in little more than a generation, we have begun to dispose of one of the most powerful sources of hatred and violence in history. And the great enabler has been the pragmatic American disinterest in doctrine in any sphere.

Paradoxically, the United States is an intensely religious country in which most of the faithful do not understand the complex tenets of their respective faiths. There is a yearning vagueness about present-day belief that disarms those who, for centuries, fought each other over the contents of the communion cup or the nature of Christ. Because of the so-recent persecution of their immediate ancestors or co-religionists, Jewish-Americans often have a better understanding of their beliefs than do others, but even in many Jewish congregations the rigor is fading, despite heartfelt attempts to reinforce it. (As a friend noted a few days ago, a third of the Christmas carolers at her office were Jewish.) Among fundamentalist Christians, the primacy of doctrine has been replaced by an obsession with behavioral forms, a full skirt in place of a full understanding, and Bible recitation as a sort of incantation. A brief visit to any Christian bookstore demonstrates that, for many devout Americans, contemporary religion has far more to do with easy sentimentality than with serious theology, and even demagogues such as Pat Robertson or Jerry Falwell, those contemporary money-changers in the temple, come across more as inspirational speakers than as theologians inspired by the Divine. An eye-rolling anomaly has been the continuing success of the *Left Behind* series of "Christian" novels—books whose focus on the apocryphal notion of the Rapture bears more resemblance to a heretical cult than to anything accepted by traditional Christian theology. American Protestantism, especially, is almost unrecognizable by historical standards, and, in the words of one Southern boy who had a way with Gospel tunes, "That's all right, mama." By making belief as convenient as a trip to McDonald's and as comfortable as a fleece pullover, we have broken down the sense of religious identity that, painfully learned and earned, separated us in the past.

Americans believe what they feel like believing. Profess what they will, they overwhelmingly choose psychological comfort and social convenience over stern principles of faith. Anathema to theologians, the fact is that it works. Our beliefs are as sloppy and as abundant as our waistlines. There are few things more revealing than trying to engage a fundamentalist on the fundamentals of his or her faith. In this one instance, ignorance—of that which would divide us—is healthy. Religious reactionaries in our society tend to be the socially fearful, not necessarily those of the most robust faith. And even the most severe among them have been declawed. While the book lovers among us may shake our heads at the sputtering fundamentalist campaign against the Harry Potter series (such condemnations are always about the parent's devils, of course, not about the child's welfare), we may take comfort in the intolerant Christian's progress from burning witches and massacring Jews to telling a disappointed child she cannot go to the multiplex with her little pagan friends.

I do not suggest that some putty-textured "world religion" is upon us, or that we are grazing among various gods as did the imperial Romans, or that we shortly will discard the formal religious identities of our ancestors. Americans are often wonderfully devout—they simply are not inclined to think much about their beliefs. (And the deepest theologians from any religion would tell you, anyway, that an excess of thought is the insidious enemy of true faith—Luther's Protestantism, especially, with its belief in salvation through faith alone, is essentially an anti-theology, perfectly suited to Americans.) We are focused upon the ends, not the process—while an obsession with process brought our more distant ancestors everything from church schisms to the Inquisition. Even the most devout Americans find ways around religious rules that prove too inconvenient, and there is among us an instinctive urge to rebel against any church or patriarch who tries to render religion too prescriptive. Americans, across all creeds, are simply making religion suit them. And so human nature changes the world.

Within my father's lifetime, tens of thousands of members of the Ku Klux Klan marched not only against blacks, but against Roman Catholics. Today, the average Protestant in America cannot tell you what tenets of faith make him different from a Catholic, apart from some vague notions about the Pope (whom most Protestants perceive as a pretty good guy). Yet, for centuries, men died over these differences. The civilizational progress indicated by a Catholic believer who unhesitatingly takes birth control pills or a Christmas tree in a Jewish household (though it may excite a bit of *Angst* among some family members) is a measure not of compromise, but of human confidence. Strict adherence to and interpretations of religious doctrine, as we see with miserable clarity in the Middle East, are the signs of a frightened human being in an undersocialized faith in a divided society. Nor do I make light of faith, which I believe is essential to our humanity. Rather, I propose that a faith that does not depend upon the crutch of obsolete doctrine is a more evolved faith. Composed by men, doctrine is, at best, a veil through which we see God darkly.

Faith enables, doctrine inhibits. In the true American grain, we are simply casting off that which has failed us. Faithless Europe meanders, while faithful Islam crumbles. We have gained an almost miraculous middle ground. The old World War II movies, with their idealized squads of soldiers or Marines representing every relevant creed, have given way to a mundane reality of tolerance. And best of all, we have found that we usually like each other.

How will intolerant societies compete with us? I have spent so much time on this particular development because it goes largely ignored when we consider our strategic advantages. Satellites and aircraft carriers are impressive, but they can be defeated. *A society that transcends its religious differences without losing its faith is invincible.*

Domestically, then, we are experiencing simultaneous revolutions in how men and women cooperate, believe, work, learn, and age. In a shocking break with the past and with other civilizations, we have made it possible for men and women to be friends, and we have created an environment in which the best qualified man or woman usually gets the job. Such developments may sound obvious and unimpressive to those who have seen little of the rest of the world or who have not studied history, but America's success today depends far less upon fiscal policy or the state of trade than it does upon our ability to see in others possibilities to which even our mothers and fathers were blind. All this accelerates and is accelerated by technological and scientific developments. Strategy relies upon power, and power springs from the strength of a society and its economy. On every single count, we lead the world, and we shall continue to do so. We have crossed the threshold of the true American Century.

Since the early days of the Cold War, much has been written and said about the United States as "the new Rome." Concentrating either upon our extraordinary strategic power or upon the dangers of imperial overreach, such comparisons generally have missed the most pertinent lesson: An empire can only afford to open its gates if it is feared beyond them. The United States is, indeed, an empire, if a newfangled one with no interest in occupying territory or ruling foreign populations.

We wish to do business around the world, to be safe, and to influence the future to our benefit. *But to be successfully cosmopolitan, we must be feared.* The Roman Empire at its long apogee could accommodate tremendous diversity because it knew how to punish its enemies and did not hesitate in doing so. Even a humane, rule-of-law state, committed to openness and opportunity, must be prepared to level Carthage and sow the ground with salt, or to level a few temples now and then. The largest arsenal is insufficient if your enemy does not believe you have the fortitude to use it. Graphic displays of power are essential to deterrence. Enemies must know that the price of attacking us will be exorbitant, and that it will be extracted no matter the outcry.

Enlightened empire requires that one fist be mailed and the other gloved in velvet. There must be rewards for good behavior and cooperation, but retaliation for abuses against the empire and its citizens must be swift and dependable. American strategic policy in the last decade of the twentieth century essentially collapsed, manifesting the very worst American characteristics, arrogance and ignorance, wrapped in a leader's personal cowardice. We convinced terrorists and their supporters that we were unwilling to fight back, leaving deadly attacks against our citizens, soldiers, and symbols unpunished. That much has changed. But we cannot leave the job unfinished. Empires are always at war, every single day of their existence. *America must accept the mantle of empire it long has found uncomfortable.* Greatness has been thrust upon us, although we like our role as little as do our jealous allies.

Of course, our empire is cultural and economic, a matter of influence and the occasional exercise of military power, and not one of conquests and exploitation. But it is an empire nonetheless. And we must always be on our guard and must do what is essential without flinching. There is nothing humane in a tolerance for monsters.

I believe we have found the will to fight the devils that walk the earth (the American people never lost it, only our leadership did). And with our great mongrel strength—ever confused as weakness by bigots around the world—we have the power to shape a century to the common good of mankind. We cannot repair all that others have broken, especially when an entire civilization appears determined to smash itself into irrelevance, nor can we be the world's policeman, ever on the beat on every block. But, as this book states elsewhere, we can and must be the world's referee, setting basic rules of conduct and limits to violent discord. Law, not anarchy, gives peace a chance. No one else can or will do it, and it must be done, although even the beneficiaries of our policies and actions will complain. (Today's Europeans always remind me of Frederick the Great's comment on Maria Theresa, Empress of Austria-Hungary, when Poland was partitioned: "She cried, but took her share.")

At a time when our wealth will continue to grow astronomically—as it certainly has since my childhood—unproductive societies, clinging to oppressive traditions, will suffer from internal battles over their dwindling wealth. Still more systems of social organization may deteriorate as the Islamic world has done. (Without intense immigration, it is hard to envision how some European countries will be able to sustain their quality of life in the future, and China is tomorrow's strategic wild card.) The discontents of the past several decades were as nothing to what is yet to come from the incompetent regions of the world.

When men and women seek to improve themselves and their societies through legitimate means, we should do all that is reasonable to help them; when they ask for self-determination, we should support them, rather than their

dictators; and when they ask for fairness, we should accommodate them, no matter the complaints of our own special interests. But when Americans are attacked, our retribution cannot
be merely "proportionate." It must be stunning even to our
allies. The occasional leveling of Carthage is the price not only
of empire, but of the international rule of law, and of peace.

On September 10, 2001, America was already well on the
way to the domestic renaissance the components of which are
described above. As of September 11, a strategic renaissance
began as well. Many legacy notions and illusions remain in the
fields of strategy and foreign policy, but these will fade in the
face of the new reality. What matters is that the United States is
prepared to fight when we must fight—and that the world is
getting an unexpected lesson in American resolve. It is the primary task of our present and future leaders not to let that
resolve weaken. The lesson must be lasting. And ferocity is the
ultimate guarantor of peace.

When Devils Walk the Earth

The Mentality and Roots of Terrorism, and How to Respond

This essay was written in October, 2001, for the Center for Emerging Threats and Opportunities, and is published here with the gracious permission of the CETO, and with thanks to the United States Marine Corps.

THE MONSTER'S MIND

There are two basic types of terrorist: the practical and the apocalyptic. While there are exceptions to each basic pattern, gray areas in between the two categories, and rare terrorists who evolve from one type into the other (usually from the practical to the apocalyptic), these remain the two most useful classifications in attempts to understand and defeat our enemies who employ terror. Failure to distinguish between the different threats posed by these two very different types of terrorists led to fatal misjudgments, such as the conviction that skyjackers should not be opposed in the air, since any action would only endanger passengers, based upon the assumption that aircraft seized by terrorists were bargaining chips, not weapons. But the actions of the practical terrorist, to whom we have grown accustomed, are calculated to change political circumstances, while for the apocalyptic terrorist, destruction is an end in itself, despite his extravagant statements about strategic objectives. For all his violence, the practical—political—terrorist is a man of hope. The religious, apocalyptic terrorist is a captive of his own rage, disappointments, and fantasies. One may be controlled. The other must be killed.

Lesser Devils

Practical terrorists, with whom we long have struggled, may behave savagely, but they have tangible goals and a logical approach to achieving them. Their logic may be cruel or cynical, but there is a rational (if sometimes extreme or tenuous) relationship between their long-term goals, means, risks, assets, and interim objectives. Ideology can dominate their thinking, but it does not break loose entirely from mundane reality; indeed, their struggle may be for elementary survival under oppressive conditions. While their convictions and techniques make them appear "fanatical" to the layman, their determination is fueled by the intellect and common emotions, not by the spiritual message or transcendent vision of the true fanatic.

Even when championing a particular religious minority, practical terrorists are concerned with rights, status, and apportionment in the here and now, not beyond the grave (the IRA, for example, or the Stern Gang). They make perceived (or real) injustice their cause, not infidelity or apostasy, and may pay scant attention to the religious rituals of those whom they see themselves as defending. While an ideology may substitute for religion in their psychological make-up, as it did for many Communist true believers, their concerns are bellies, wallets, security, land, and authority, not souls. They often bitterly reject the otherworldly promises of organized religion, which they may view as a tool of the established order, even as they develop their own secular liturgies. They may be at once the self-appointed representatives of a religious minority and opponents of that minority's prevailing religious hierarchy (the Molly Maguires in the Pennsylvania anthracite fields in the nineteenth century, or Quebecois separatists in Canada's more recent history).

Even when practical terrorists routinely invoke their religious affiliation, they tend to think in terms of birth and bloodlines (as did virtually all terrorist paramilitaries in the former Yugoslavia, no matter their confession). Critically, they view their own deaths as a misfortune, however necessary or noble, and not as an embrace of the divine. They would rather live than die, and regard death as final, not as a promotion. They approach the theological plane only in the cloudy belief that they will "live on" in the people whose cause they have made their own. They want rewards on earth, and do not expect them in heaven.

The practical terrorist may have ambitious dreams—the overthrow of a state or the institution of a radically new political system—and may be willing to undergo great hardship and sacrifice in pursuit of those dreams—but he (or she) is rarely suicidal and does not view death and destruction as goals unto themselves. He is conservative in the sense that he wishes to preserve a party organization, or just his small cell, for the day when he imagines he or his fellow conspirators will "take over." Suicide attacks are extreme tools to him, employed only in desperation and against targets of great value or prestige.

The practical terrorist may be convinced of his beliefs and embittered toward society and "the system," but his goals are always the re-creation of the society or state, not its total annihilation. He may be willing to kill thousands, to use torture, and to subject others to his brutal will, but the environment he wishes to inhabit in the bright future he foresees is of this earth, and there are other flesh-and-blood human beings in it. The practical terrorist may attract helpers who enjoy destruction and cruelty for their own sakes, but the overall terrorist organization remains focused upon political goals that the terrorist leadership judges to be attainable.

While some practical terrorists may be such die-hard believers that they will fight to the death (or undertake desperate suicide missions), others may mature beyond their terrorist backgrounds, prove open to compromise, even become capable of a degree of give and take with the very authorities they once single-mindedly demonized (consider how the image of Yasser Arafat has changed with the years). Some are implacable and obsessive, but others will settle for incremental change—or be co-opted into an evolving political system (one thinks of those contemporary European politicians, exemplified by Germany's brilliant foreign minister, Joschka Fischer, who grew from left-wing street-fighter or conspiratorial backgrounds into surprisingly adept and conscientious statesmen). There are many subdivisions of the practical terrorist category, and it is the task of law enforcement and intelligence services to differentiate among them. For some individuals, affiliation with a terrorist group is a thrilling fad they later abandon; for others it is an all-consuming mission from which they can never extract themselves psychologically. Some can be frightened, persuaded, or bought, while others must be killed, and it is a very sloppy, foolish state that neglects to distinguish the transient helper from the hardcore killer.

There usually are lines the practical terrorist will not cross—some groups he wishes to protect, certain tools he will not employ, some self-imposed limitations upon the scale of his actions. It is extremely unlikely that such a terrorist would employ biological or nuclear weapons, although he might make limited use of chemical weapons. A domestic terrorist who employed NBC weapons, for example, would likely be a psychotic or a member of a delusional group with an apocalyptic vision. Germ warfare, especially, is most liable to be waged along apocalyptic, racial, or religious lines. While the practical terrorist may commit certain deeds to create an atmosphere of terror among a target group or audience, the good opinion of at least a portion of the public remains important to him. He may misread public sentiment and deceive himself about his image, his effect, and the ultimate possibility of attaining his goals, but he does not detach himself entirely from the day-to-day world and its concerns, nor does he fully escape the psychology of popular morality. He may commit atrocious acts—setting off car bombs in public places, kidnapping the innocent relations of his chosen enemies, committing assassinations—but the scale of his actions is usually limited, despite the attendant drama. Perfectly willing to demolish police stations or government offices, he does not destroy entire cities, which he would rather rule than wreck. He wants to lead "his people" to power or to independence, not to their deaths.

The practical terrorist's morality may be very different from that of the average American, and he may even be psychologically unbalanced, but he does not disregard the value of human life entirely. He may commit grand gestures in frustration or desperation (or because he possesses a flair for exploiting the media), but he continues to see himself as the representative of an earthly agenda, not as a divine missionary. He tends to see history as a progression which requires his assistance—not as a collapse toward a longed-for Armageddon. Though subject to bouts of depression, he is ultimately the more hopeful and less pessimistic terrorist. He is concerned with his own failures and those of his group, but not convinced that all those who believe otherwise are eternally damned and condemned to annihilation, or that a sinful world must be consumed by fire. In his dark way, he believes in redemption of the masses, in the possibility that they can, through example, education, or force, be convinced that his way is the enlightened way. The practical terrorist always sees more to be captured than destroyed. He wants prizes. Willing and able to dehumanize specific targets, he is often surprisingly sentimental about specific objects, individuals, or those human types or classes whom he idealizes.

The practical terrorist's commitment to his cause may remain relatively constant, but his actions can be inconsistent—now violent, now passive, violent again, then accommodating. He may be capable of an abrupt change in his perception of who constitutes the "enemy" and how that enemy should be opposed. He is deadly, but usually a greater threat to individuals he deems "guilty" than to the masses. Setbacks can be difficult for him to rationalize and he may undergo periods of despair, which transform his perception of how best to further his cause. He is usually the terrorist of lesser strength, and always the terrorist of lesser menace. Although we may, in our outrage, term him a madman, his mentality often remains recognizably like our own. There is logic to his actions.

The practical terrorist's hellish counterpart, the apocalyptic terrorist, is mentally divorced from our world and its values and from any respect for flesh and blood. The practical terrorist has dreams. The apocalyptic terrorist is lost in a nightmare.

The Original Smart Bombs

The "pure" practical terrorist is an idealist, sometimes very well educated (historically, secular universities have been excellent recruiting grounds for terrorists who want to force improvement upon the world). While it may seem counter-intuitive, the apocalyptic, religious terrorist tends to be recruited from the ranks of the fearful and threatened, from among the worried,

not the confident; he is a coward in the face of life, if not in the
face of death (this is absolutely applicable to the key operatives
of the September 11, 2001, plot).

Despite the media-driven image of Islamic terrorists representing hordes of the Faithful, apocalyptic terrorists, such as the
members of al Qa'eda, tend to act out of intensely personal disaffection and a sense of alienation from social norms, while the
practical terrorist is more apt to feel driven by group grievances
(though he, too, is rarely a "successful" member of society
before his conversion to terror). The apocalyptic terrorist "wants
out," while the practical terrorist wants "back in," although on
much-improved terms of his own dictation (another aspect of
this psychology is that practical terrorists, even when involved in
international movements, prefer to focus on the locale of their
personal grievances, while apocalyptic terrorists view the greater
world as their enemy and are far more likely to transpose blame
from their own societies onto other cultures).

While both types find comfort—a home and brotherhood—in the terrorist organization, the practical terrorist
imagines himself as a representative of his people, while the
apocalyptic terrorist sees himself as chosen and apart, despite
his occasional rhetoric about protecting the masses adhering to
his faith. The practical terrorist idealizes his own kind—his
people—while the apocalyptic terrorist insists that only his personal ideals have any validity. The practical terrorist is impassioned and imagines that his deeds will help his brethren in
the general population, while the apocalyptic terrorist is
detached from compassion by his faith and only wants to punish the "sinful," whom he finds ever more numerous as he is
progressively hypnotized by the dogma that comforts him.

Except for the most cynical gunmen, practical terrorists
believe that mankind can be persuaded (or forced) to regret

past errors and make amends, and that reform of the masses is possible (although a certain amount of coercion may be required). But apocalyptic terrorists (such as Osama bin Laden) are merciless. Practical terrorists may see acts of retribution as a tactical means, but apocalyptic terrorists view themselves as tools of a divine and uncompromising retribution. Retribution against unbelievers, heretics, and even their own brethren whose belief is less pure, is the real strategic goal of apocalyptic terrorists, even when they do not fully realize it themselves or cannot articulate it. Even among average Americans, there is often a great gulf between what they consciously think they believe and the "slumbering" deeper beliefs that catalytic events awaken—such as the frank thirst for revenge felt by tens of millions of "peaceful" Americans in the wake of the events of September 11. It is considerably less likely that a morally crippled, obsessed, apocalyptic terrorist cocooned in an extreme religious vision will be able to articulate his real goals; we cannot know apocalyptic terrorists by their pronouncements so well as by their deeds, since much of what they say is meant to make their intentions seem more innocent or justified than they are.

Often, apocalyptic terrorists are lying even to themselves. Apocalyptic terrorists are whirling in the throes of a peculiar, malignant madness and barely know what they believe in the depths of their souls—in fact, much of their activity is an attempt to avoid recognition of the darkness within themselves, a struggle to depict themselves as (avenging) angels of light. Centuries ago, we might have said they were possessed by devils. Today, we must at least accept that they are possessed and governed by a devilish vision.

The practical terrorist punishes others to force change. The religious terrorist may speak of changes he desires in this world, but his true goal is simply the punishment of others—in the largest possible numbers—as an offering to the bloodthirsty, vengeful God he has created for himself. This apocalyptic terrorist may identify himself as a Muslim or a Christian, but he is closer akin to an Aztec sacrificing long lines of prisoners on an altar of blood (one of the many psychological dimensions yet to be explored in terrorist studies is the atavistic equation of bloodshed with cleansing—an all-too-literal bath of blood).

No change in the world order will ever content the apocalyptic terrorist, since his actual discontents are internal to himself and no alteration in the external environment could sate his appetite for retribution against those he needs to believe are evil and guilty of causing his personal sufferings and disappointments—for such men, suicidal acts have a fulfilling logic, since only their own destruction can bring them lasting peace. Above all, they need other humans to hate while they remain alive; this is the only release for the profound self-hatred underlying the egotism that lets them set themselves up as God's judges—as imitation Gods themselves—upon this earth. In theological terms, there is no greater blasphemer in any religion than the killer who appoints himself as God's agent, or assumes a godlike right to judge entire populations for himself, but the divine mission of the apocalyptic terrorist leaves no room for theological niceties. Pretending to defend his religion, he creates a vengeful splinter religion of his own.

The health of any religious community can be gauged by the degree to which it rejects these bloody apostles of terror, and the Islamic world's acceptance of apocalyptic terrorists as heroes is perhaps the most profound indicator of its spiritual crisis and decay. Make no mistake: The terrorist "martyrs" of September 11, 2001, and Osama bin Laden will be remembered by Islamic historians and by generation after generation of Muslim children as great heroes in the struggle for true religion and justice. No matter what Islamic governments may say to please us, many millions of Muslims around the world felt tremendous pride in the atrocities in New York, Washington, and Pennsylvania. This makes it all the more vital that the United States kill Osama bin Laden, exterminate al Qa'eda, destroy the Taliban, and depose any other governments found to have supported their terrorism. If Osama bin Laden survives to thumb his nose at an "impotent superpower," he will attract hundreds of thousands of supporters, and tens of millions more sympathizers. He is already a hero, and he must not be allowed to remain a triumphant one. He is an apocalyptic terrorist of the worst kind, and his superficial agenda (deposing the government of Saudi Arabia, expelling U.S. troops from the Middle East, imposing Sharia law) is nothing compared to his compulsion to slaughter and destroy.

Although his vision is closer to the grimmest passages of Christianity's Book of Revelation than to anything in the Koran, Osama bin Laden has been able to convince countless Muslims that his vision is of the purest and proudest Islamic form. This should be a huge warning flag to the West about the spiritual crisis in the Islamic world. Logic of the sort cherished on campuses and in government bureaucracies does not apply. This battle is being fought within the realms of the emotions and the soul, not of the intellect. We face a situation so perverse that it is as if tens of millions of frustrated Christians decided that Kali, the Hindu Goddess of death and destruction, embodied the true teachings of Jesus Christ. We are witnessing the horrific mutation of a great world religion, and the Islamic world likely will prove the greatest breeding ground of apocalyptic terrorists in history.

Small and Vicious Gods

The belief systems of practical terrorists are often modular; some such men can learn, evolve, synthesize, or realign their views. But the apocalyptic terrorist cannot tolerate any debate or dissent—all divergent opinions are a direct threat to his mental house of cards. The apocalyptic terrorist embraces a totality of belief and maintains it with an ironclad resolution attained by only the most extreme—and psychotic—secular terrorists. First identifying himself as a tool of his God, he soon begins to assume his right to godlike powers. The practical terrorist is in conflict with the existing system, but the apocalyptic terrorist sees himself as infinitely superior to it. The practical terrorist looks up at the authority he seeks to replace, but the apocalyptic terrorist looks down on the humankind he despises. Despite enforcing rigorous discipline within the terrorist organization, the practical terrorist nonetheless retains a sense of human imperfection. The religious, apocalyptic terrorist believes that those who are imperfect deserve extermination (in one of terrorism's gray area anomalies, the "secular" Nazi regime took on an essentially religious vision that embraced state terror— Hitler's attitude toward the Jews was astonishingly similar to Osama bin Laden's view of Jews, Christians, and even secular Muslims; of course, the desire to please God or authority by slaughtering unbelievers has a long tradition in many religions, from medieval Catholicism to contemporary Hindu extremism).

Scared of the Girls

Both types of terrorists draw accomplices and foot soldiers from the uneducated masses, but the leadership in each type of movement tends to have at least a smattering of higher education and may even be highly intelligent and learned in terms of the host society's norms. In both cases, however, their vanity cannot satisfy itself with what the system offers. The terrorist is always an egotist with a (desperate, fragile) sense of unappreciated superiority, aggravated by his inability to establish satisfying social, personal, or vocational relationships. The terrorist is convinced that he is right, but is not much concerned with being just. He wants to "show" the world or even God. At the core of many a terrorist leader is a spoiled brat disappointed by the failures of adulthood.

Perhaps the most routine commonality between the practical and apocalyptic terrorist is the male terrorist's inability to develop and maintain healthy, enduring relationships with women—although the practical terrorist is more apt to idealize members of the opposite sex, who then disappoint him, and to imagine himself re-created as a storybook hero of the sort he believes would appeal to his fantasy woman (Timothy McVeigh), while the apocalyptic terrorist fears, despises, and hates females (Mohammed Atta, whose testament perfectly captured the Islamic fanatic's revulsion toward women).

Practical terrorists may be puritanical, but they are much more likely to accord women admission to and high status in their organizations (from numerous historical left-wing terrorist groups to the Tamil Tigers). Practical terrorists may even show an egalitarian attitude toward the sexes, though by no means always—it very much depends on societal context—while the apocalyptic terrorist usually mistrusts and shuns women (al Qa'eda and other Islamic terrorist organizations are classic examples, although some Christian fringe groups also seem to believe that the word "evil" is derived from the root word "Eve"). There is great cultural variation in the attitudes of terrorists of both kinds toward women, and a few apocalyptic cults have even been led by female prophets, but apocalyptic terrorists generally denigrate or actively humiliate women far more often than they value them, while practical terrorists, at worst, relegate women to the status customary in the society in which they operate.

Nonetheless, the statistical inability of terrorists of both kinds to form enduring sexual relationships with a beloved partner is an aspect of terrorist psychology that has gone largely unexplored—we are so determined to be "serious" and to be taken seriously by our peers that we may have missed the forest for the trees. A review of historical terror cases makes it startlingly clear: Terrorists rarely have successful dating histories. Sexual fears and humiliation as young adults—and the consequent loneliness and alienation—may be the single greatest unrecognized catalyst in the making of a terrorist (whether Mohammed Atta or Timothy McVeigh). A terrorist's passion for political reform or preserving rain forests, or his compulsion to serve God through colossal destruction, may be more of a final symptom than a root cause.

Terrorists are disturbed, unhappy men. We have done an inadequate job of asking what has made them so unhappy that they seek release in killing their fellow human beings. We look for answers in economic statistics, while ignoring the furious power of the soul.

There have been plentiful exceptions, but the general rule is that the more repressed the society and the more fervent its rejection of reciprocity in sexual relations, the more terrorists it produces; and the greater the gap in social status between men and women in the society, the more likely it is to produce suicidal male terrorists. Societies that dehumanize women dehumanize everyone except those males in authority positions—and the ability to dehumanize his targets is essential to the psychology of the terrorist. While those who will become terrorists may wed to accommodate social norms or familial insistence, the rarest form of human being may be a happily married terrorist.

Avenging Angels

Apocalyptic terrorists are a far more serious matter than even the deadliest practical terrorists, and these religion-robed monsters are at war with the United States and the West today. Jealous of our success and our power, terrified and threatened by the free, unstructured nature of our societies, and incapable of performing competitively in the twenty-first century, they have convinced themselves that our way of life is satanic and that we are the enemies of their religion and their God. Nothing we can do will persuade them otherwise (it is a dangerous peculiarity of the West to imagine that we can "explain everything" satisfactorily to those who hate us—apocalyptic terrorists and their masses of sympathizers don't want explanations, they want revenge).

Muslim apocalyptic terrorists do not understand the reality of our society or our daily lives, and they do not want to understand. They can live among us and see only evil, even as they enjoy a shabby range of pleasures, from video games to prostitutes. Their extreme vision of the world constructs evil even from good and easily rationalizes away the virtues of other societies and civilizations. They *need* to hate us, and their hatred is the most satisfying element in their lives. Death and destruction delight them. They cannot be reasoned with, appeased, or even intimidated. No human voice can persuade the man who believes that God is speaking in his other ear. Apocalyptic terrorists must be destroyed. There is no alternative to killing the hardcore believers, and it may be necessary to kill thousands of them, if we are to protect the lives of millions of our own citizens.

We still fail to recognize that the atrocities of September 11, 2001, composed the most successful—and dramatic—

achievement of the Islamic world against the West in centuries, greater than the Ottoman victory at Gallipoli, the establishment of Arab states, the nationalization of the Suez Canal, or the Iranian Counter-Revolution of 1979. It was a great day in Muslim history, and it will be remembered as such, no matter what tribulations we visit upon the terrorist networks and their state accomplices in retaliation. This was their big win, and let us hope it is the only one.

THE FERTILE FIELDS OF TERROR

But Don't We Have Our Own Fundamentalist Terrorists?

There are certainly domestic terrorists in the United States who claim religious justification for their deeds, such as those who bomb Planned Parenthood clinics, murder doctors who perform abortions, or perpetrate vicious hoaxes. But such men and women usually are practical terrorists, not apocalyptic, and have tangible social goals. They do not seek to destroy entire populations, but to alter specific practices within a society of which they are otherwise hopeful. While the acceleration of societal (and technological) change and the attendant psychological disorientation may spark the rise of domestic apocalyptic cults that seek to jump-start Armageddon, we have been lucky thus far—a tribute to the opportunities offered by our society and to our cultural robustness.

At present, the greatest domestic danger remains the lone psychotic triggered into action by the hate-filled rants of televangelists and other demagogues, by the insidious false communalism of the internet, or simply by a self-constructed vision. Abroad, the globalization of information has been the single most destabilizing factor in foreign cultures, and even here the information revolution has had its dark side, making the propaganda of prejudice and blame available as never before. Accusations that draw only laughter from the rest of us may spur the waiting madman to commit horrendous deeds, and, in the future, we who profit so richly from the free flow of information may find ourselves compelled to a more vigorous censorship of hate speech and the paraphernalia of bigotry. Much of the Islamic world has been poisoned by false, but wonderfully comforting information, and we do not yet know the degree to which the same thing is happening here. The man of no prospects, in any culture or civilization, is always glad to be told that his failures are not his fault and that there is a target he can blame. Individual and group success disarms hatred more effectively than laws or lectures, and we must hope that our continued success is ever more inclusive of those citizens now relegated to the social fringes, from whose ranks the commandos of domestic terror are drawn.

Some of our domestic cult groups already have veered across the border toward apocalyptic behavior, but most of these bands of believers are *introverted* millenarian movements that seek to inaugurate the "end of days" and the Kingdom of God by suicidal gestures, rather than by mass attacks on outsiders. We must be on guard against small groups who buckle psychologically under the pressures of modern life and take refuge in *extroverted* millenarian movements that lash out in attempts to bring down the heavens upon us all, but, for now at least, the greatest risk from apocalyptic movements comes from abroad—and overwhelmingly from the Islamic world. Christian extremists may yet turn to direct action to bring on the "end of days," as they did five centuries ago (see below), but our society appears to be sufficiently inclusive and promising to content all but a few alienated individuals and small cells with limited goals. Nonetheless, we are playing the odds, with no guarantee that events will not trigger greater domestic threats from those convinced that God requires them to kill.

Consider a few patterns of domestic religious "terrorism" to date, with their American twists and heritage:

The "Reverend" Jim Jones and the grape Kool-Aid mass suicide and murders in Jonestown, Guiana, a generation ago; David Koresh's Branch Davidians; or the odd If-I-kill-myself-God's-spaceship-will-carry-me-away cult are introverted millennial variations of terrorist movements, but are not usually classified under "terrorism" because their acts are directed against their own followers and themselves. They are as close as Americans have come, in our time, to domestic apocalyptic terrorism (even the Unabomber, who made a secular religion of his crusade against technological progress, targeted specific individuals in his attempts to "alert" our society and did not use his abilities to attack undifferentiated citizens in a broad manner). Fortunately, the tendency in contemporary Western cults with Christian roots is to retreat from society, rather than to try actively to reform it—withdrawal from the world long has been a tradition in the American grain, dating to the earliest New England settlements, whose inhabitants sought to build exclusive "cities on a hill" and who sought to divorce themselves from the perceived corruption and very real persecution of the Old World (the benign Shakers or the gentle Brethren of the Ephrata Cloister strike more responsive chords in the American psyche than do bloody cults).

As an aside, one of the reasons Eastern religions have a special resonance with many Christians—although not with Muslims—may be our conditioning over centuries to revere ascetic withdrawals from the world on the part of saints and lesser believers, from Saint Anthony to the Shakers. Such retreats bear recognizable similarities to the Buddhist and Hindu traditions of the renunciation of mortal things. Islam certainly has its ascetics and renunciations, but, as practiced today in the realms of Sharia law (as opposed to those subregions where the far less menacing Sufi traditions dominate belief), it is much more of an applied religion, with a much greater focus on efforts to censor and discipline the world that is—reminiscent of medieval Catholicism. Contrary to recommending that believers "render unto Caesar what is Caesar's," Muslims expect Caesar to render unto their faith, an attitude the Protestant Reformation blessedly deconstructed in the West.

Americans who sincerely believe that a remarriage of government and religion is just what the cosmic doctor ordered should be very careful what they wish for, since states wed to single religions consistently find that the relationship is bad for both the religion and the state—although profitable to demagogues, as in Iran. The practice of religion is always most free where its relationship with government is least adhesive, and, in every society, those who wish to impose one religion's dominance on the state tend to be authoritarian in disposition. Osama bin Laden's vision of a properly run society is much closer to John Calvin's oppressive Geneva than to the brilliance and humanity of Moorish Cordoba or the flowering of Samarkand—before the murder of Ulug Begh by the "mad mullahs" of the day. In fact, the intellectual and spiritual calcification of Islam can be dated precisely to that assassination five and a half centuries ago.

In one of the many ironies of history, two great religions have swapped places over the last half millennium, with Christianity breaking free of medieval intellectual and social repression, while the once effervescent world of Islam has embraced the comforts of shackles and ignorance. Today, at least, the Judeo-Christian world faces forward, while the Islamic world looks backward with longing and wallows in comforting myths.

About Those Myths . . .

Myth is far more powerful than fact, not only in the Islamic world but wherever men and women seek absolution for their individual and collective failures. For all the Muslim world's rhetoric about the damage done by the Crusades, internal Crusades within Europe—against heretics and Jews—took many more lives over the centuries than did pre-Renaissance Europe's small-scale adventures in Palestine. Today, more Muslims live in the greater Washington, D.C., area than the total number of Crusaders who marched east over two centuries, and Washington does not feel under siege from these local residents. The power of the Crusader myth in today's Middle East has far more to do with the perception of collective failure and vulnerability than with reality—after all, the Islamic Ottomans conducted a centuries-long, much more successful crusade against Europe thereafter, and Islamic warriors threatened the marches of Europe well into the nineteenth century. Islamic invaders did far more damage to the Ukraine and Poland than the Crusaders did to Palestine. Those in the Middle East who cite the Crusader conquest of Jerusalem as an act of peerless historical viciousness might do well to remember Islam's conquest of Constantinople and Budapest, and the Ottoman progress to the gates of Vienna. If the streets of Jerusalem ran with blood, so did the streets—and churches—of Constantinople. There is plenty of historical guilt to pass around. We are blessed to live in a civilization that has moved on—but we face threats from a civilization that clings to a cosmetically enhanced past. While well-intentioned Westerners have gone to great lengths to refute Samuel Huntington's thesis of a "clash of civilizations," the man in the street in the Islamic world believes, intuitively, that the clash has been going on for a very long time, and no argument will dissuade him from his delicious belief in Western malevolence. How better to explain his wasted life in a ravaged state?

Until September 11, 2001, the most appalling terrorist act on American soil since British atrocities during our Revolutionary War was the Oklahoma City bombing, which was the deed of a practical terrorist who had deluded himself into believing America was ripe for another revolution that required only a catalytic event. It was about as vicious as an act of practical terrorism ever gets, and the difference in scope and scale (as well as intention) between the attack on one mid-sized Federal building in Oklahoma and the attacks on the World Trade Center provides a very good measure of the relative dangers of practical versus apocalyptic terrorism. Indeed, we may find that apocalyptic terror is capable of deeds far in excess of those in New York (especially employing weapons of mass destruction), while practical terror always has a ceiling. Admittedly, that ceiling may be much higher in other cultures, especially when speaking of ideology-based, regime-sponsored terror employed against the regime's own population during an era of transition, as in Stalin's Soviet Union, Mao's China, or Pol Pot's Cambodia, but this essay will confine itself to international and anti-state terrorism, in the interests of pertinence and brevity. One concern we should have about practical terrorists, though, is the copycat effect—will they think bigger now that they have seen what apocalyptic terrorists achieved on September 11, 2001?

While a few of the most extreme fundamentalist Christians in America have committed terrorist acts to achieve explicit goals, they tend to be "off-the-reservation" individuals or small groups who interpret doctrine with obsessive rigor and whose parent churches, though sometimes vociferous, do not encourage or support their acts of terror. Despite the cloak of religion, these terrorists have more in common with the

Weathermen or the Symbionese Liberation Army than they do with al Qa'eda. They want to change society's rules, not to destroy society. The behavior patterns of these domestic fanatics are, as stated above, those of practical terrorists, even in the way some of them idealize "unborn children" and mothers, while demonizing those women whose behavior they find anathema. Apocalyptic terrorists demonize plenty of their fellow human beings, but idealize none except their own leaders and martyrs to the cause. The idealization of a segment of humanity is a consistent hallmark of the practical terrorist.

Anti-choice terrorists in the United States are not trying to jump-start the Book of Revelation. Whatever we may feel individually about the issue of pro-life versus pro-choice, the extremists who indulge in terrorizing behavior have a practical agenda that hopes to change behaviors and laws. Their greatest similarity to apocalyptic terrorists is that they long to turn back the clock to a past they have idealized, as did the decidedly secular Unabomber. In the past, much terrorism sought to modernize decaying societies; today, terrorism increasingly seeks to restore past strictures on behavior. Much of the terrorism of the nineteenth and twentieth centuries was revolutionary, but, increasingly, both practical and apocalyptic terrorists are reactionary. And the issue of the role of women in society almost invariably plays a role in their agendas. (Women seem to get the worst of it in every religion, and it is likely that only the splintering of Western churches allowed the productive liberation of women in our own societies; wherever a single orthodoxy prevails, women occupy a subordinate position in society. Even in the United States, a geographical plot of the regions that maintain the strongest insistence on "traditional" roles for women consistently highlights those regions that are the least developed economically and culturally, and the most religiously homogeneous.)

Perhaps the closest figure to Osama bin Laden that America has ever produced was John Brown. Millions of people thought he was right, too. And we have to wonder what that cherished American "saint" might have done had he possessed twenty-first-century technology. He too reveled in a "cleansing" bath of blood. Perhaps our saving grace today is merely that successful economies and flowering societies spawn fewer zealots. But should apocalyptic terrorists from the Islamic world ever manage a truly devastating attack upon America, they might find a new John Brown waiting in our wings—with twenty-first-century technology. Certainly, no sane person in the West wants the current conflict with terrorism to become a religious war. But the apocalyptic terrorists and their supporters already consider it to be one. And we in America probably underestimate our own capacity for savagery against another religion, if sufficiently provoked. Abraham Lincoln may be the greatest figure in American history, but John Brown is the most haunting.

Longing for the End of Days

The apocalyptic terrorists of the Islamic world are the most menacing individuals in the world today. And they intend to be. It is difficult for citizens in a successful, secular society to grasp the degree to which these men see themselves as God's avengers. In the aftermath of September 11, 2001, numerous analysts and commentators have attempted to discover coherent goals and logical behavior in the actions of such terrorists. But we lack the vocabulary or knowledge of the human psyche to cleanly describe the motivations, impulses, and visions of such men.

One way to visualize the difference between the more familiar practical terrorists and these apocalyptic terrorists is to describe their archetypes in terms of painting. The exemplary practical terrorist is like a classic representational painter, a

Poussin or even a da Vinci: The canvas is coherent at a distance, and, the closer you come to the surface, the more fine detail and granularity you see. But apocalyptic terrorists are like the high impressionists—Cezanne, for example. Their "work" is only coherent when viewed from a certain distance. As you approach the canvas, the forms dissolve into splotches and lose their apparent definition. So, too, the apocalyptic terrorist may seem to have explanations, even justifications, for his attacks. He "wants the U.S. out of all Islamic countries," or reviles the invasive corruption of the West, or desires the establishment of a Palestinian state (on his own strict terms). But, upon closer inspection, all these relatively rational purposes begin to blur and dissolve. It is impossible to content the apocalyptic terrorist. His agenda is against this world, not of it. Viewed closely, his vision is inchoate, intuitive, and destructive without limit. It is reality that has not pleased him, and he wants to destroy reality.

Although he views the world as sinful and corrupt, the apocalyptic terrorist's vision of an afterlife is ecstatic. He is absolutely certain that his deeds will be rewarded in the heaven of his particular god. This model is by no means limited to Islamic terrorists—it enraptures apocalyptic terrorists in every susceptible religion. Our problem is that today the failures and psychological debilities of the Muslim world spawn an increasing number of these deadly visionaries and their sufficiently convinced accomplices.

Aggressive religious cults are a predictable aberration of troubled societies struggling through periods of profound change. Some human beings simply cannot deal with the sudden fracturing of their verities and the inadequacy of their long-held, cherished beliefs. Particularly for the apocalyptic terrorist, belief is all or nothing. If his earlier beliefs—either in a particular form of religion or in a cultural milieu—fail to answer his practical and, above all, psychological needs, he tends to rush to another extreme. The appearance of suicidal Islamic terrorists who, earlier in their lives, seemed well-integrated into society and even fond of Western things is a perfect manifestation of this phenomenon. We fail to recognize the difficulty those from other cultures face in internalizing the extremely complex, synthetic value system that allows Americans to operate in our very challenging, apparently contradictory, supercharged society. An outsider can take pleasure in a pair of Nikes or Hollywood films, even revel in the sexual freedom he finds among some segments of Western societies, only to find that his cultural background has not armored him for the disjunctions of the "American way of life."

Americans are masterful at social improvisation and evolution (obviously with many individual exceptions), but this is not a developed skill in more traditional societies. A single, ill-timed rejection, a number of real or perceived humiliations, a gnawing sense of inadequacy and anomie, a failed university course, a lost job, or a nasty touch of venereal disease all can turn the seemingly Westernized visitor from a traditional society into a rabid hater of all things Western as he turns for emotional comfort to the verities of an idealized version of his root culture (from which he earlier had thought to escape). Others need no direct contact with the West to feel immensely threatened by its implications of moral lawlessness (as perceived by the outsiders) and ruthless competition (which they suspect they cannot outface).

Whether the terrorist has an old immigration stamp in his passport or has never left the alleys of Cairo or Karachi, the unifying factor is the fragility of his "cradle," the inadequacy of cherished Islamic traditions to cope not only with the postmodern, but even with primitive versions of the modern world. A religio-social society that restricts the flow of information, prefers myth to reality, oppresses women, makes family, clan, or ethnic identity the basis for social and economic relations, subverts the rule of secular law, undervalues scientific and liberal education, discourages independent thought, and believes that ancient religious law should govern all human relations has no hope whatsoever of competing with America and the vibrant, creative states of the West and the Pacific Rim. We are succeeding, the Islamic world is failing, and they hate us for it. The preceding sentence encapsulates the cause of the terrorism of September 11, 2001, and no amount of "rational" analysis or nervous explanation will make this basic truth go away.

The last time a "world" and an all-encompassing way of life failed in the West was during the early years of the Protestant Reformation. (Of note, economic failures alone do not seem to drive people to apocalyptic behaviors. The Irish Potato Famine, the eviction of Highland crofters, the collapse of the Silesian weaving industry, the destruction of the artisan's way of life by mass manufacturing, and the breakdown of coal mining all failed to spawn millenarian movements; apocalyptic behavior is spawned by cultural failure in the broadest sense.) The "great chain of being" worldview that comforted a majority of the European population during the Middle Ages could not withstand the stresses of nascent modernity and, above all, the explosion of information after Gutenberg's development of the movable type printing press in the mid-fifteenth century. Although the theological and social issues took centuries to resolve (and some *still* have not been laid to rest), the fate of the Protestant Reformation was essentially decided in its first dozen years. The subsequent hundred and twenty-odd years of interconfessional warfare was about the boundaries of

Protestantism, not really about its existence—although contemporaries saw it otherwise. In that initial "long decade," a way of life developed over centuries, a sequence of beliefs and behaviors that had withstood near-constant feudal warfare, recurrent famines, and the unparalleled slaughter of the Black Death collapsed with astonishing speed north of the Alps. Certainly there long had been fissures in the fabric of society and state, and economic burdens helped trigger the assault on the old, uniform system, but what matters for our discussion is that the deepest verities—issues of salvation, sanctity, and the very nature of worship, as well as elementary questions of how church power is vested and which behaviors find divine favor— were suddenly open to debate not only by learned theologians but also by common men and women (and a great many not-very-learned men of the cloth). As the old, monolithic structure of belief and prescribed behavior broke down—with a speed that would bewilder even today's mentally agile Americans— millions of human beings lost their bearings. Some quickly found refuge in a new mainstream of Protestant churches, while others never let go of, or quickly re-embraced, the Roman church. But many thousands could not content themselves with either the old way or the more temperate of the new ways. And they initiated the greatest outbreak of popular terror the West has ever known, the Peasants' Revolt in the Germanies in the 1520s. Bloodier than any revolutionary movement prior to the Russian Civil War, its impulses were apocalyptic in the extreme.

The Peasants' Revolt, or Peasants' Wars, is misnamed to a degree, since the rebellious leaders were extreme-radical theologians, lesser knights, and some members of a fractious, often impecunious nobility. The peasants and some disaffected townsmen provided the mass, not the minds—although some hallucinatory visionaries did emerge from the lower levels of society. And, as East German historians anxiously pointed out during the Cold War, the outbreak of millenarian terror in the mid-1520s had secular antecedents in the *Bundschuh* movement and disparate local revolts that preceded the Reformation. But it was the crisis of faith and the loss of the certainty of salvation as a reward for traditional behavior (and a new calculus for damnation) that catalyzed disparate local movements with concrete grudges into a horde of impassioned killers chasing redemption with swords, scythes, and torches.

Although the East Germans of the old German Democratic Republic tried to repackage him as a proto-socialist, the revolutionary and theologian Thomas Muentzer may have been the Western figure closest to Osama bin Laden (the practical terrorists of the Counter-Reformation and the Inquisition don't even come close). Muentzer, who led his rebels behind a blood-red cross (alternatively reported as a blood-red sword), left a trail of devastation across the middle of the Germanies that only ceased when a coalition of the nobility and knights brought him to a final, apocalyptic battle that ended with an uncompromising pursuit and massacre of the insurgents, followed by the ingenious torture and executions of their captured leaders.

The suddenness and scale of the rebellion had caught all of the authorities of the day by surprise, and it took time to organize an effective response. In one of the paradoxes of history, the decisive revolutionary in the history of the West, Martin Luther, was terrified by the insurgency's embrace of social chaos and the lack of obedience to traditional authority (which he wrestled with rather successfully himself), as well as by the explicit threat to the security of his own reformed church, which was still struggling for legitimacy. In what many consider the greatest blot upon his life and work, Luther wrote a vitriolic public manifesto justifying the extermination of the rebels by any means necessary. To be fair, Luther always saw himself as a loyal, if misunderstood reformer of a true church, not as a revolutionary, but few men know themselves of their effects. Luther condemned that which he himself had unleashed. (His situation bore at least a superficial similarity to the U.S. role in fostering fundamentalist extremism in Afghanistan and Pakistan, the excesses of which now appall us.)

In the meantime, the various ill-disciplined bands of peasants and townsmen, some attracted to charismatic leadership and others simply delighted by the opportunity for revenge and destruction, had sacked castles and towns, tortured, raped, and slaughtered any members of the elite who fell into their hands, devastated churches and iconic art, and reveled in destruction. While there was a great deal of simply "having their own back" in all this for the peasants and the poor of the towns, Muentzer and the other charismatic extremists preached an "end of days" and a sort of purification through destruction that absolved their followers in advance. Muentzer and his familiars read messages in the Heavens, heard God's voice on a private line, and interpreted the Scriptures (especially the Book of Revelation) in a manner that gave their followers license to almost any excess. Their mentality of dragging heaven down to earth through violence, of helping God bring on His Day of Judgment, and of avenging the oppressed through the slaughter of real or imagined oppressors provides the last, five-centuries-old shred of evidence for the campus leftist's argument that "We're really all alike." Indeed, Osama bin Laden is Islam's Thomas Muentzer—a hero to many, a demon to the rest of us. Like John Brown, Muentzer lacked our ultra-modern technology of destruction. But had he possessed nuclear, chemical, or biological weapons, he doubtless would have used them. The authorities he attempted to bring down with terror realized that he had to be killed, and they killed him and as many of his followers as they could track down. The soil of Thuringia, northern Franconia, Eastern Hesse, and the foothills of the Harz were soaked with blood. But Central Europe never suffered another apocalyptic uprising of a similar scale. And the chastened followers of Muentzer and his co-believers who survived, though they long nursed grievances, turned inward, forming, among others, the Anabaptist movements from the Rhineland that helped pioneer America.

Dying for God

An obvious counterargument to the suggestion that apocalyptic terrorists are possessed by a suicidal impulse is that Osama bin Laden seems to want to stay alive. But the desire for self-annihilation takes many forms. In the case of the operational leaders of the September 11 attacks, there was, indeed, an impatience with this world and a readiness to embrace a self-justifying excuse for leaving it behind. Although each of those terrorists would have rejected out of hand the suggestion that they were suicidal or that their discontents were primarily of an inward nature, the fact is that few such men willingly recognize their own motives—or have either the wish or the ability to do so. Often, motive is more easily identified from without. But men who are at peace with themselves and the world do not destroy themselves and as large a portion of the world as they can take down with them.

As dangerous as the "martyrs" of September 11, 2001, were, those of the Osama bin Laden cast are much more worrisome. With or without weapons of mass destruction, the foot-soldier terrorists rushing to kill themselves in a dramatic, annihilating gesture may create plenty of horror and havoc, but the "long-run suicides," those who judge themselves too important to throw away in a "minor" episode, are more dangerous by far. The do-it-now personalities attack specific targets, but the apocalyptic masters seek to destroy vast systems. (Of note, the demands of practical terrorists sometimes diminish over time, as they gain perspective on what is or is not possible, but the demands of apocalyptic terrorists only increase and grow ever more fantastic.)

Osama bin Laden is willing to die—but he wants a commensurate effect when he goes. He is in no hurry and takes great pleasure from the rising crescendo of destruction he can effect through his underlings. But he is not a survive-at-any-cost figure (unlike bureaucrat-terrorists, such as Saddam or Milosevic). Osama bin Laden will, indeed, die for his beliefs—and he will do so with great willingness if he believes he can extract a cataclysmic price in return for his own life. While it would be inaccurate to say there is nothing at which he would not stop, the things that would give him pause are inconsequential to us—taboos in daily behavior, notions of physical pollution, and the corruption of religious rituals. The totems of belief and reassuring behavior are more important to him than complex theological arguments—no matter how much Islamic commentary he may have memorized to use to support his position. He may know all of the Koran by heart—but that, too, is a ritual function. His theology cannot be penetrated by argument, though it can be bolstered by agreement. In terms of religion, he imagines himself as Allah's humble servant but is, in fact, an extreme egomaniac, "leading God from below." When he imagines his own end, it is less a vision of entering a physical paradise and more a sense of merging with his god. He wants to go out with a very big bang.

This is not to suggest that Osama bin Laden is plotting his own end, or that he is eager to die. Rather, he is *willing* to die, and he finds the notion of transcendence through death enticing rather than forbidding. The world reaches him only in negative senses, and, unless the biology of fear kicks in as he faces his own death, he will not much regret leaving this world behind. The corollary, of course, is that he is never reluctant to sacrifice others to his vision and his will. As of this writing there is a theory making the rounds that Osama is, in fact, a very clever manipulator who has a complex, rational plan to get what he wants. This is probably true—but only reflects the least, most superficial part of his character. There are many varieties of madness, and a Hitler can plan very well under congenial circumstances; so, too, does Osama bin Laden. But he cannot be dealt with as a rational actor, since, under the cunning surface, he is irrational in the extreme. His methods make cruel sense, but his goals are far beyond the demise of a particular regime or the recognition of a Palestinian state. He wants to destroy, at the very least, a civilization he has cast as satanic. He does not want to defeat the West—he wants to annihilate us. If he had the technology today, he would use it.

Evidence and the Believer

One of the most frustrating things for Westerners since September 11, 2001, has been the demands throughout the Islamic world for "proof" that Osama bin Laden was behind the attacks. At the same time, "friendly" Arab governments condone or even quietly support suggestions that "Zionists" directed the attacks, that American Jews were warned before the strikes on the World Trade Center and that 4,000 of them did not show up for work on the fateful day. We cannot believe that anyone could believe such folly and we want to extend proof of the truth. But empirical reality is almost irrelevant within the Islamic world—comforting myths are much more powerful. The mental processes at work are so fundamentally different from our own that we literally cannot comprehend them.

Were we to provide a videotaped confession by Osama bin Laden, Muslims would insist that Hollywood had staged it. Were we to provide multimedia records of Arabs committing the deeds of September 11, the response would be the same. Statistics, facts, evidence, proof—none of this has much weight in the Muslim consciousness. I have personally never quite gotten used to the stunning ability of even educated people between the Nile and the Himalayas to believe with deep conviction and passion that which is patently, provably false.

Another aspect of the Islamic mind is its ability to disaggregate and compartmentalize. One moment, a Pakistani or an Egyptian might tell you that Israel staged the attacks on the World Trade Center and the Pentagon, then, a moment later, tell you what a great hero Osama bin Laden is and that the Muslims who piloted the planes were great heroes. We see an obvious lapse in logic, but our Muslim counterpart sees nothing of the kind. He can comfortably believe both "truths."

Part of the problem is that empirical truth comforts us, since we're a success story. The Joe-Friday facts support our satisfying view of ourselves. But few facts support a positive self-image within the Islamic world. The flight into fantasy has been going on for a very long time—at least since the expulsion of the Moors from Spain in 1492—but the impact of globalization, modernity, and now postmodernity has driven hundreds of millions of Muslims into a fabulous refuge of their own collective construction. Powerful myths may be the only thing the Islamic world is any longer good at building.

What it means for us is that we should not waste too much effort trying to prove that which will never be believed, no matter how much supporting data we offer. We can convince through our deeds alone—and even then only partially. When we kill Osama bin Laden, millions will refuse to believe in his death (even if we should put the corpse on a Middle East tour, complete with on-the-spot DNA sampling). And the talent for overlaying conspiracies on even the most benign Western actions will always override the reality of any good we seek to do or accomplish. (Of course America has its own conspiracy fanatics, but in our society they exist on the margins, while the belief in complex, malevolent Western and "Zionist" conspiracies is integral to middle-of-the-road discourse in the Muslim world.)

We are dealing with a delusional civilization. This is a new problem in history. Certainly the degree of delusion varies from individual to individual, to some extent between social classes, and somewhat between peoples and states. But it means that the American and Western tradition of reasoning with opponents, of convincing doubters, and of marshalling evidence has far less potency—often none—in dealing with the Islamic world.

We may believe with great satisfaction that we have the truth on our side, but myth is on their side, and myth can be more powerful than truth. Some noble or hapless souls may sacrifice their lives in service to the truth. But millions will rush to die for a cherished myth.

Only physical reality, brought home with stunning force, can make much of an impression. Even that will be rationalized away in time. But where the truth cannot make headway, punitive or preventive violence must protect us.

We too have our comforting myths, among them that all the people of the world are really "just like us," that all men are finally subject to reason, and, most perniciously, that violence is a desperate measure that solves nothing. In fact, billions of people are not "like us," surprisingly few men are subject to reason when reason threatens their most precious beliefs, and violence is often the only meaningful solution.

Palestinian Terrorists and the Dark Transformation

We are worried about the Palestinian problem for many of the wrong reasons. Beyond our appalling double standard of criticizing Israel for killing known terrorists and their commanders while tut-tutting at Palestinian suicide bombings that intentionally kill and maim dozens of innocents, we are making the classic American error of pursuing short-term comfort over long-term benefits, pursuing the impossible goal of placating the Islamic world (impossible, at least, without countenancing the destruction of Israel). In theory, the goal of a Palestinian state makes sense and, in reality, its creation appears inevitable, so doubtless we must make the best of it. Our error is to imagine that the creation of that state will bring peace. On the contrary, it will only elevate the struggle to another level. Too many Palestinians are now the enemies of any peace that allows Israel's continued existence, and, beyond the near-Babel of rhetoric, for many militants the ultimate destruction of Israel is a far more captivating goal than the establishment of a rule-of-law Palestinian state that will require them to deal with an unsatisfying daily reality. We do not have to like everything the Israelis do to recognize that our long-term interests and theirs coincide. We will never find a resolute ally on the other side, and this new cockpit of crisis, from the Nile to the Hindu Kush (and perhaps beyond) consumes concessions with an insatiable appetite.

What is immediately relevant to a discussion of terrorism, however, is the metamorphosis that has been under way in the ranks of Palestinian terrorists. Over the past few decades they have evolved from a mostly secular, practical outlook with finite (if sometimes extreme) goals to an increasingly apocalyptic orientation. The shift is still under way, and terrorists of the more secular variety still exist, but fervent Islam increasingly trumps political calculation. A cardinal symptom is the increasing percentage of suicide bombers. Palestinians have long been willing to die for their cause (in many ways an easier alternative to devoting a life of hard work to the construction of a state and its infrastructure), but the terrorist who *might* die in the course of a daring operation is giving way more and more to the terrorist who *intends* to die as a consequence of his action. And if you compare the rhetoric of the 1970s and 1980s to the fevered declarations of contemporary Palestinian terrorists, their supporters, and advocates, the intensifying embrace of religion is unmistakable.

An analyst with no other knowledge of the situation would assume that this radicalization into apocalyptic religious behavior must be the result of the failure of the secular approach, but the actual situation is the reverse: The Palestinians have made impressive progress toward complete self-government and a state of their own; they have won an astonishing legitimacy in the eyes of the world, including the United States; and, except for the destruction of Israel, their original aims are well on the way to fulfillment. Another analyst might say that the pace has been too slow, that discontents were allowed to boil over. In retrospect, however, Palestinian progress has been relatively swift in historical terms. The source of the radicalization lies elsewhere.

The Palestinians, who are in many respects the most successful, educated, secular, and "Westernized" Arabs since the shattering of Lebanon a generation ago, have been catching the contagion sweeping the Arab world, if more slowly than in more backward regions. Increasingly, Israel is more of a mythologized object than a tangible reality (although for Palestinians the reality admittedly can be pretty harsh), more a demon to be slain than a state to be challenged. The thorough demonization of Israel is now the single biggest obstacle to any peace plan. While there always was a religious and civilizational element to the conflict in Palestine, the change over the past decades has been profound. No matter how generous the terms offered to a future Palestinian state, a substantial, deadly portion of the Palestinian population (to say nothing of Arabs of other nationalities) will never be satisfied, materially or, more importantly, psychologically. The Arab world's spiritual crisis, born of a generalized failure, needs the demon Israel (and the demon America) far more than it needs peace in the West Bank or Gaza. Israel is the great excuse for failure, and it will never be viewed as a mere tolerable neighbor.

The roots of the fervor that transmutes all too easily into an apocalyptic vision lie in the general failure of the Islamic world to compete. What had been a political crisis is now a massive psychological crisis. Some years ago, a popular work of history was entitled *The Madness of Crowds*. We are now dealing with the madness of a civilization. Of course, many readers will dismiss this as hateful or vicious thinking—and I personally wish the reality were otherwise. But the doubters have only to wait. Islam's sense of failure is only going to intensify (because its counterproductive behaviors and values will not change), and the apocalyptic, vengeful impulse will intensify in turn. It is one of the tragedies of the Arab world that a deadly, crippling segment among the Palestinians—who had at least a chance of performing competitively—has been collapsing backward into a medieval vision of religion just as they approach their long-championed secular goals. While it is impossible to predict the pace and scope of this transformation—and it may yet be stymied by Palestinian secularists, who increasingly realize that they, too, are in a battle with religious extremism—we may find ourselves hoping the blander forces of corruption, greed, and selfishness in the Palestinian Authority will somehow trump the fervor of the rising generation of believers. It is not only an unattractive position in which to find ourselves, but an almost hopeless one.

Elsewhere, the same phenomenon of transformation from practical to apocalyptic terrorism has taken hold broadly. Where once Islamic terrorists espoused sloppy versions of socialism, communism, Nasserism, Arab nationalism, or many another fuzzy-ism, they are now increasingly *Islamic* terrorists. It is a long way down into the darkness from the once-feared terrorists of Black September to the mass murderers of September 11. For all of us who have lived through the last half-century, it is astonishing to note that George Habash now looks moderate in comparison to the hypercharged, god-intoxicated terrorists of today.

As the Israelis have already learned, even if they cannot openly acknowledge it, there is no solution to this challenge, only a determination to survive on the most advantageous terms possible. A friend of mine commented, shortly after September 11, that "We're all Israelis now." He was correct, in the sense that our lives are no longer inviolable. But we have far greater power and wealth than does Israel, and better geography, globalization notwithstanding. We have the power to set the terms strategically, and even to fix the terms of most tactical encounters. But before we can do so, we must recognize how the world and terrorism have changed. And then we must have the strength of will to do what must be done.

FIGHTING TERROR: DOS AND DON'TS FOR A SUPERPOWER

1. *Be feared.*

2. *Identify the type of terrorists you face, and know your enemy as well as you possibly can.* Although tactics may be similar, strategies for dealing with practical versus apocalyptic terrorists can differ widely. Practical terrorists may have legitimate grievances that deserve consideration, although their methods cannot be

tolerated. Apocalyptic terrorists, no matter their rhetoric, seek your destruction and must be killed to the last man. The apt metaphor is cancer—you cannot hope for success if you only cut out part of the tumor. For the apocalyptic terrorist, evading your efforts can easily be turned into a public triumph. Our bloodiest successes will create far fewer terrorists and sympathizers than our best-intentioned failures.

3. *Do not be afraid to be powerful.* Cold War–era gambits of proportionate response and dialog may have some utility in dealing with practical terrorists, but they are counterproductive in dealing with apocalyptic terrorists. Our great strengths are wealth and raw power. When we fail to bring those strengths to bear, we contribute to our own defeat. For a superpower to think small—which has been our habit across the last decade, at least—is self-defeating folly. Our responses to terrorist acts should make the world gasp.

4. *Speak bluntly.* Euphemisms are interpreted as weakness by our enemies and mislead the American people. Speak of killing terrorists and destroying their organizations. Timid speech leads to timid actions. Explain when necessary, but do not apologize. Expressions of regret are never seen as a mark of decency by terrorists or their supporters, but only as a sign that our will is faltering. Blame the terrorists as the root cause whenever operations have unintended negative consequences. Never go on the rhetorical defensive.

5. *Concentrate on winning the propaganda war where it is winnable.* Focus on keeping or enhancing the support from allies and well-disposed clients. Do not waste an inordinate amount of effort trying to win unwinnable hearts and minds. Convince hostile populations through victory.

6. *Do not be drawn into a public dialog with terrorists—* especially not with apocalyptic terrorists. You cannot win. You

legitimize the terrorists by addressing them even through a third medium, and their extravagant claims will resound more successfully on their own home ground than anything you can say. Ignore absurd accusations, and never let the enemy's claims slow or sidetrack you. The terrorist wants you to react, and your best means of unbalancing him and his plan is to ignore his accusations.

7. *Avoid "planning creep."* Within our vast bureaucratic system, too many voices compete for attention and innumerable agendas—often selfish and personal—intrude on any attempt to act decisively. Focus on the basic mission—the destruction of the terrorists—with all the moral, intellectual, and practical rigor you can bring to bear. All other issues, from future nation-building, to alliance consensus, to humanitarian concerns, are secondary.

8. *Maintain resolve.* Especially in the Middle East and Central Asia, "experts" and diplomats will always present you with a multitude of good reasons for doing nothing, or for doing too little (or for doing exactly the wrong thing). Fight as hard as you can within the system to prevent diplomats from gaining influence over the strategic campaign. Although their intentions are often good, our diplomats and their obsolete strategic views are the terrorist's unwitting allies—and diplomats are extremely jealous of military success and military authority in "their" region (where their expertise is never as deep or subtle as they believe it to be). Beyond the problem with our diplomats, the broader forces of bureaucratic entropy are an internal threat. The counterterrorist campaign must be not only resolute but constantly self-rejuvenating—in ideas, techniques, military and interagency combinations, and sheer energy. "Old hands" must be stimulated constantly by new ideas.

9. *When in doubt, hit harder than you think necessary.* Success will be forgiven. Even the best-intentioned failure will not. When military force is used against terrorist networks, it should be used with such power that it stuns even our allies. We must get over our "cowardice in means." While small-scale raids and other knife-point operations are useful against individual targets, broader operations should be overwhelming. Of course, targeting limitations may inhibit some efforts, but, whenever possible, maximum force should be used in simultaneous operations at the very beginning of a campaign. Do not hesitate to supplement initial target lists with extensive bombing attacks on "nothing" if they can increase the initial psychological impact. Demonstrate power whenever you can. Show, don't tell.

10. *Whenever legal conditions permit, kill terrorists on the spot* (do not give them a chance to surrender, if you can help it). Contrary to academic wisdom, the surest way to make a martyr of a terrorist is to capture, convict, and imprison him, leading to endless efforts by sympathizers to stage kidnappings, hijacking, and other events intended to liberate the imprisoned terrorist. This is war, not law enforcement.

11. *Never listen to those who warn that ferocity on our part reduces us to the level of the terrorist.* That is the argument of the campus, not of the battlefield, and it insults America's service members and the American people. Historically we have proven time after time that we can do a tough, dirty job for our country without any damage to our nation's moral fabric (Hiroshima and Nagasaki did not interfere with American democracy, values, or behavior).

12. *Spare and protect innocent civilians whenever possible, but do not let the prospect of civilian casualties interfere with ultimate mission accomplishment.* This is a fight to protect the American people,

and we must proceed, whatever the cost, or the price in American lives may be devastating. In a choice between "us and them," the choice is always "us."

13. *Do not allow the terrorists to hide behind religion.* Apocalyptic terrorists cite religion as a justification for attacking us; we cannot let them hide behind religious holidays, taboos, strictures, or even sacred terrain. We must establish a consistent reputation for relentless pursuit and destruction of those who kill our citizens. Until we do this, our hesitation will continue to strengthen our enemy's ranks and his resolve.

14. *Do not allow third parties to broker a "peace," a truce, or any pause in operations.* One of the most difficult challenges in fighting terrorism on a global scale is the drag produced by nervous allies. We must be single-minded. The best thing we can do for our allies in the long term is to be so resolute and so strong that they value their alliance with us all the more. We must recognize the innate strength of our position and stop allowing regional leaders with counterproductive local agendas to subdue or dilute our efforts.

15. *Don't flinch.* If an operation goes awry and friendly casualties are unexpectedly high, immediately bolster morale and the military's image by striking back swiftly in a manner that inflicts the maximum possible number of casualties on the enemy and his supporters. Hit back as graphically as possible, to impress upon the local and regional players that you weren't badly hurt or deterred in the least.

16. *Do not worry about alienating already hostile populations.*

17. *Whenever possible, humiliate your enemy in the eyes of his own people.* Do not try to use reasonable arguments against him. Shame him publicly, any way you can. Create doubt where you cannot excite support. Most apocalyptic terrorists come from

cultures of male vanity. Disgrace them at every opportunity. Done successfully this both degrades them in the eyes of their followers and supporters and provokes the terrorists to respond, increasing their vulnerability.

18. *If the terrorists hide, strike what they hold dear,* using clandestine means and, whenever possible, foreign agents to provoke them to break cover and react. Do not be squeamish. Your enemy is not. Subtlety is not a superpower strength. The raw power to do that which is necessary is our great advantage. We forget that while the world may happily chide or accuse us—or complain of our "inhumanity"—no one can stop us if we maintain our strength of will. Much of the world will complain no matter what we do. Hatred of America is the default position of failed individuals and failing states around the world in every civilization, and there is nothing we can do to change those minds. We refuse to understand how much of humanity will find excuses for evil so long as the evil strikes those who are more successful than the apologists themselves. This is as true of American academics, whose eagerness to declare our military efforts a failure is unflagging, or European clerics, who still cannot forgive America's magnanimity at the end of World War II, as it is of unemployed Egyptians or Pakistanis. The psychologically marginalized are at least as dangerous as the physically deprived.

19. *Do not allow the terrorists sanctuary in any country, at any time, under any circumstances.* Counterterrorist operations must be relentless. This does not necessarily mean that military operations will be constantly under way—sometimes it will be surveillance efforts, deception plans, or operations by other agencies. But the overall effort must never pause for breath. We must be faster, more resolute, more resourceful—and, ultimately, even more uncompromising than our enemies.

20. *Never declare victory.* Announce successes and milestones. Never give the terrorists a chance to embarrass you after a public pronouncement that "the war is over."

21. *Impress upon the minds of terrorists and potential terrorists everywhere, and upon the populations and governments inclined to support them, that American retaliation will be powerful and uncompromising.* You will never deter fanatics, but you can frighten those who might support, harbor, or attempt to use terrorists for their own ends. Our basic task in the world today is to restore a sense of American power, capability, and resolve. We must be hard, or we will be struck wherever we are soft. It is folly for charity to precede victory. First win, then unclench your fist.

22. *Do everything possible to make terrorists and their active supporters live in terror themselves.* Turn the tide psychologically and practically. While this will not deter hardcore apocalyptic terrorists, it will dissipate their energies as they try to defend themselves—and fear will deter many less-committed supporters of terror. Do not be distracted by the baggage of the term "assassination." This is a war. The enemy, whether a hijacker or a financier, violates the laws of war by his refusal to wear a uniform and by purposely targeting civilians. He is by definition a war criminal. On our soil, he is either a spy or a saboteur, and not entitled to the protections of the U.S. Constitution. Those who abet terrorists must grow afraid to turn out the lights to go to sleep.

23. *Never accept the consensus of the Washington intelligentsia, which looks backward to past failures, not forward to future successes.*

24. *In dealing with Islamic apocalyptic terrorists, remember that their most cherished symbols are fewer and far more vulnerable than are the West's.* Ultimately, no potential target can be regarded as off limits when the United States is threatened with mass

casualties. Worry less about offending foreign sensibilities and more about protecting Americans.

25. *Do not look for answers in recent history, which is still unclear and subject to personal emotion.* Begin with the study of the classical world—specifically Rome, which is the nearest model to the present-day United States. Mild with subject peoples, to whom they brought the rule of ethical law, the Romans in their rise and at their apogee were implacable with their enemies. The utter destruction of Carthage brought centuries of local peace, while the later empire's attempts to appease barbarians consistently failed.

The New Strategic Trinity

Parameters, Winter 1998–99

At the end of the twentieth century, the more successful the state, the less important its military. In the early nineteenth century, Carl von Clausewitz, the greatest philosopher of war the West has produced since Machiavelli, created a strategic model based on the interplay of the state, its people, and its military. The concept was robust and useful, although it never applied to the United States, where the military was kept to a subordinate role unimaginable to a Central European of the Napoleonic era. Today, that Prussian theorist's model applies only to cankered, coup-prone countries, such as Congo or Paraguay, or to military-braced states such as Turkey and Pakistan. Every country in which the Clausewitzian model remains relevant is a failure. For successful states, where the military is only a tool of occasional or last resort—and not a domestic actor—the new strategic trinity describes the creative tension among the state, its people, and information.

Like all philosophers who gain public notoriety, Clausewitz has been simplified and often twisted in practice. A German Romantic forever misread as a rationalist, his core trinity examined the interplay of reason, passion, and chance, made manifest by the state, the people, and war. But even this more subtle distinction breaks down in our time. While chance still influences the battlefield, cultural determinism dramatically reduces the role of chance at the strategic level. An informationally empowered culture such as our own can be defeated by an information-deprived culture only if we choose to be, as we did in Somalia.

The Clausewitzian model was designed with balance-of-power Europe in mind, not the lopsided world of the new millennium. An archetypal German of his time, Clausewitz was forever torn between chaos and clockwork, between the drill field and the darkness of the soul. His death from cholera—in the same epidemic that killed Hegel—must have been a relief to him, absolving him of the need to finish his impossible work. While he remains worth studying, his value today lies more in his high-Romantic appreciation of the role of will in human affairs than in his interpretation of state-military relations (even his assumption of the state's rationality has crumpled—who would claim that today's Russia is a rational state, to say nothing of the Germany that immolated its soul in the ovens of Auschwitz?). And, if nothing else, Clausewitz whoppingly underestimated the importance of information in war, dismissing even the need for reconnaissance. He would have been baffled by America, and by America's success, in which the First Amendment leads directly to military victory.

We are the sum of that which we are allowed to know, and American citizens and soldiers are allowed to know more than any human beings in history.

This essay is not a commercial for computers, which are only one (albeit important) factor in the cognitive revolution dividing the world into winners and losers. Our sloppy rhetoric about the Information Age is ever short on specifics, and generally cites the wonderful volume of data now available to the average citizen as revolutionary. But that flood of information has the quality of an act of nature—immense, uncontainable, and irreversible—and, as with a natural flood, some countries and cultures prove better prepared than others to cope with the consequences. There are two salient factors that determine the success or failure of states and peoples in the postmodern age: the *quality* of information available to the population, and the *ability* of the population to discern quality information.

That sounds simple. It is not. Using the United States as the benchmark, only a handful of nations come close to the informational veracity of our society and the interpretive genius of our population. Our concept of objective facts, the complex cross-referencing within our culture that verifies facts, and the average citizen's ability to identify, accept, and exploit facts are the products of at least five centuries of social development—and possibly of a much longer period.

Consider a recent debacle internal to the American media. CNN, the world's most powerful news selector, broadcast a claim that U.S. forces employed nerve gas in Indochina. Even allowing for a general resentment of CNN within media circles, the speed and thoroughness of the self-correction process was remarkable. CNN had not respected the available facts, and the network's peers took them to task. CNN had to apologize publicly and fire at least a few minor players in penance.

Such a scenario would be possible only in North America above the Rio Grande or in Northwestern Europe. Elsewhere, it either would not have occurred at all because the government controlled or suborned the media, or, when it broke, other local media outlets would have jumped on the bandwagon and made even more extravagant claims.

This matters. Our "trivial" respect for the truth enables our economy, our government, and our society to function in the manner we Americans take for granted. We are a measuring culture, from gross national product down to the number of Americans who now prefer salsa to ketchup. We can't get enough factual data, and we demand that it be as accurate as possible.

Other cultures do not want to know. Consider our drug problem, which is certainly real. When I worked at the Office of National Drug Control Policy, we routinely heard complaints from drug source and transit countries that the United States was the world's greatest drug consumer, with the highest per capita addiction rate, and so on. As I visited country after country, it became evident to me that, along with select European and East Asian countries, we were the only ones attempting to keep honest books. Drug consumption and addiction rates appeared far higher in Burma, Thailand, India, Pakistan, Mexico, Brazil, the Caribbean, and a host of other countries (Myanmar/Burma may have not only the highest rate of heroin addiction in the world, but the world's highest HIV infection rates in its northern provinces). But in each of these countries, the empirical reality conflicted with their representational needs, or simply had no utility, and nobody bothered with it (Thailand is an exception). Each government and population found it more convenient to think of the United States as both the greatest victim and greatest victimizer.

The CNN Operation Tailwind/sarin-gas story also comes into play here, since no level of apologies and explanations will kill the story in the less-developed world. We may have moved on, but the belief that the United States used nerve gas against its enemies will live on through our lifetimes in countries where a lurid story is more appealing than cold truth (especially if the story "reveals" American wickedness). This includes not only countries such as Iraq and Libya that will use the instant-myth to justify their own actions, but most of the world. CNN has done irreparable damage to efforts to contain the chemical weapons threat.

Yes, there are Americans who believe the *National Enquirer,* or that our government is nothing but a layer-cake of conspiracies. But they are proportionately few—and they are almost always from the least-educated, least-successful elements of our society. In failed or superseded cultures, even elites believe the CIA is responsible when the plumbing doesn't work.

Consider Egypt. While a great deal of data is available to literate Egyptians, those individuals are not "truth literate." If you read the Egyptian papers, you will be astonished at the difference with which they interpret the world. The media is about cultural and national self-justification, not about reporting facts. In one brief stretch this year, Egyptian papers reported that Israel was behind the attacks on local tourist sites (a fabrication created by the government to avoid admitting a domestic terrorist problem); that Princess Diana had been murdered by British intelligence so that she would not deliver a half-Arab, Islamic half-brother to the heir to the throne (this story has astonishing credibility throughout the Islamic world); and that Egyptian schoolchildren were suffering convulsions because Israelis had slipped them poisoned pencils that infected them as they did their lessons (perhaps the best excuse for nonperformance since "The dog ate my homework").

A country or culture that cannot tell fact from fiction cannot succeed in the postmodern era, with its dependence on data to create wealth.

Our national ability to identify, accept, and absorb high-quality data may be our most underappreciated characteristic as a people. Consider the effectiveness with which Americans have learned to invest in stocks and mutual funds in the last decade or so. Starting from an initial distrust born of a lack of understanding and middle-class fiscal conservatism, a majority of our working citizens learned to exploit sophisticated investment instruments to improve their personal wealth and security, either through private investments or through retirement plans at their place of employment. Now there will certainly be market downturns and disappointments—but we have seen a revolution in the way our citizens develop wealth (as well as realizing Karl Marx's dream of the workers owning the means of production—through stocks and mutual funds). This has further enabled American business to expand investment and enhance productivity and profitability. While the total model is far more complicated than the outline given here, the description captures the essence of what has happened. The ability of our citizenry to learn something new, while largely avoiding false steps, is remarkable.

In much of the rest of the world, investment models either lag—concentrating on savings stashed under the mattress, or in passbook accounts, or held in physical property—or go entirely off the rails. As Americans were growing richer with reasonable security, Russians and Albanians fell for massive pyramid schemes—the Russian variant shook Moscow, while the Albanian one brought down a government and unleashed a civil war.

If a culture does not assign a high value to the unimpeded flow of factual information, it cannot make competitive decisions.

Informational dysfunction generally cripples two types of states or cultures. First, those which embrace comfortable myths over painful reality—such as most of the Islamic world and much of the former Soviet Union—and, second, those which attempt to restrict the flow of information, such as China or North Korea. Often, as in the cases of Saudi Arabia or Nigeria—and even otherwise-promising Turkey—states manifest both failings: the forcible exclusion of threatening information and the propagation of comforting myths. This amounts to volunteering for failure.

Information is a liberating tyrant. It insists on universal access and enforces an often-painful mental sobriety; in turn, it allows receptive states and cultures to compound their success. It is difficult to bring the vital importance of informational freedom home to Americans simply because it is taken for granted. Even those who would remove Darwin from our schools comparison shop for automobiles and expect that the available information will be accurate. We are so informationally privileged that it is difficult to get a perspective on the richness that pervades our daily lives. The news in the papers, on radio, or on television will be amazingly accurate by international standards, and even the most lunatic talk show is constrained in the lies it can proclaim. From stock market reports to the contents list on cereal boxes, information disseminated by business will be accurate. We even learn from television commercials—which today have an amazingly high standard of factual presentation, thanks to the competitive nature of our economy, our laws, and watchdog agencies. Our textbooks are as factual as we imperfect humans can make them, and even our politicians are usually forced to tell the truth. Our waking hours are passed in the most *accurate* environment in history, and access to the information that enables us to operate in our professions and improve our lives is nearly universal. When we choose, we can make informed decisions. We are part of a small minority of present-day humanity.

Economic data is the most difficult to accumulate and verify, and the speed of today's national and world economy makes the problem ever greater, despite our marvelous informational tools. Yet, we do a superb job of measuring that which can be measured. When Alan Greenspan makes a decision, the data on which it is based is imperfect—but superior to anything previously accumulated and filtered by mankind. Elsewhere, societies are designed to conceal data, or to obfuscate. Consider Russia, with its insurmountable economic problems. A concealing peasant culture formed the basis for the dishonest Soviet regime—and now "capitalist" Russia is plagued by inaccurate reporting and hidden assets at all economic levels. A state cannot move forward without sound data on which to base developmental and fiscal decisions. With its addiction to mythic data, Russia has no hope of gaining full economic health in our lifetimes—since each day it falls farther behind in relation to the states with which it must compete. We may, in the coming decades, see a return to autarchy among failing states, which may provide the highest level of poverty available to them.

Since at least the Civil War period, our economy has towered over our military. In time of crisis, that economy has enabled the creation of military establishments other states could not afford or sustain. While the paradigm has changed to the extent that the technological sophistication of some forms of warfare forces us to maintain a more substantial force-in-being than we did prior to the Second World War, even that larger force is dwarfed by the post-industrial, information-driven economy it serves. We will continue to need a strong, ready military. But our military today is less important to our nation than is our banking system—to say nothing of our educational system. Our military is essential—but it is essential only for limited purposes. It is the medicine we keep in the cabinet for emergencies. On a daily basis, our media has a vastly greater effect on the world than does our military.

Yet even our military is information-based and, when it is allowed to fight, its informational adeptness is a force multiplier so strong it cannot be measured (even by our measuring culture). A long time ago technologically, in Operation Desert Storm, we fielded an information-based military and won a victory so lopsided historians strain to find a precedent. Although our casualties could have been greater had we made worse decisions in some areas (and we could have been even more successful, given other potential decisions), the outcome of the conflict was never in doubt—not because we had the better troops or training or equipment (although we did, and each of these things matters), but because we had fielded a new kind of military. The fighting in Mesopotamia was as lopsided as any engagement of Maxim guns against spears.

Consider the way we handled information. In our Desert Storm force, junior enlisted personnel, from air planning staffs down to artillery battalions, had access to data of unprecedented volume and accuracy; had such data been available in the past, it would have been restricted to a few generals and staff officers. We shared data throughout the force, moving it with astonishing speed (although there were the inevitable gripes and real glitches). We have, without fully realizing it and certainly without planning it, *democratized* information within our armed forces. Of course there is still classified and restricted data, but from the reintroduction of "commander's intent" twenty years ago to the proliferation of computer terminals today, we are closer to "playing on the same sheet of music" than any military establishment in the modern age. This unity of vision facilitates independence of action. It is a devastating combination for an opponent to face.

We are already masters of information warfare, and fail to realize it.

Consider our opponent in Desert Storm. Saddam not only had access to far less information, but he hoarded what he got. Military reporting (inaccurate, in any case) went up stovepipes, and not only were services unwilling or forbidden to share data with each other, individual units would not pass data laterally. Saddam got distorted reports and clutched them against his chest. Orders went down the chain, but little useful data accompanied them. Saddam's subordinate commanders lacked the information to make intelligent decisions, even had they been permitted to do so. His forces did not know what was coming, and afterward they did not know what had hit them. It wasn't only the Iraqi military that was defeated, it was an entire culture.

Certainly, there are other factors that contribute to the success or failure of states and cultures, from their willingness to extend opportunities to their full populations to their appreciation of contract law. But that relationship between the state, its population, and information is the crucial determinant in our time.

This will be difficult for less adept countries and cultures to face. First, because it threatens their pride. Second, because the situation takes generations to put right. Examine the informational chaos in the former Soviet Union, where data had been falsified and restricted for seventy years. Sudden access to quality information in great volumes has not instantly redeemed any of the descendant states (although the Baltic states, with their different traditions, cultures, and shorter occupations, are making the most progress). For many citizens, unaccustomed to sorting the informational wheat from the chaff, the sudden flood of information has been unwelcome, psychologically destabilizing, and threatening. If a population has not been acculturated over generations (if not centuries) to an instinctive evaluation of the quality of information, it will lack decisionmaking criteria, will make bad decisions, and will blame its new-found freedom. This is exactly what is happening in Belarus, within the Russian right and left, and in the struggling populations of every other regional state. Instead of embracing facts, disappointed citizens are fleeing into comforting myths, from the Transcaucasus to the Polar Circle.

I do not suggest that the United States is perfect. I am astonished, almost daily, by the ability of some of my countrymen to believe incredible fantasies. Yet, on average, we are informationally empowered to a degree other states can only envy. Only the other English-speaking states approach our fact-wielding power, and only a few European and East Asian states are in the competition long term. The gap between these comparatively few successful nations and the many states and peoples failing to adapt—culturally, psychologically, or practically—to the demands of the postmodern world, with its informational foundation and uncompromising insistence on facts, will increase throughout our lifetimes. It will make for a very jealous, unstable, and violent world.

In Clausewitz's most famous dictum, "War is simply a continuation of policy through other means." We can update that claim as well. Today, information mastery is the enabler of both war and policy.

The Hourglass Wars

A version of this essay originally appeared in The Role of Naval Forces in 21st Century Operations, *edited by Richard H. Shultz and Robert L. Pfaltzgraff, Brassey's, 2000.*

The profile of our future enemies has begun to emerge from the fog of peace (contrary to Clausewitz, war is a great clarifier). With increasingly rare, anachronistic exceptions, these enemies will not be so foolish as to attempt to compete with us in the heavy-metal combat of ships, aircraft, and tanks. They will not bankrupt themselves in a conventional arms race or expose themselves to defeat in "honest" battle. They will arm themselves with the most basic killing tools and with sophisticated information technologies: sidearms and cell phones, machetes and modems, incisive low-density technologies and genocidal masses of humanity, child warriors and weapons of mass destruction. They will wage psychological and information warfare campaigns on levels we do not credit as military areas of responsibility. They will fight not for the transient human romance with statehood, but for belief systems, blood ties, clans and tribes, nationalisms exclusively defined, personal gain, revenge for incredibly imagined wrongs, and for the ineradicable joys of subjugating, destroying, and killing.

A graphic depiction of these enemies would look like an hourglass—the bottom broad with that most expendable resource of bullies, excess population. Simple armaments, from personal weapons to antiaircraft missiles and bombs, will be widely available to them. At the top of the hourglass, our most capable enemies will concentrate their resources on off-the-shelf technologies for communications, information manipulation, and cyber-attack; on lawyers and propagandists; on media coercion; on eliciting sympathy from third parties who can impede us in international fora; and on weapons of mass destruction. Their Pattons will be programmers, their Jacksons men of iron will, obsessive vision, and enthusiastic cruelty. From drug lords to warlords, and from charismatic nationalists to religious furies, the common trait of these enemies is that they will not present suitable targets for the military we have constructed.

Our forces are designed to strike where this new breed of enemy does not exist. For all of our intelligence and targeting capabilities, we will be shooting at thin air. We are aimed at the middle of the hourglass, at a mirror image of our own force. Despite recent technology purchases, our heavy combat systems remain so dominant in our thinking and practice that our information systems automatically become slaves to yesterday's combat tools instead of being used to expand the horizon of combat. Also, we are bound by extremely conservative, state-limited notions of the legitimate parameters of military activities. We are focused on boundaries—between states, between departments of government, between units. Yet, the state with its component institutions—no matter the degree of federalism—remains a hierarchical unit that reached its apogee in the late nineteenth and first half of the twentieth century. Today, some enemies we face are unrestricted by bureaucracy, charters, or laws.

Because of our dominant conventional power in all spheres—and our growing cultural-economic power—we feel no pressing need to change. Yet, the world is changing, and our own country is changing. There is evidence of our government's inability to adapt to this accelerating pace of change on many fronts. Congress has transitioned—without realizing it—from a proactive legislative body that shaped the country to a reactive body that struggles to catch up with the dynamism of our culture, economy, society, and technology. Our organs of justice are incapable of maintaining basic civility in our cities. The Immigration and Naturalization Service is increasingly part of our national security and has become a defender of our shores. We cannot even measure our economy accurately. Our private sector and culture are the most advanced, creative, resilient, and successful on earth. America dominates the world—our government muddles through, looking backward with longing.

Our new enemies, by contrast, are creatures of change—although they are by no means uniform in the changes they desire. Some seek regressive change, a return to an imaginary golden age. Others want to impose an unprecedented local dominion over their neighbors. Some just want the gold, while others cherish messianic dreams of a collective destiny. But they all will do whatever it takes to reach their goals, without counting the cost in human misery. Timothy McVeigh, not Albert Schweitzer, is the international model of the committed man.

We will fight saints and opportunists and everyone in between. Greed tends to be cleverer than Belief, but Belief is more enduring. We will encounter remarkable combinations: enemies intoxicated by medieval religious practices who nonetheless employ brilliant software programmers, mass murderers who understand the manipulation of our humanitarian impulses, and international gangsters whose most

effective defenses are our own laws. But our laws and humanitarian affectations otherwise mean nothing to men who will be
delighted to employ weapons of mass destruction so hideous
they are ultimately suicidal. The elation of man at the suffering
of others—especially, but not only, that of his enemies—is just
one of mankind's dirty little secrets. (It is difficult to find a
moral difference between yesteryear's gleeful spectators at public tortures or burnings and the audience spikes when CNN
covers genocide, mass rape, or terrorist attacks—we find horrors inflicted on others titillating, life-affirming, entertaining,
and satisfying on a level for which the English language, at
least, does not have a term.)

We are at the end of the Western conceit of rational man.
The Enlightenment—coincident with the largest-scale wars in
European history—is finished as a philosophical or sociological
model. Future historians will see it as a foolish and futile
attempt to match the social sciences to the Newtonian revolution, an endeavor equivalent to expecting men to behave with
the predictability of beams of light. Well, we are the darkest of
creatures, by far the most destructive, and we revel in it. The
most powerful weapon our future enemies will bring to bear
against us will not be submarines, or strike aircraft, or tactical
missiles, or software viruses—or even nuclear weapons. Their
most powerful weapon will be hatred.

Man loves, men hate. While individual men and women
can sustain feelings of love over a lifetime toward a parent or
through decades toward a spouse, no significant group in
human history has sustained an emotion that could honestly be
characterized as love. Groups hate. And they hate well. Despite
the lurking evidence in today's society, the unique quality of
the American experience and its galvanizing myths has dis-
armed our understanding of the enduring, invigorating power

of group hatred. In many societies, it is the fundamental human bond outside of the family.

While psychology—an infant discipline that is little more than astrology for the educated classes—has not begun to explore the layered paradoxes of mass behavior, firsthand observation makes several things clear: While individuals can readily sustain love for years or even a lifetime, it is rare for an individual to sustain hatred, which tends to wither quickly into mere dislike. We might even blurt out that we want to kill the boss, but we only rarely get around to it, occasionally even developing a perverse retrospective affection for him or her as we suffer under a successor.

Masses hate. In turn, hate bonds the masses. Love is an introspective emotion, while hate is easily extroverted. Americans—cultural descendants of religious zealots who survived only because of their ability to hate rigorously—reject this out of hand, conditioned by a heartless liberalism of culture that ignores human reality until its devastations begin to touch our elites. We refuse to believe that the "civilized" peoples of the Balkans could slaughter each other over an event that occurred over six hundred years ago. But they do. Hatred does not need a reason, only an excuse. Until Americans begin to grasp the depth, extent, and seductive appeal of the hatreds revived in our grave new world, we are unlikely to fashion an appropriate or fully effective military policy.

We have chosen not to examine mass behavior. Our dying century was one of mass *mis*behavior, of illogical descents into madness: brilliant Germany celebrating the most hideous cult of death since the Aztecs, Russia exterminating its natural leaders and culture, Japan embarking on a national killing spree, divided India's confessions painting themselves with blood upon independence, African tribes slaughtering each other until the death toll reached millions—these are just highlights. But such events have been so horrible, so inexplicable in terms of notions we cherish, that we have done our best to ignore them, studying the facts in neutered atonement, but avoiding the least serious study of the underlying causes. The truth is that we do not want to know the truth about ourselves.

And the truth is that human beings are different in mass. Our primitive level of science cannot yet differentiate the psychological from the biological changes when humans group together, but profound changes do occur. That is why military organizations work. We take an eighteen year old; condition him or her to our organizational values, norms, and goals; and accelerate group bonding through stress and ritual differentiation from human beings who are not members of the club. As a result, we can get that eighteen year old to do things under the intoxication of group identity that he or she would never do if left to his or her own devices. Psychologically, at least, masses are much greater than the sum of their parts.

Anyone who has ever been part of a mob, or who has observed one firsthand, has experienced sensations beyond the power of language to articulate. We change in groups, and the stronger the group focus, the richer the change, taking us to Srebrenica and Rwanda. There is a programmed longing for the group's approval—for belonging—that trumps biological self-interest as well as those values taken for granted over a lifetime. Fools, heroes, and monsters are all creatures of the mass.

Group behavior is self-accelerating until sated. That is why we see noble self-sacrifice, and that is why we see a half-dozen average college boys get drunk and commit a rape. There is a rapture in dynamic participation in group activities, from team sports, to warfare, to the slaughter of the innocents. While group behavior is too intertwined with other basic impulses—

still little understood—to explore further here, it appears that mankind is a violent herd animal hardly more domesticated than the wolf. Our understanding of our bodies, brains, and souls remains so primitive that future specialists will laugh at our ignorance the way we mock Renaissance plague doctors. And mass behavior is only part of the bad news.

Men like to kill. Not all men like it, and not all of those who do kill like it to the same degree. Some are surprisingly indifferent to it. Others dislike it and suffer from their participation in the act. But the latter are few; tearful regrets and self-pity do not equal repentance. We need to get past the lecturing of those who have never experienced violence to face the world as it is. Violence is psychologically rewarding for the victor, and it is addictive. It is cathartic and exhilarating, and lying about it will not change any of this. Violence and killing are as addictive as heroin and as intoxicating as crack cocaine. That is why spouse abusers do not commit abuse just once; it is why child warriors rarely can be redeemed; it is why gangs flourish and prisons fill; and it is why agreements signed in Bosnia bring pauses but not peace. For many men, there is no more empowering act than taking a human life. For some, it is the only empowering experience they will ever have. Just as junkies often do not have more attractive options than heroin in their lives, so do the killers among us lack competitive satisfactions. The Balkan bullies were losers or also-rans in peacetime. Civil war is the best thing that ever happened to them.

Many men—especially those who have lived privileged lives under conditions of peace—have had the killing impulse subdued. It is dormant, if not deadened. Likely the great majority of human beings today are not natural born killers. Only future science will determine the proportions of popular tendencies, but it is enough to rupture continents if only a small part of mankind remains psychologically "uncivilized." Conflicts, such as those in the wreckage of Yugoslavia or in Central Africa or in the Caucasus, are not triggered by well-organized mass movements, but by smaller groups of men unsatisfied with the recognition life has given them. Most men have something to lose; the most dangerous do not. Before catalytic events, the masses gossip and meander. Then the hard core of misfits begins the killing, and the spirit of violence proves contagious, activating the lethargic mass. The murder in an alley at night turns into the next morning's pogrom.

In the cathartic mass-violence phase, the misfit often becomes the messiah. And messiahs are best sustained through killing, through the creation of a threatening opposition that can be imagined as a force of evil, through fear. Nothing sustains collective violence like the individual's fear of retribution. After the mass intoxication, reality sets in. So does self-knowledge. In the former Yugoslavia, the biggest obstacle to an exhaustion we might pass off as peace is the individual's fear of what he or she has done, and the group's shame at its actions—a shame impossible to admit, which is why the shouting continues. As of this writing, Karadzic and Mladic survive, defended by their people, because to admit their wrongs would be to admit "our" wrongs.

We Americans are amazed again and again that others could continue to believe for so long in Hitler, or Stalin, or Pol Pot, or the media's thug of the week. We have been blessed by a lack of leaders who devour our individual identities. But those enemies with whom we must deal today and tomorrow cannot bear their inherited identities and will sacrifice themselves to alter them.

Even in the pogroms and slaughters, the majority rarely participates in direct physical violence. The crucial violence is usually perpetrated by a smallish number of actors, with lesser violence enacted by a larger circle, with still a larger group enjoying the spectacle of the violence and, perhaps, looting. Even in the atmosphere of the mob, different personalities crave different satisfactions. Mobs—and mass movements—can be uniform in their effects without being uniform in their behavior; although they desensitize members to behavioral standards and fears, the degrees of courage and energy still vary from individual to individual—and from mob to mob, from cause to cause, from upheaval to upheaval.

Usually, when the eruption is about deeply held values and supernatural convictions, the violence is worse and participation fuller. Fights between religious parties or groups of different racial or blood identities tend to excite the broadest participation—especially if the different parties have long coexisted in the same space, since nothing excites jealousy, hatred, and fear as does the mystery of the different neighbor (even if the differences appear inconsequential to outsiders). We expect foreigners to be foreign; we demand that the folks next door conform to our beliefs, values, language, and appearance—and damn them for the slightest transgressions. Interestingly, one of the most enduring and pervasive themes in the ignition of human conflict is the myth of the abducted child taken for ritual purposes by members of an evil minority come among us, from horrid medieval fantasies of Jews kidnapping Christian infants for blood worship to contemporary propaganda about third world children kidnapped so that the rich can use their body parts for transplants or arcane cures. (The story that AIDS is a Western tool to ravage the third world is a reverse play on this—and it has been given remarkable credence abroad; a related confabulation is a Malaysian leader's recent insistence that financier George Soros "diseased" his region's economic success; yet another is the Russian and Romanian conviction that Westerners willing to adopt disabled orphans are out to weaken the local gene pool.) We may dehumanize those whom we do not know, but those we do know are more likely to dehumanize us.

There are near-infinite variations in the details of mass behavior, and the phenomena must be explored scientifically, dispassionately, and honestly. For initial purposes, however, the commonalities are key: men like to kill; humans change in mass; masses hate instinctively; a small number of instigators can lead the mass to commit atrocities its individual members would shun in isolation; violence is addictive and cathartic; the fear of retribution long outlives the joy of action. Perhaps worst of all, the most effective ways to deal with mass behavior are either to let it run its course or to kill so many of the participants the effect is debilitating and intimidating for a generation. Both options are unacceptable to the Western conscience (at least as embodied by our elites). We will continue to focus on human rights, while our enemies enjoy an excess of the human commodity.

The next century will be one of excess population in the least absorptive regions; of destabilizing informational availability decoupled from the capacity to understand it; of continued sociobiological revolution; and of enraging wealth for a minority of the earth's peoples, with real or perceived deprivation elsewhere.

Information is already the most destabilizing factor in our world, and the situation will worsen. Exacerbating the confusions of information overload, we are engaged simultaneously in altering patterns of human behavior—the relationship between men and women, and the content of work—that have existed largely unchanged since human beings began to self-organize. We live in a period of such powerful change and dislocation—physical and psychological—that the collapse of the Roman Empire looks glacial by comparison. The grail of individuals and masses alike will be the quest for an excuse for their failures. They will find it in a return to crude, intoxicating systems of belief and valuation—wronged gods and stolen patrimonies. The result will be intermittent euphorias of hatred, stunning violence, and ultimate failure that then begins the cycle again. Much of humanity is returning to the days of witches, anti-Christ, and self-willed apocalypse. Only today the forces of evil are associated with female emancipation, computers, and satellite television. And, to a great degree, these neo-traditionalists are accurate in their fears. While we concern ourselves with markets and quality of life, much of humanity will imagine itself engaged in a struggle between good and evil. Even if the entire world learns English, we will never understand one another.

The broad pattern of discontent, disruption, and violence is predictable. Specific events often are not. Violent mass movements develop after the pattern of epidemics, not classic wars. The visible build-up period may be only a matter of weeks or months, or perhaps a few years. Governments tend to believe it is in their self-interest to hide the symptoms until it is too late. The infection breaks out—usually in a densely populated urban area. (Villages are capable of great cruelty, but it takes a city to get genocide moving efficiently.) It spreads rapidly, if not ruthlessly contained, and the pattern of its spread is not fully predictable with present tools. The "epidemic" feeds on itself, with intercommunal violence taking ever more victims on both sides (or on multiple sides), constantly upping the ante. You go from a backstreet confrontation, to a pogrom, to an ethnic cleansing campaign and civil war, to attempted extermination and regional destabilization—roughly the pattern in the former Yugoslavia, in the multiple murder fests in the Caucasus and Transcaucasus, in the Indian neighborhood. The alternative pattern is state- or leadership-sponsored genocide, as in much of Africa, in the Armenian holocaust, in Germany's culturally suicidal campaign against the Jews, in regional efforts against the Kurds, in Chinese efforts against minorities, in Indonesia.

An objective examination of these phenomena might find them far more predictable than present analytical tools allow. We eventually figured out where plague and cholera originated. Far from examples of spontaneous combustion, these disturbances tend to occur in societies that have slipped from or have been thrown out of equilibrium. Intercommunal violence appears to be the programmed response of unbalanced societies seeking to "right themselves." The formula may prove as simple as high school physics.

When, as during the Cold War, cultural ecosystems are kept artificially in disequilibrium through the exertion of external pressure, they are apt to react explosively in a self-correcting action when that pressure is finally removed. (Freedom can very quickly become the freedom to kill.) The notion is so crude and fundamental it is probably true. If so, inserting large foreign entities—such as the 10th Mountain Division—into the system, seeking a new balance, will only delay resolution. Should this model be correct, the success of our interventions would be statistically predictable: The greater the degree of resolution achieved by the target society before our arrival, the likelier we are to facilitate recovery. Intervention in a society in the fits of disequilibrium would be wasted effort, except to the extent it made us feel good about ourselves or we were willing to remain as occupiers.

There are a great many related issues deserving study, from the devaluation of human morality that occurs with urbanization to the anthropology of normative behaviors and their regulatory role in restricting individual and mass violence. The issue of appropriate—and necessary—weaponry is vast in its possibilities, import, and moral dilemmas, from crowd control weapons to new weapons capable of altering human behavior. But the fundamental requirement is for an open confrontation with ourselves that demands truth seeking as to who we really are and why we behave as we do. We must begin by overcoming our vanity about the level of our self-knowledge. If it is to deal with humanity's violent diseases and not merely their topical manifestations, our military must study mass behavior.

Heavy Peace

Parameters, Spring 1999

Peace is expensive. When the peace is our own, no expense is too high. Peace is the cradle of our greatness. Although we Americans freed ourselves through war, we formed ourselves in peace. But when the peace is the peace of others, far from our shores and faint in its relevance, cost matters. Usually, the financial price is minor compared to other national expenditures. But the cost to our military establishment, already slimmed to fragility and poorly structured for missions short of war, can be exorbitant.

It is a calculus our military feels, but fails to adequately understand and explain. The world we knew is gone, replaced by ferment, confusion, and contradiction, and no comprehensible global order is likely to reemerge in our lifetimes. In this age of opportunity and danger, our military clings to traditional solutions based upon a romantic and superficial reading of history. We praise a past we do not understand, imagining rare virtues where there were only struggling human beings like ourselves. The reality of America's military past was too often one of institutional mediocrity redeemed by wealth, courage, and blood.

That mediocrity is again apparent in our approach to new technologies and consequent institutional change. Instead of exploring the possibility that new technologies might change the way we organize for war and conflict, we limit ourselves to the selection of technologies that allow us to improve traditional organizations. Our military is accumulative, not innovative. We graft laser designators onto muskets. It is as if America's surgeons were to insist that yesteryear's operating techniques remain indisputably the best, and that, although they welcome sharper scalpels, all further innovation would imperil the health care system. In this era of American triumph, only two major American institutions continue to resist the future: blue-collar unions and our armed forces. The unions have a better case.

The mathematics of readiness have altered radically, but we have not deciphered the new formula. The deployment of a reinforced brigade cripples multiple corps. Instead of reforming dysfunctional structures, the Pentagon tries to avoid missions, with little regard for differentiation between their importance. Thus, our national leadership sees the military as stubborn and willful, when our generals and admirals are, in fact, bewildered.

This situation will worsen.

Although history is littered with treaties cobbled together from ill-matched parts, marking pauses between rounds of violence and not true peace, the forms of "peace" have rarely, if ever, been as various and uncertain as they are today. The subsequent Cold War notwithstanding, World War II ended in exultant clarity. We knew who won, and the losers knew, unmistakably, that they had lost and must submit. Then came Korea, with notions of modulation and fantasies of diplomatic nuance alien to our national soul. Korea made Vietnam inevitable.

Meanwhile, a sliver of Asia has enchained American troops and policy for nearly half a century. We may unreservedly support South Korea while nonetheless asking if the peace on the 38th Parallel was well wrought.

Still, the times were such that Korea was our fight. Our involvement in Indochina, too, made strategic sense—it was the execution that was botched, at every level above tactical combat. But while we focused on the final manifestation of our century's contest between good and evil—and it was no less than that—another face of conflict reemerged all around us, sculpted by unleashed desires and ineradicable hatreds.

The "little" conflicts of the 1960s and 1970s, erupting while America was otherwise engaged or licking its wounds, established the new paradigm. From the Congo to Cyprus, from Northern Ireland to the Indian subcontinent, the best peace was uneasy, and the rest had to be enforced and then guarded. Focused mightily on the Soviet Union—and ever fearful of another Vietnam—the American military looked away as nations decayed and slaughters spread. Our peacekeeping deployments were treated as exceptions, aberrations. We died in Beirut, uncomprehending to the last, but stayed in the Sinai. We descended on impoverished islands like tourists with guns, and soon went home as tourists do.

Then came the 1990s. Somalia. Haiti, poorest of the poor. Macedonia. Rwanda and eastern Zaire. Bosnia. After the squandered triumph of Desert Storm, we lingered in the Persian Gulf, watching as the dictator we spared tormented his people and played peek-a-boo with the UN surrogates we supported only with a hollow presence and hollower rhetoric. On a lesser scale, we sent observers to Cambodia and Abkhazia, and to the contested border between Ecuador and Peru. Of all these problems, only Haiti directly affected the United States—

because of a wave of desperate migrants whose longings shamed and worried us—and only our Gulf engagement had an economic rationale. The rest were Cabinet conflicts in which we deployed because diplomats and their camp followers persuaded the President that engagement was either in our political interests or a moral requirement. But our military went, as it will go again and again. Meanwhile, the average American could not readily locate a single one of these territories on a map—and, frankly, he or she is none the poorer for it.

We live in an age of "heavy peace." What passes for peace now might be a temporary exhaustion of warring parties, or a clever move by one side to buy time, or a new status quo that no one will admit. Each demands military observers and, increasingly, troops to guarantee the peace that blood has made.

The Department of Defense has deceived itself, hiding from the truth, and then, in the case of Bosnia, it deceived Congress, for motives still obscure. Bosnia's peace is one of mutual unhappiness, of corruption and stagnation, in which even those who do not want a renewal of conflict would be swept along by a sense of inevitability, were our troops to leave today. For the Serbs, unhappy and unsated, the situation is akin to Trotsky's "Neither peace nor war." For the Bosnians, it is a chance to build an army while living on charity, and the provisional temper of the Dayton Accords allows the Sarajevo government to postpone all difficult choices. The Croats are consolidating gains that were disallowed by the spirit, though not the reality, of the Dayton Accords. And we have convinced the warring parties that our military's presence is essential to their peace. Nonetheless, in 1996, an election year, the Chairman of the Joint Chiefs of Staff told the elected representatives of the American people that our troops would be home by Christmas—while, in the Pentagon, the contours of a follow-on force were already under discussion. We may be in Bosnia as long as UN elements have been on Cyprus—for a generation.

A border away, we insist that the question of Kosovo will not be answered by U.S. ground forces. That claim may prove to be correct. But there will be other Kosovos, and, whether for strategic or humanitarian reasons—or just muddled impulses—we will not be able to resist them all. I do not seek to judge morality or human obligation here (I am myself as uneasy with inaction as with action). This essay seeks only to highlight the price our military is paying and will continue to pay, with interest.

We cannot enter upon such commitments under the assumption that they will be temporary and brief. Some may last only a few months (or the day it takes to evacuate U.S. citizens). But in this troubled, hate-filled era, we will witness more civil wars, more state and regional dissolutions, more fragmented borders, and more factional strife than our consciences will be able to absorb or our military able to cover. Presidents, frustrated or inspired, will send our military to address some of these problems, if only because the military is usually the only tool left on the shelf (and always the most impressive). The next century will, indeed, be an American century, but it will be a century of difficult American choices, and it is unlikely that we will always choose wisely. Military readiness is essential—but the military must be ready for reality, not for its fantasy war.

We tolerate a self-deluded, "no-mores" military—as in no more Vietnams, no more Task Force Smiths, no more hollow forces, no more sexual harassment, and now, no more Bosnias. We might as well attempt to solve the crime problem by declaring that there will be no more crime. It is useful to learn from your mistakes, but abject foolishness to define yourself by them. And no matter how loudly we shout these negative battle cries, the willingness of Americans, or at least of their elected leadership, to intervene is loosely cyclical—just eccentric enough to prevent forecasting—and it is not dependent on military readiness or willingness.

Sometimes, indeed, our military will get lucky and avoid undesired commitments. I am only afraid that it will avoid them at the wrong times. The Pentagon is much more apt to acquiesce to minor efforts that do not much matter than to major involvements that make a strategic difference, or that prevent a significant regional threat from emerging. Our national tendency is to delay doing the inevitable until the cost soars.

One way or another, we will go. Deployments often will be unpredictable, often surprising. And we frequently will be unprepared for the mission, partly because of the sudden force of circumstance but also because our military is determined to be unprepared for missions it does not want, as if the lack of preparedness might prevent our going. We are like children who refuse to get dressed for school.

Yet in an age when those who make our national decisions have not served in uniform and do not understand either the technical or human dimensions of military operations, our forces consistently look capable in ways they are not—and too expensive and powerful to be left on display when the President is out of options and key interest groups or foreign leaders are clamoring for American action. We are going to go to school, whether or not we have learned our lessons.

To be fair, this problem transcends the military sphere. The U.S. armed forces are the victims of a world that won't hold still—a bloody, hate-drunk world that refuses to make sense to those charged by election or appointment to determine America's role in it. Perhaps the saddest loss of our time is the destruction of the Liberal myth of innate human goodness. That myth was noble, if naive. Yet, before its destruction, that myth shaped the generation that dominates Washington today, a blessed generation untouched by physical danger, and the policies they attempt continue to reject all evidence of man's fallibility. It is the inevitable disarray of those policies that leads both to the frequent use and the frequent misuse of our military.

It is hard to watch the stumbling of those men and women who imagined—or continue to imagine—that a "peaceable kingdom" might descend upon this globe. They are reduced to what we might christen a Charles Dickens foreign policy. Like the feckless Mr. Micawber in the novel *David Copperfield,* they simply keep hoping that something will turn up.

In this era of heavy peace, the United States does not really have a foreign policy, only a shifting array of prejudices and infatuations, habits and hopes. And the grim truth is that we may never have an integrated foreign policy again, no matter who sits in the Oval Office or which party sets the terms of government. While we may reasonably expect a more mature grasp of international reality from a future administration, the world may have grown too complex for a classic, "unified field" foreign policy in the style of a Metternich, Bismarck, or Kissinger. One size no longer fits all—consider how swiftly the Clinton administration's "universal" support for democracy and human rights broke down, defeated by trade priorities and global economics, by strategic calculations and cronyism (our government has not made a peep about human rights or democracy in Saudi Arabia, for instance), and even by the administration's ludicrous, destructive infatuation with a vision of Russia that has nothing to do with Russian reality.

At the risk of using a technoid cliché, our traditional hierarchical, pin-striped image of foreign policy is giving way to interactions webbed in a complex-adaptive system. Our foreign policy establishment no longer shapes the world, but responds to it, too often in confusion and haste. Our difficulties arise because we have not recognized the profound nature of change. We keep longing and striving to do things the old way. At present, the best-integrated of our multiple foreign policies are those crafted by the Secretary of the Treasury and the Chairman of the Federal Reserve, while the Secretary of State plays on the margins. Even our media have a vastly greater effect on the world than does Foggy Bottom. Yet, the Department of State will not change without a fight. And that fight will be waged with our military forces, in broken countries and in hopeless foreign streets.

The future will not depend upon which mission a coy military condescends to accept, but upon those missions—often intractable—that will be thrust upon it. Ours is a disproportionately small force relative to its requirements, yet disproportionately expensive relative to its capabilities. It is small in its one-deep (sometimes none-deep) ranks of special skills and painfully short of human capital in general, and it possesses ever less flexibility and staying power. It is expensive because we buy the wrong systems with such enthusiasm. We prepare for our ideal missions, while the real missions must be improvised at great expense to readiness, unit integrity, and the quality of life of our service members.

Although the thought grates in the face of current wastefulness in the realm of procurement, our defense budget is too small. Yet, recent increases may hurt rather than help. While a very real personnel crisis continues to deepen, the military refuses to make hard organizational and acquisition choices. It is likely that only Congress has the capability to force change at this point—yet Congress bears much of the blame for the current situation, as the Hill continues to favor defense procurement over military personnel and meaningful reform. The soldier will always be the subject of patriotic rhetoric, but he or she is rarely the object of enduring concern. The soldier contributes blood to military campaigns, not dollars to political campaigns or boun-teous contracts to voting districts, and that will forever be his or her undoing. To a lurid extent, our military has turned into a business endeavor, and its business is not readiness.

So when we deploy a force to patrol ethnic or religious divi-sions—this heavy peace that weighs upon our times—the drain upon troop strength, and the stress upon a criminally austere supply and maintenance system that must support fickle, over-engineered military technologies, is crippling. One middling deployment rules out any possibility of responding to two major regional contingencies and constricts our ability to mount one full-blown expeditionary effort in a timely manner.

Yet, if these peacekeeping and peacemaking, policing and observing missions cancer our readiness, it is because we have done nothing practical to fight the cancer. We fight against the missions, instead of facing the shortcomings inherent in a force that has contracted, but has not changed with the times. There is no adjective harsh enough for a bureaucracy that places legacy systems and legacy organizations above the recruiting, training, welfare, and numerical adequacy of the men and women in uniform. While we continue to need heavy forces, their current configuration is fit for a museum, not for our likely missions. And most of our operational requirements for the coming decades will be for adequate numbers of well-trained, smart, fit, and psychologically robust soldiers. How can we fail to recognize the absurdity of a situation in which the most expensive military in history is chronically short of people?

In the 1980s, the U.S. Army fell in love with a dumbed-down version of the "culminating point," a sort of coloring-book approach to Clausewitz. Clausewitz was often quoted, but generally unread. In the original text, the explanation of how an army reaches its culminating point describes campaigns in which, as the army advances, it sheds numbers to man garrisons and guard its lines of communication. Eventually, as it progresses deeper into hostile territory, the attacking army becomes so weakened by its successes—by the requirement to leave ever more forces in its wake—that it loses both adequate mass and decisive momentum. The enemy has grown stronger not in absolute, but in relative terms. That is the culminating point.

While dreary wargames spawn imprecise discussions of tactical or operational culminating points, the U.S. armed forces, and especially our Army, are on the way to a strategic culminating point—without even fighting a war. If we do not reverse negative personnel trends and expand our practical forces, we will be so pared down by noncritical commitments over the coming years that we will defeat ourselves. Again, this is not an argument against executing the missions—we have no choice when the President orders us to go—rather, it is an argument against dismissing the strategic reality in favor of our professional desires.

Numbers matter. And we don't have them. Even the systems we plan to buy come in ever smaller numbers, as their cost, specificity, and complexity increase. Lobbyists and retired generals employed by defense contractors argue that it takes a decade or more to bring a new system into the force and that we cannot delay. But how long do they think it takes to build competent officers, warrants, or NCOs? Who will do the commanding, planning, training, and mission execution that employs our outrageously expensive, slightly improved systems? And who will walk the foreign streets and patrol the back roads where those systems are useless?

It bears repeating that the conflicts of the coming century will be human conflicts, and that these will require a human response. Even in Iraq, where the fruits of victory turned out to be an elaborate game of hide and seek (except for the Kurds and the Marsh Arabs, for whom our victory meant ill-placed hope, then massacre), our best technologies were inadequate to ferret out a dictator's deadly secrets. While proponents of airpower claim it can accomplish every military mission by itself, infantrymen keep the muddy watch in the Balkans. Technology is seductive, but frequently irrelevant in the clinch. This age of heavy peace is the age of the skilled, disciplined soldier (and we may hope he will be backed by a firm and wise national leadership). And it is the soldier, above all, who is in short supply.

Various proposals to reduce the burden of peace operations on our forces have been floated along the Potomac. None is convincing. Certainly, contracted civilians (usually military veterans) can do a great deal where the threat level is low and firepower is not an immediate requirement. But issues ranging from legal status to enforcement credibility limit their potential in more dangerous situations. Essentially, military contract employees can provide a fig leaf for warring parties looking for an excuse to quit fighting, but they cannot stop or prevent violence. Contract employees can also serve in "gray area" jobs in which we do not want our service members to appear. But they are not going to take over responsibility for general peacemaking and peacekeeping. They are useful tools that expand our national capability, but they cannot be allowed to veer off the rails and become private armies.

Another proposed solution, offered in various forms, involves a two-tier military establishment: ready, fully developed elite forces to fight our wars, and a secondary, cheaper, constabulary military to do the jobs the "fighters" don't want to do. Apart from the impossibility of recruiting international garbage collectors, the argument founders on cost analysis (it would not, in fact, be cheaper), inevitable jealousies, and the damage that consequent reductions in the number of combat units would do to our forces. Besides, we already have a "B-team" of less and less ready forces on active duty.

Our forces are respected as peacekeepers specifically because of the combat power that stands behind them. A secondary force, unprepared to conduct sustained combat operations, would not only prove ineffective, but unwanted internationally. UNPRO-FOR, the United Nations Protection Force, offers a classic example of the inefficacy of such a force. The paradox of successful peacekeeping is that it relies upon a recognized warmaking ability (as well as upon the will to employ that ability).

Lastly, some academic theoreticians have proposed saving money by hiring foreign forces—either recruiting individuals or hiring existing units—to do our dirty work for us. This is the kind of "thinking" that comes from sedentary, overnourished males who have read too much soft-core military history. First, the legal ramifications would be insoluble. Second, such forces would have neither the practical capabilities nor the moral force of U.S. troops. Third, we would not be able to recruit or hire by unit from nations that shared our values and level of behavioral development (the Swedes aren't going to play—want some Liberian troops?). Fourth, it would drain money from our own defense and play into the hands of extreme liberals and defense contractors, both of whom would be glad to cut our military personnel accounts. Fifth, it would be politically impossible. Proponents of such nonsense picture a sort of Raj military, with loyal sepoys and tough Gurkhas doing the dirty work for our nation. But if the U.S. government ever recruited Gurkhas, we would take away their knives and warn them never to hurt anybody. It isn't even worth going on to the arguments that nations that must rely on mercenary forces are nations in decline—the image of darker-skinned foreign hirelings enforcing America's will in ravaged countries is not one we are likely to embrace.

At the end of the day (and for countless days to come), this will leave us with unwanted missions and an ill-matched military. Although our military leadership imagines it can change the missions, it would be far easier, and ultimately more useful, to change the force to fit the times. This does not mean discarding all heavy weapons and turning soldiers into policemen, as the Pentagon's staff drones characterize all efforts to reduce our military's structural obesity. Rather, it means fielding deployable forces, concentrating on the core issue of personnel, avoiding the purchase of new systems that perpetuate our deployment difficulties, focusing research and development on innovating the weapons of the future instead of perfecting the weapons of the past, and reforming our thought, doctrine, and training to better reflect the world as it is and will be.

But the crux of the problem is people. We must have soldiers of adequate quality in sufficient numbers, and they must be well-trained and appropriately equipped. When we think about the Army of the future, for instance, we must stop thinking from the division down and start thinking from the soldier up—the middle level of the force is the anachronistic level. We must learn to embrace the missions that are inevitable if we want to avoid the missions that are hopeless. Through our honest participation in our nation's struggle to modulate foreign crises, we must rebuild the trust our military has lost because it has insisted that rescuing poor Eliza from the ice flow inevitably leads to another Vietnam.

In this age of heavy peace, hatred, genocide, displaced populations, and iron intolerance, our military will face enormous and repeated challenges that clash with our ideal of a military's use. We must stop pretending those challenges will disappear—that "something will turn up"—and prepare to meet them.

The American Mission

Parameters, Autumn 1999

We, the American people, have reached the end of a two-and-a-half-century crusade that defined us and changed the world as profoundly as any event in history. For a quarter of a millennium, we fought empires. Now, those empires are gone—every one—and we do not know what to do with ourselves. Our present enemies are vicious, but small. They cannot excite us to a new national purpose. The United States is suffering from victory.

Pentagon officials struggle to justify the purchase of $350 billion worth of unnecessary aircraft, while our diplomats sleepwalk through atrocity and our foreign policy is an incoherent shambles. None of our outward-looking institutions has grasped the dimensions of change. We need to break 250 years of habits we did not even realize we had. Our national cause, never articulated or even consciously realized, was to break the imperial hierarchies that held mankind in bondage. In 1989, as the last and worst of the old empires fell, we won a complete victory, and found ourselves unprepared for the fractured world the struggle left behind.

The verities and cherished villains are gone, and we have entered an age of small-scale evils. We crave a great, new American mission, and policy circles feel confusion and malaise in the new threat vacuum. The mightiest American foreign policy tradition is gone—a tradition that predated our existence as a country. We are a people formed in opposition, and that opposition was always to empire. Now there is no mightiness to oppose, no galvanizing evil, but only hard-to-locate countries where bloody shreds of mankind butcher neighbors.

We began under English dominion, opposing the French empire in a struggle that culminated in the mid-eighteenth century. If America's independence began at Lexington and Concord, it found its inspiration on the Plains of Abraham before Quebec, where colonial militiamen learned how easily an empire might fall. Next, we fought the greatest empire of the age, Britain itself, to champion the political and economic rights of man. A first war drove the British out, while a second confirmed their relegation to the Canadian margins of our continent.

Then we fought the Mexican empire and cut it in half. Our subsequent Civil War was an internal purge, cleansing from our soil the last European notions of hereditary authority and human subjugation. It was an Americanizing bloodbath that ended the first phase of our anti-imperial struggle, consolidating the physical shape of the United States we know.

The second phase of our crusade began with the Spanish-American War, a globe-spanning conflict whose brevity and relative lack of suffering have always obscured its importance. This time, we not only defeated a European empire, but destroyed it. It was not a local revolution against colonial overlords, but an international assault upon colonial possessions. No matter that Spain's imperium was little more than a carcass—this was a watershed in history, the death knell for the old European empires. The Spanish-American War was note-worthy, too, because it was our first war against a distant "evil empire." Spain's treatment of its Cuban and other colonial subjects both moved us and gave us an excuse to grasp its treasures. It proved an addictive model.

Japan observed the low price we paid, then emulated us half a dozen years later, when it attacked the other decayed European empire with dominions in East Asia, the Czar's Russia. Japan won brilliantly, then launched itself as an upstart empire that would end forty years later, in humiliation, on the deck of an American battleship.

The First World War was a conflict of discontents that were not ours, a hacking off of Europe's diseased limbs by the afflicted body itself. That great European civil war fatally weak-ened the remaining empires, while spawning new ones. America's late entry aligned us against three more empires: the Second Reich of Germany, Austria-Hungary, and the Ottoman Empire. Although we hardly engaged the latter two, we guar-anteed their destruction.

In the Second World War, America saved the world from unspeakable tyrannies. This is an unfashionable, but absolutely accurate way of putting it. For all the valor of crumpled Britain and agonized Russia, the United States decided the outcome. In doing so, we destroyed the Japanese and Nazi-German empires, as well as the operetta empire of Fascist Italy. Fatally weakened, the British and French empires collapsed of their own weight after the war. Only the Soviet incarnation of the Russian empire, a domain of figurative and literal darkness, remained to represent the imperial idea of human subjugation.

In 1945, we found ourselves guarantors of a world we barely knew. It is not surprising that we made tragic mistakes, but that we made so few. During the Cold War, the complexity of our struggle increased. The force of arms proved weaker than the force of ideas—ours or theirs. In Korea, then Vietnam, we found ourselves engaged with a grisly empire of ideology. Yet, the populations against whom we fought were fighting their own anti-imperial struggles. The United States fought anti-imperial wars against anti-imperialists fighting to expand a totalitarian empire. The Cold War was an age of paradox and moral erosion—as dark as it was cold—overshadowed by the ever-present threat of nuclear cataclysm.

At the end of this last struggle, those who believed that man should govern himself from below had defeated those who believed that man must be governed from above. In that sense, 1989 marked the end not of a mere quarter millennium of human history, but the climax of man's entire previous history of governance. Certainly, many a local tyranny remains around the world, but they will not prosper. The future belongs to citizens who control their own governments. All else is a vestige.

When the Berlin Wall fell, we were triumphant and at a loss. We opened the door to mankind's future, but closed the door on who we had been for so long. Along the way, we had become an empire ourselves, if of an unprecedented kind. Ours is an empire of culture and economic power, not of military occupation and physical enslavement. Nonetheless, the nation that defined itself as David has become the last Goliath.

We destroyed the old world, but lack a useful vision for a new order. Since 1989, too much of humanity has failed to live up to our ennobling rhetoric. Our victory over the last of the old empires unleashed forces we failed to anticipate, the zealous butchers wrapped in religion and ethnicity. Perhaps all that is left to us is a long minding of brute children.

We destroyed or helped destroy eleven empires in this 250-year epoch, while the remaining few—Portuguese, Dutch, Belgian—died of decay. The fundamental difficulty remaining, apart from mankind's innate tendencies, is that those empires twisted the world into unnatural shapes. Although the empires are gone, the treacherous boundaries they established remain. Empires drew borders based not upon popular preference or human affinities, but as a result of conflicts, competition, and compromise with other empires. Often, borders were defined in ignorance of local affairs or even of geographical detail. Lines inked—or sometimes crayoned—upon a map determined the fate of millions. Those borders remain a plague upon our times.

The United States, history's most powerful force for human liberation, now finds itself in a perverse and ill-considered position. Due to inertia and the fears of bureaucrats, we have slipped into the role of defending inherited, utterly dysfunctional imperial borders. Our Department of State, administrations drawn from both parties, lawyers, and academics all oppose "violations of sovereignty" and even the most logical and necessary amendments to borders. Future historians will be amazed at America's actions across the past decade. One administration initially tried to convince the Soviet Union to remain together, while successive administrations opposed the breakup of Yugoslavia, an entity as unnatural as any cobbled-together state could be. In our addiction to stasis and our obsession—for it is nothing less than that—with "inviolable" interstate boundaries carved out by imperial force in a different age, we are putting ourselves on the side of the empires we destroyed. America thoughtlessly supports oppression because we find the lines on the map familiar and convenient. The ghosts of kaisers, kings, and czars must be howling with glee in hell.

We must rethink this blind and destructive policy. Instead of using our might in vain attempts to force those who hate one another to live together—our "no-divorce" approach to foreign policy—we should lead the way in developing mechanisms to amend borders peacefully—or as peacefully as possible. Of course this will be difficult to do, for many of those in power profit from the present arrangement, and the sufferings of the powerless do not move them. And justice will be relative, for the redefinition of many borders will involve population transfers: Even when statistically just, such changes will prove unfair to many individuals. Amending borders is not a formula for a perfect world, only an approach to improve the present one and lessen slaughter.

The alternative is ethnic cleansing, genocide, and violence without end. We cannot force a man to love his neighbor. And, most important, redrawn borders and population transfers work. Those conducted at the end of World War II in Europe resulted in the longest period of peace in European history—until the disintegration of Yugoslavia, where borders had *not* changed.

Certainly the least mention of just borders will bring howls from every scruffy dictatorship in the United Nations. But should the nation that changed human history for the better and shattered the imperial model quake at the protests of Balkan thugs, African strongmen, or Asian authoritarians?

Of course, it will not be possible to impose effective changes in every case. Strategic interests will have their due, while some demands for independence arise only from a minority of the championed minority. At times, the ethnic mixing will be too complex, the claims too layered and contradictory. And in some cases the local populations will still have to settle their differences in blood. There will be no universal formula for success. Each case will have its own dilemmas. Yet, who believes that the present system is functional, or acceptable, or decent? As we prepare to enter a new millennium, it is time to discard those foolish prejudices that have come to pass for wisdom in world affairs. Bad borders will change. The only question is how those changes will occur.

Our American mission is not over. Although it is ever a temptation to withdraw from this troubled world and celebrate our own wealth and comfort, isolation is an impossible dream. The world is now too much of a piece, its interlocking systems too complex and binding. American interests are everywhere, or nearly so. We are condemned to work for global betterment.

This does not mean our current penchant for plunging thoughtlessly into random crises that happen to get our attention is a wise one, or that we must engage always and everywhere. On the contrary, a consideration both of where our greatest national interests lie and of what is actually achievable (and affordable) should always shape our web of policies—economic, diplomatic, and military. But there are two worthy goals that we might bear in mind:

First comes the practical matter of borders. We must either foster the creation of mechanisms to fix those that do not work or at least side with those seeking self-determination and not with dying, repressive regimes that cling to every inch of their "sovereign" territory. This world is changing, whether we like it or not. A fundamental change is occurring in the forms, shapes, and sizes of statehood, reflecting national downsizing in the aftermath of empire and the simultaneous development of transnational modes of cooperation. Although horrified diplomats and professors declare the impossibility of changing borders, they are wrong. Borders are already changing, from

Colombia's internal borders to the inevitable independence of Kosovo, from Central Africa to Indonesia. Our current position is at best naive. Because we do not support the legitimate aspirations of other human beings to live peaceably among those for whom they feel a natural affinity, we find ourselves time and again on the wrong side of history. It is time to come to our senses and lead the way to freedom once again.

The second worthy goal is support of universal human rights. The present administration, despite its deplorable failure to pursue that goal, began with appealing rhetoric. Long after the glare of scandal has dulled, America's enduring support for monstrous dictatorships will fascinate those who study our history. The mechanics of the present administration's failure were simple. Coming to office with a genuine desire, but not a commitment, to support human rights, the administration quickly found that it owed too much to too many interest groups—support for human rights was not compatible with business or diplomatic convenience. Early on, during a meeting of the National Security Council staff, the decision was taken to "give" Burma/Myanmar to the human rights advocates to appease them—anathematizing it for its human rights record and banning new American investment—while continuing to conduct business as usual with more important states such as China and Saudi Arabia, where human rights abuses were and remain far worse.

Support for human rights need not involve constant engagement on all fronts, with U.S. troops deployed each time a bully kicks a dog. Rather, we simply should consider this moral and practical factor when making diplomatic decisions. Strategic requirements will not always allow us to put human rights first in every case and country. But their consideration must never be fully absent. Further, dependable support for human rights—and a range of penalties for abusers—would bring our country both renewed respect and practical advantage. Respect for basic human rights forms the basis for both sound policy and good business. The partner state that respects the needs and aspirations of its own citizens is apt to be a dependable partner, but the dictator always comes down in the end.

We have too often been on the wrong side of a popular revolution. We no longer have even the excuse of Cold War polarities to explain our penchant for supporting oppressors. When the Russian government slaughtered tens of thousands of its own citizens in Chechnya, we hastened to assure Moscow of our unreserved friendship. In the Balkans, we cut deals with dictators time and again, only to watch the torrent of blood expand. In Indonesia, we clung to yesterday's corrupt regime even as the people pulled it down. Especially in the Middle East, we kowtow to regimes that oppress and abuse women, torment and even kill those of different faiths, and utterly reject democracy. These are inexplicable cases of the strong allowing the weak but intolerant to set the terms of engagement. We garner no respect, but are despised for our hypocrisy and fecklessness. We desecrate our heritage each day.

Americans attempt to defeat proposals they do not like by simplifying them to death. The propositions sketched above will be misinterpreted—purposely—as a call for sending in the Marines, or launching a quixotic global crusade, or even supporting the bogeyman of world government. I advocate none of these things, but only an intelligent approach to change, a moral stance where one is possible, and a recognition that wishing away the desires of oppressed populations will not keep foreign borders intact.

As for sovereignty, it is the privilege of the just, successful state. Any state that butchers, or even oppresses, its own population forfeits any claim to sovereign rights. Recently, we heard repulsive arguments that attempts to stop mass murder and ethnic cleansing in Kosovo infringed on sovereign territory. By that logic, Hitler would have been acceptable had he killed only German Jews. States exist to protect and benefit their populations. That is the rationale for these United States. Shall other human beings be condemned in order to keep our atlases intact and embassy receptions on schedule?

If a state cannot control criminality, terrorism, or ecological devastation on its own territory and those problems adversely affect its neighbors—or the entire planet—may it still claim sovereignty? This is the argument of kings, not of the common man. At present, we pretend that ineffective or even criminal regimes are legitimate because we "know no other way." It is time to forge another way.

This world is one in which we cannot stand alone. While we must protect our own sovereignty, which is legitimate, earned, and beneficial to all, we must also recognize the need for teamwork. NATO served American interests well—and still does, despite that organization's need to evolve. The United Nations, pathetic, inept, and indispensable, has also brought us more advantages than disadvantages, from providing an umbrella for some necessary actions to giving discontented minor states the illusion of a voice. But NATO is a regional alliance, and will not span the globe. The United Nations remains ineffective in the clinch, not only because of its dreadful bureaucracy (which may, in fact, be a blessing, since it prevents the organization from doing much damage), but because it is too inclusive. No organization in which backward, vicious regimes, such as those of China or Russia, have veto power will change much of anything—least of all unjust borders, a digestive ailment from which both these gobblers of minorities suffer.

It is time to form a Union of Democratic Nations, of globe-spanning, like-minded states whose people live under the rule of law and choose their own leaders. We need a grand alliance that can act, diplomatically, economically, and, when necessary, militarily, for global betterment. Such an alliance would include only true democracies, such as most European states, our own country, and others such as Japan, South Korea, Brazil, Argentina, Chile, Israel, South Africa, and the sturdy English-speaking states down under and to our north. It would exclude false democracies, such as Russia or Malaysia. Corrupt democracies and those in which religious prejudice or ethnic favor is dominant would also be excluded, until they reform. This would leave out for now India and Pakistan, Mexico and Nigeria. The purpose would be to unite in an alliance those states whose behavior has earned them the right to support positive change in troubled regions.

It would also have to be an open alliance, in which a two-thirds majority and not unanimity would be required for action, and in which no member would be required to participate in a specific embargo or deployment against its will. It would, in short, be truly democratic and utterly voluntary. Such an alliance might even prove capable of timely action. At a minimum, it would be the richest, most powerful, and most desirable club in the world.

On the threshold of a new millennium, Americans can be proud. We have led the world a long way out of the darkness. But there are still miles to go. We destroyed the old hierarchies that wasted human aspirations and talents as surely as they squandered human blood. We broke the tradition of rule by fiat that stretched from Babylon to Moscow. It is hard not to see these United States as blessed and chosen.

We are very fortunate. And with good fortune comes responsibility. We are condemned to lead. This means we must stop clinging to the past, whether antiquated notions about the sacrosanct nature of a butcher's borders or the belief that what goes on beyond our neighbor's customs barrier does not concern us. It is not a matter of seeking "foreign entanglements," or compromising our own hard-won freedoms, but of doing what is best for ourselves, as well. A world in which men and women live freely and enjoy secure rights is the world in which our own greatness is likeliest to endure.

Killers and Constables

The Future of Conflict and the Continuity of the American Military Experience

Strategic Review, Spring 2000

The structures of conflict are changing, but the substance within endures. Obscured by technological developments that affect the strategic and operational levels of warfare—and even the architecture of some tactical encounters—we forget the human being at the core of all violence. He waves his bloodied arms, but we stare past him.

When American ideologues insist that "Guns don't kill people, people do," they make this point unwittingly—although people with guns kill considerably more of their fellows than those armed with pocketknives. The causes and executors of violence remain human. Killing tools enable, increasing the efficiency of violence, and their possession can be a temptation to use. But the drive to the deed is within us. War and its sibling murder are fundamental human endeavors. For the worst among us, they are fundamental pleasures. It has been so since the days of killers with rocks in their hands, and so it will remain. Any model of future conflict that does not place flesh and blood at its center is frivolous. The bloody-handed man will shape our future, as he has shaped our past.

And yet, ours *is* an age of rupture. Accustomed forms of conflict wane. New variants of warfare appear and old patterns of mass violence reemerge. This is an era of the destruction of old forms not only in the military sphere, but in cultures, societies, and economies. Future historians may term our centuries "The Great Change."

Nowhere are the changes more profound than in the field of political organization. The model of government that prevailed across humanity from Ur and Nineveh to imperial Europe and, ultimately, the Soviet Union is dissolving. The collapse of the Soviet empire marked not only the end of the Cold War, but a tidal turn in history. From now on, those regimes that rule a voiceless people from above, whether in Beijing or Baghdad, are on the defensive. We have entered the age of the popular will. This may not mean American-style or parliamentary democracy for the world, but it does insist that dictatorial rule by an individual or an elite group is outmoded and broadly noncompetitive—although its death throes may be long and bloody.

Nearly a decade ago, Francis Fukayama published an audacious book predicting the "end of history," meaning the triumph of democracy over other forms of government. He was more right than wrong, and only off a century or so on the timelines. From elections to the internet, innovations erode traditional forms of social control. The new millennium (we must remember, of course, that our millennia are a Western form of measurement) will begin with the People in the ascendant—although we cannot see how it will end.

Popular force is a cause for hope and fear alike. Given the savagery of history, which William James described perfectly as "a bath of blood," we may hope that power vested in common men and women will bring us closer to the peaceable kingdom (and without kings, at that). But the jury is still out on human nature, and the last decade of the twentieth century does not provide a promising example. At best, we may see a collective resistance to the great wars that reached their apogee in the industrial age. But we would be foolish to assume an innate human goodness for which there is no historical evidence. Indeed, many of the worst slaughters of the past decade resulted from group hatreds reignited. We may only have passed from mass wars to modular conflicts—to which our industrial-age military structures and idealistic worldview are ill-suited. Even the stylish notion that democracies do not fight other democracies should be handled gingerly. Democracy is too new a form for us to comprehend any deep liabilities that may be obscured by the prosperity of the past two centuries (and, especially, of the past few decades).

Even our imprecise language is a danger. "Democracy" is but a shorthand word for systems ranging from the painstakingly equitable, through the spotty but congenial, to those in which the largest tribe or ethnic group dominates the balloting and reads its victory as a license to oppress those of lesser power and number. Democracy—at its best the most decent form of government yet devised—is a promising child, but we cannot guarantee its adult performance, and democracy *as we know it* may yet prove a hothouse flower that cannot be transplanted between civilizations without suffering hideous mutations. We comprehend so little of the phenomena of mass behavior that we dare not assume that no human collective will vote for Armageddon.

Under the press of our day-to-day concerns, it is difficult to gain even a slight perspective. The crisis of the moment clouds our vision and heats our judgments, while the power of technology—less tested than democracy—inflates our sense of capability beyond reason. It is a paradox of our age that this era of mighty science is also one of resurgent human problems unleashed by systemic breakdown. We need not yet regret the death of kings, but cannot assume the masses will behave better. Casting off the chains of old hierarchies has accelerated the human experiment. But this greatest of experiments may yet go awry.

Meanwhile, Cain slaughters Abel in the Balkans and in Chechnya, in Kashmir, Aceh and East Central Africa, in Colombia and in Kurdish villages. While Western leaders dream of bloodless war, the knife and gun remain the currency of political decision in much of the world. We are Prospero surrounded by a thousand Calibans, hoping that our incantations work.

Never underestimate the savage, or the human love of comforting lies, or the power of irrational belief. The fundamental weakness of American foreign policy is that it is made by educated, like-minded men and women who cling to a rational model of human affairs against all evidence to the contrary. If you want to grasp the uproar in the world—and begin to cope with it—you need to consult those who would ban the teaching of evolution in Kansas, or who bomb family-planning clinics and drag mentally handicapped black men to their deaths behind pick-up trucks, or who believe their lives have failed because of government storm-troopers in black helicopters. Study Waco. Learn from Timothy McVeigh, the avenging angel of personal failure. *Ecce homo.* The soul in secession, not the government minister, is the threat of today and tomorrow. Whether armed with a sniper rifle or weapons of mass destruction, John Brown has replaced the cabinet minister as the threat to world peace. And John Brown is compelling, as no bureaucrat will ever be. The great wars of our fathers were waged between states competing for success. Tomorrow's conflicts will be spawned by failure and blind hatred.

One verity in all this is that, for the foreseeable future, civilized nations will need good soldiers and police to control human excesses. We may arm them with precision-guided ordnance and, ultimately, with killer satellites, but we had best insure they have muscles, bullets, and combat skills, as well. Man is ingenious. He will always find a way to martyr his neighbor. Until our weapons prove able to alter the human soul for the better, we must be ready and able to kill the killer.

In this age of change, I stress the continuity of human behavior and, perhaps, human instinct (issues of biological or cultural or complex causation remain unresolved, and those among us vain about the state of contemporary knowledge had better read Aristotle or Oswald Spengler to learn how wrong intelligent men can be about the wisdom of their age). We are primitives, and have barely begun to understand who we are. Ignorance is our lot. Yet, a few things are knowable. There is, for example, an obvious continuity relevant to the military future of the United States: Amid the tumult of change, the roles of the American soldier are a constant.

FROM FORT KEARNEY TO KOSOVO

Those who assail our present peacekeeping commitments attack America's military tradition. I do not suggest that all of these commitments are wisely conceived, only that America's land forces have far more years of constabulary experience than they have of combat—and the constabulary model increasingly includes our sea and air power as well.

Although they may be separately described, the American soldier's dual roles of combatant and constable are of a piece. Clearest on the Indian frontier, this was also the model for many of our foreign adventures, once we had begun the destruction of European empires in earnest. The Spanish-American War was brief, if epoch-making (the first destruction of a European empire by a non-European power), but our resultant "peacekeeping" operations, from peacemaking on

Mindanao to the occupation of a base at Guantanamo, have spanned a hundred years. Perhaps our most costly error of the twentieth century was too rapid a disengagement from Europe after World War I, abandoning a bad peace to vicious and myopic Europeans.

Indeed, benign peacekeeping is largely an American invention. Even on the Great Plains or in the Desert Southwest, the Army's role was far nobler than revisionist historians and present-day Hollywood will have it. The Army massacred (as did its enemies), but such events were rare. Frequently, bluecoats protected Indians against encroachment and violence. The settlement of minor quarrels punctuated slow careers, and the drabness of garrison life is unimaginable today. Repeatedly, the War Department argued for more equitable treatment of the tribes and the observance of treaties but could not win against the political force of settlers, concessionaires, the venture capitalists of the day, and congressmen unconcerned with matters of human decency. The dull and dusty role that occupied the frontier Army was the maintenance of peace. It often served as referee—and with tougher antagonists than the Balkans have produced—and negotiations with the "warlords" of that time occupied many an officer. Sadly, the Army also oversaw population transfers and the dispatch of refugees on a scale as tragic as that in Bosnia or Kosovo.

Even Reconstruction, following our Civil War, was an exercise in peacekeeping and nation-building, if uneven in its success. Federal troops faced precisely the problems American forces face today in the wreckage of Yugoslavia—resistance to the rule of law, mass psychosis, and ethnic (racial) hatred. But our greatest achievements in this field were the occupations of Japan and the American Sector of Germany following World War II. In Japan, the U.S. military wielded remarkable power—

and employed it remarkably well. In Germany, the American military set the standard of military-political behavior and, although the French and British regimes were harsher, the result was the integration of Europe's problem nation into a community of its neighbors.

The anomalous size of America's Cold War military establishment, sustained by a peacetime draft, obscured its sense of identity. Just as the ability to preposition unit sets of equipment in Europe created an Army mindset that ignores the need for swiftly deployable organizations and equipment, so, too, did the Cold War condition us to think of ourselves as a big-job military, meant only for titanic clashes of heavy metal, while lesser efforts were but a distraction from our purpose. Enamored of scope, scale, and grandeur, our military suppressed the memory and lessons of our Indochina wars as swiftly and fully as mankind suppresses the memory of pandemics. We saw ourselves preparing for a clash of giants. Now pygmies embarrass the lethargic titan we have become.

The traditional model of the U.S. military—and the one to which it largely is returning—is a compact professional force augmented, in times of crisis, by reserve forces and federalized militias, and then, if need be, by citizens with no previous military experience. Indeed, the greatest differences between the United States military of 1800, 1900, and 2000 are the current force's wealth, the smaller proportion of immigrants in its ranks, the crippling percentage of married junior enlisted soldiers, and the respect accorded it by the average citizen. Otherwise, the frontier trooper from Fort Kearney wears a flak jacket in Kosovo, the valiant men of Malvern Hill reappeared in Mogadishu (where their generals proved as near-sighted as they did on the peninsula), and the private who followed Scott to Mexico City awaits his deployment to Bogota. Even the whining from the Pentagon about the unsoldierly nature of Gen-Xers falls within the tradition of American officers complaining of the men who would redeem their battlefield errors.

The American fighting man—and now woman—has always been quick to question, irreverent toward folly, loyal in the clinch, and consistently underestimated by his superiors and enemies. Were we to pluck a soldier from behind the cotton bales at New Orleans or from a regimental garrison in warlord China and drop him into a U.S. platoon in Bosnia, he would (briefly) be impressed by the equipment, then he would sit down with the guys, bitch about the food and the stupidity of his lieutenant, square off with the man from the next platoon who dared criticize the same lieutenant, and fight like a devil, if the need arose.

He is a splendid peacekeeper. And he still patrols America's frontiers—no longer the national frontier we had assumed, but the international frontiers we have inherited—and where he once kept safe the settler, today he guarantees the order beneficial to America's strategic interests and, not least, oversees the transition from yesterday's hierarchies to popular rule. The complaints against his employment in this capacity that have merit are only these: Our forces are too few for a troubled globe; fighting skills do atrophy in occupation and constabulary forces (Custer's men could not shoot as well as their Native American opponents); and not all assigned missions have a reasonable chance of success. More infantrymen and selected increases in the number of support troops would reduce the first two problems. The third is political in nature and has to do with the naiveté and willfulness of our national leadership, which has come to see the military as an all-purpose tool to be used when the world does not behave as ivy-league universities teach that it should. Indeed, the political leadership's ignorance of our military's capabilities and limitations has become the number one obstacle to military effectiveness.

THE AMERICAN WHY OF WAR

The other strand in the American military tradition is, of course, fighting big wars. Russell F. Weigley's classic historical analysis of *how* those wars were fought stands up well, although it may need fine-tuning in the future. What we have failed to recognize, however, is the American *why* of war, the causes that brought us to the battlefield. Traditional explanations drawing upon sociological, political, or economic theory (each "discipline" more akin to astrology than to a science) are utterly insufficient. Nor do topical issues—ever more symptomatic than causative—drive a nation to sacrifice the lives of hundreds of thousands of its citizens.

Those who reach into the realm of human passions come closest to explaining the fundamentally irrational decision to go to war, but no single theory of causation suffices. Collective behavior is far more complex than any DNA code yet unraveled, and it is less understood than the structures of distant galaxies. Chaos theory and complexity studies, with their willingness to break down disciplinary firewalls, may move us closer to an understanding of why masses of men kill while their women collectively acquiesce to the dying of their men. In the meantime, only an interdisciplinary approach that examines both the component parts and the greater-than-the-sum-of-those-parts totality of a culture can shed even a faint light on the timeless endeavor of warfare.

My personal suspicion is that nineteenth-century thinkers were closer to the mark than we are, and that war is biologically ingrained, with the impulse aggravated or tempered by cultural environments. But I can no more prove this than others can disprove it. In our nascent understanding of the human beast, such issues are reduced to musings and emotional exchanges.

Yet, a few things can be known. On the most prosaic and obvious level, wars can be triggered by the action of an enemy, whether the attack on Pearl Harbor or the bombardment of Fort Sumter—yet, even here, the complexity of the response remains incalculable. Why, in 1812, did a weak American state go to war with mighty Britain over minor provocations, while superpower America cowered at the takeover of its Teheran embassy and the imprisonment of its diplomats by a mob? Leadership is not the only answer. We may generalize about behavior patterns; for example, Clausewitz's dictum that "War is a simple continuation of policy with other means" is a European, not an American, truism—for us war means that policy has failed. But the will to fight one war and not another, or to fight at all, goes deeper than any explanation yet offered.

Perhaps the problem lies in attempting to apply rational analysis to a most irrational act; indeed, the madness of war is closer to the phenomenon of religious hysteria than to any other collective experience. It is likely that future historians, looking back on the elaborate "predictive" models of conflict devised in the Cold War era, will find them hilariously quaint. Our strategic models bear no more resemblance to war and conflict than a mannequin does to a flesh-and-blood human being. We measure outward forms and ignore the essence within. When do our theorists of international relations use the word "soul"? We are a measuring culture, based on engineering, and what we cannot quantify we ignore.

To identify the roots of warfare—to barely glimpse them—leads us from approved academic paths, for the gulf between campus and combat is unbridgeable. We must enter the realm of the unknown, where intuition honed by experience is a better guide than any theoretical knowledge, and we must accept the probability of error. Indeed, the present trend in military exercises—structuring the wargame to produce a desired conclusion—may advance careers, but it will not advance our understanding. The path to wisdom leads through error, whether we speak of science, religious enlightenment, or a lieutenant maneuvering his platoon for the first time. Our fear of being wrong blinds us to our possibilities.

In seeking the "American why of war," a grand pattern suggests itself. I suspect that evolutionary theory applies not only to the individual, but to the vast human collective (and, as with evolution, involves many wrong turns—dinosaur civilizations—and consequent extinctions), and that the effect of human mass is to increase developmental velocity (far more Darwin than Newton there, and developments are by no means strictly linear). I find no other explanation for the comparatively rapid development of social organization, while the individual's qualities remain largely the same as they have been since the days of mythologized history—religious and secular myths resound because we have changed so little, when we have changed at all. There is such a striking difference between human organizational progress and the lack of development of the individual human's behavioral range that the lack of attention paid to the discrepancy is baffling. While individual behavior, apart from table manners and dress, has changed little since the days of myth, social and political organization has made clear, if uneven, progress. Boston *is* better than Babylon.

For better and for worse, the human collective is more than the sum of its parts. We in the West focus exclusively on the parts, and bar ourselves from understanding. In mobs and masses, the individual submerges. We resist this elementary fact.

Without conscious realization, though with an inchoate sense of destiny, Americans have gone to war under remarkably consistent circumstances. As I have written elsewhere, it appears there was a collective American mission to destroy hierarchies. Perhaps wiser men will find a better explanation for our warmaking patterns, but the consistency with which the American people have attacked, defeated, and ultimately destroyed empires captivates me. Apart from our constabulary efforts and minor interventions, it is all we have ever done.

Even before we were a nation, we fought the French empire and its Indian allies. Under British tutelage, we helped defeat a global empire on the Plains of Abraham. Next, we twice engaged the greatest empire since Rome's, the British imperium, and twice defeated it, seizing and guaranteeing our independence. Next, we dismembered the Mexican empire. Our Civil War cast off the vestiges of empire on our soil, human bondage and a landed aristocracy. (The surrender of Lee's army is as clean a dividing line between an old age and a new as can be found anywhere in human history—the world changed with that signature in rural Virginia.)

Then we ventured outward, dismantling the remnants of the once-great Spanish empire. That started the dominos falling, and, in less than a century—historically, the blink of an eye—we destroyed or guaranteed the destruction of two successive German empires, the Austro-Hungarian and Ottoman empires, Japan's upstart empire, the adolescent Italian empire, and, finally, the Soviet empire founded on that of the czar's. Those empires we did not fight against were fatally weakened by the wars that smashed the others. Even our Indochina wars were waged against an imperial ideology.

Perhaps all this was an accident, a quirk of history. Maybe our ferocious destruction of the European empires that climaxed millennia of arbitrary rule was only a statistically explicable winning streak on the roulette wheel of time, a variant of the infinite number of monkeys at an infinite number of typewriters (computer keyboards?) eventually producing the works of William Shakespeare. But even for those who would refuse or refute a grand pattern, the problems left behind by the destruction of those empires are real.

Now that the empires against which we fought are gone—every one of them—what is our mission? Not long ago I mused that all that was left to us was the minding of brute children, but that missed the complexity of the imperial wreckage. The geostrategic problems facing the United States today, and which will continue to face us for at least another century, are the result of imperial collapse. The ballyhooed "new world order" is, indeed, on the way, and we are destined to play the part of midwife, at least some of the time. But we cannot predict the ultimate shape of that new order, and its birth will be long and hard. We will not live to see the infant.

When political scientists speak of the "post-colonial era," they generally mean the period between the end of the Second World War and the fall of Saigon in 1975. This is as wrong a historical judgment as any ever formulated. The post-colonial era has barely begun. Five hundred years of European imperial domination, with its attendant deformations of global organization and cultural confusions, could not be redeemed in three decades. The post-colonial era is here and now and will endure beyond our lifetimes. If a new order emerges within the next century, that will be a remarkably swift resolution of today's problems. Around the world—even in the old imperial homelands—the human ecological systems we call cultures and civilizations were kept out of balance artificially for centuries. And, as in the laboratory, when a system is forced out of balance by external pressures, there is a dynamic reaction when those pressures are removed. The collapse of Europe-centered empires, from 1898 to 1991, removed the outside force. Now those human systems are seeking a new balance. It is a turbulent, difficult, and often bloody process.

The evolution of a post-colonial order is impeded by the residue of empire—above all by artificial borders. The frontiers Europe imposed upon the world, most notoriously in Africa but equally arbitrary from the Andes to the Caucasus or Kashmir, divide those who would live together and force together those who would live apart. Whether Hutus and Tutsis in Africa, or the peoples of the Balkans, the human mixes created by imperial horse-trading and imperial ignorance are the most volatile factor in the world today. While human hatred and attendant discontents cause violence around the globe, bad borders trigger the action.

Until the world community develops a more peaceable mechanism for correcting borders to reflect the popular will and, when necessary, overseeing population transfers, there will be no end to the ugly "little" conflicts pocking the globe. And there is, of course, no such mechanism in sight. On the contrary, one of the few things upon which the world's diplomats agree is the sanctity of even the worst borders. But those borders will change. The masses will change them. The only issue is how much blood will be shed and how many hatreds reawakened or deepened in the process.

There are a few hopeful signs, for the beleaguered, re-grouping nation-state cannot forever resist the thrust of history. Recently, the Secretary General of the United Nations took a major step toward recognizing that a claim of sovereignty is an inadequate defense for genocide or atrocity within the borders of a state, thus laying the groundwork for future humanitarian interventions. But the diplomatic processes will be slow and reactive, while the world's problems are highly dynamic. Diplomacy as presently practiced is a nineteenth-century institution encrusted with an elaborate twentieth-century superstructure. It is inadequate to the challenges of the coming century and cannot stay a butcher's hand before he kills.

The American mission continues, although with the emphasis shifted toward constabulary efforts. Mongrel whelps of the old regimes remain, and the Russian Federation bays over the corpse of Moscow's empire. Transitional "mini-empires," such as those of Indonesia, China, Iraq, Nigeria, Congo, Sudan, India, the former Yugoslavia, or Canada, are spinning apart or struggling to resist centrifugal forces.

The first challenges for Americans are mental. With our foreshortened view of history, we—and especially our diplomats—tend to assume that any country that exists today must always exist. (We even tried, albeit briefly, to persuade the Soviet Union to remain together, then argued for a unified Yugoslavia.) Yet, entire civilizations disappear. In our time, some states may break up—notably Indonesia, Congo, Nigeria, Iraq, Sudan, or even Colombia—while others will see their boundaries shrink—as they have in Yugoslavia and may in Russia and Canada. Some states, such as Rwanda or Venezuela, may see their boundaries expand.

Elsewhere, frontiers have begun to mean different things, whether in the European Community or in the world of e-commerce. The deluge of available information has sounded the death knell for hermetic states. While the world of 2050, when viewed on a map, may look largely the same as the world of 2000, such an appearance of stasis would be deceptive—the blood flows on the margins, both on Samuel Huntington's intercivilizational fault lines and within troubled cultures. A slight change on a map may represent a seismic shift in history, and, until maps reflect the evolving nature of regimes, the development of citizenries, and the local history of violence, they will be a weak measure of change. Boundary alterations will prove inevitable and often bloody, although they may appear relatively small when considered in a global context. But their impact will be disproportionate, and boundary issues, ethnic divisions, and regime transitions will spur the majority of American military deployments. Now that the empires are gone, we must put down their ghosts.

Certainly, the possibility of conventional war remains, but, statistically, such conflicts will be fewer than ever in human history. In our lifetimes, no power will challenge American fleets and air armadas with like forces of its own. If we fight a conventional war, it will be on land, with U.S. air and naval power contributing. But no state, not even eternally ill-tempered Russia, is trying to compete with America's conventional power. We have triumphed our way out of that part of our job.

Our combats will be *Kleinkriege,* for the most part, the little wars and uproars that will continue to punctuate mankind's ongoing transition from hierarchical rule to popular dominion. The term "asymmetrical warfare" is much in vogue, and it is appropriate—though appropriated for some very unlikely scenarios. To the extent that asymmetrical warfare means non-traditional strategies encompassing new disciplines, or enemies with a rusty Kalashnikov in one hand and a cell phone in the other, or the growing (though presently overstated) threat from weapons of mass destruction, the term is valid and useful. It only falters when it falls victim to fashion and is used to validate utterly ungrounded notions that cyber-warfare—dueling computers—will soon obviate the need for soldiers and Marines. This folly demands a brief discussion.

Without aligning ourselves with the English farm hands who destroyed the first threshing machines or the weavers who wrecked early mechanical looms, we may express some skepticism that a human owl at a computer will win the next war. While all dimensions of information warfare, traditional and innovative, must be rigorously examined and—when helpful— exploited, the current claims made for cyber-warmaking exceed the extravagant claims made for airpower by early theorists. Computer warriors are not yet even at the Giulio Douhet level of capability, but their claims exceed his by an order of magnitude, for even that Italian apostle of strategic bombing recognized that humans only resolve their greatest disagreements in blood.

Despite a few information-warfare monkeyshines during the Kosovo conflict, the computer advocates have not yet fielded their Lafayette Escadrille, and the 8th Air Force is a very long way away. Perhaps some sudden technological breakthrough will change the equation—and we must be ready to seize it, if and when it comes—but even should we develop the means to control or destroy every computer in an enemy's hands, it does nothing for us if the enemy does not have computers or does not rely upon them. Still most useful in the intelligence field, cyber-power has yet to find a means to stop the killer with the pistol or knife, and I am not certain it ever will.

Without ignoring cyber-war's potential, we must beware premature conclusions of the sort that led to the "nuclearization" of the Army in its Pentomic reorganization—on the eve of our decidedly non-nuclear Indochina wars—a period of good intentions and whopping misjudgments definitively analyzed by Andrew Bacevich. The fundamental problem remains human violence and physical destruction, not computer hacking. Cyber-war will doubtless expand the modalities of warfare in the future, but it will not replace the sticks and stones that break our bones until our own bones are rotting in the grave.

So we are left with an empire-breaking force and no empires left to break. Apart from combat itself, the greatest challenge facing America's armed forces is the need to cast off industrial-age convictions as to how a military should be structured and equipped. And only the military itself can carry out the nuts and bolts of reform—critics without experience in uniform only muddle the problem, with outlandish demands to cut the supporting "tail" that fail to understand how much of that tail has grown up to support the metastasizing complexity of contemporary forces, or that a dangerous degree of support structure already has been cut, and that arbitrary reductions in the rear cripple the "tooth" units that interest armchair strategists so exclusively. The only effective way to cut logistics requirements is to re-create the combat forces so that the demand for support is reduced. Meanwhile, a soldier who is hungry and out of ammunition, whose combat vehicle cannot be repaired for lack of spare parts, and who must rely on dubious medical care is hardly a sharp tooth.

Other critics argue that forces could be reduced across the board—at a time when our commitments are expanding and will continue to do so, despite partisan desires. Certainly, intelligent reorganization, especially of the Army, could increase the efficiency achieved within current end-strength. Ultimately, though, our forces are simply too small in terms of manpower, no matter how personnel are reallocated. This most-expensive-military-in-history is chronically short of people.

It has been said elsewhere, and often, that we need swift, lethal, expeditionary forces that can deploy without the need for lengthy build-up phases. The military, although its worldview is evolving, remains convinced that a weight-loss program for our matériel and organizations would sacrifice essential capabilities. That is the Cold War speaking from its grave. Lighter, swifter forces would return us to the American tradition—that of the frontier cavalry, or Smedley Butler's Marines in Central America, or the Navy that took on the Barbary pirates. We need a bigger smaller force, not a smaller bigger force.

If I am right and there has been a deep American mission, then it is only half accomplished. To finish it, we need vision, will, and a return to an expeditionary military.

ABOVE ALL, THE PEOPLE

While it may seem incongruous to end an essay on military roles and the strategic environment with a discussion of the domestic perception of our military, I believe the matter is integral. Our military, more than any in history, reflects the will of the people behind it. In war, it relies on popular support as no army under king or czar or dictator ever did. Far from existing apart from American society—as some current pundits would have it—our military, despite its Indochina interlude and the end of the draft, resonates more positively with the American people than it ever did in peacetime. It is the people's military, and the appreciation accorded it by the public is a remarkable development.

Indeed, a gulf does exist in our society, and it is dangerous, but it lies not between the people and a professionalized military, but between American society and a professionalized, increasingly hereditary government elite that despises the common man nearly as much as it does the common soldier. We have moved from an age in which government leaders sought to do what was best for the people to one in which the political leadership is convinced it knows what is best for the people, whether they like it or not. We suffer under the arrogance of those (in both parties) who have not worked for wages or served their country in uniform, but who are convinced they understand the workplace and warfare better than the lesser beings condemned to labor or fight could ever do.

Those who worry about a novel gulf between the U.S. armed forces and the American people have not bothered to open a history book. Do they imagine that the frontier Army, condemned to long years of service at remote locations, was part of the nineteenth-century American mainstream? How can they look at today's outwardly mobile, indelibly middle-class officer corps without comparing it favorably to the insular officer corps of the 1930s, with its undercurrent of crypto-fascism and its hatred of Franklin D. Roosevelt that far exceeded the shrug-shouldered disgust today's officers feel for the current Commander-in-Chief? Even the political conservatism that is undeniable in the officer corps is benign, patriotic, and non-doctrinaire. (In twenty-two years of service, I never encountered an officer as mindlessly conservative as the Budweiser Khomeinis currently plaguing Capitol Hill with their isolationist celebration of social discrimination, religious bigotry, and firearms.)

On the other flank, it has always seemed disingenuous to me that liberals, who decline to serve in the military and leave that tough job to more conservative citizens, whine about the military's conservatism. Liberalizing our military's political composition would be the easiest thing in the world: Those whose worldview tilts left have only to volunteer for uniformed service in sufficient numbers to shift the balance. Otherwise, it would become them to be quietly grateful to those who defend their lives of safety and privilege.

A few of the worst commentators imply that our military is somehow coup-prone. Evidently, they have not met any of today's top generals or admirals—officers so timid in the presence of their civilian superiors that they fail to give the forthright advice necessary for informed decisionmaking by our nation's leaders. Nor does the U.S. military have any tradition whatsoever of coup attempts. We never produced a man on horseback, not even McClellan or MacArthur, whose ego was Napoleonic in scale. Of those generals elevated by the electorate to the Oval Office, not one pursued a militarist policy or stayed a moment beyond his allotted term. Indeed, it was Washington who warned of wars of conquest, and Eisenhower who tried—unsuccessfully—to alert the nation to the rapacity of the "military-industrial complex."

Our military's tradition of loyal service is a worthy precedent for the world. Nor can I imagine the American soldier, with his built-in bullshit detector, following a would-be coup leader around the block. What we are hearing is not cogent analysis, but the ignorance of an intelligentsia that considered itself too valuable to serve in uniform and, steeped in prejudice, cannot comprehend the values and virtues of those who did and do join the military.

Indeed, except in the Marines, where discipline and a martial atmosphere still prevail, the danger is that our services too fully reflect the negative qualities of the society from which they are recruited—physical weakness, witless social accommodation, and a lack of moral courage—without demonstrating that society's positive qualities, such as creativity and openness to change. A military *must* be different from society in some important ways and, as John Hillen has written, we should celebrate the people willing to accept the burden of those differences instead of slandering the patriotism of our most obvious patriots.

Fortunately, the American people demonstrate more innate intelligence than the intelligentsia. The kindest of the discontinuities in the American military experience mentioned above is the unprecedented regard in which the average

American holds our military and the degree of trust placed in it as an institution. Poll after poll has demonstrated that the average citizen's trust in the military is as high as or higher than that in religious institutions—and far higher than that in other branches of government. This has never happened before in peacetime, and it is a gift of which our military must learn to make more effective use, whether in recruiting or in requesting judicious increases in the size of the force.

The American tradition has been to despise and distrust the military. Our founding fathers debated and debated again the wisdom of maintaining a standing army of even a few battalions, and the founding of West Point—perhaps the most valuable educational institution in America's history—was accompanied by warnings of the rise of a professional officer caste. Soldiers were regarded as incapable do-nothings with their snouts in the national trough (except, of course, in wartime), and the peacetime ranks of our regiments, from the Federalist period to the First World War, depended heavily upon impoverished immigrants. The middle- and lower-middle-class youth who join today in substantial numbers would not have dreamed of signing up for military service in a previous century—or even earlier in the twentieth century.

Ulysses S. Grant, America's greatest memoirist and, along with Winfield Scott, one of our two greatest generals, recalled how he proudly went for a ride in his brand-new lieutenant's uniform, only to have a "little urchin, bareheaded, barefooted, with dirty and ragged pants" howl in a crowded street, "Soldier! will you work? No, sir-ee. I'd sell my shirt first!" When, as a boy, I mentioned to my own father an interest in a military career, his response was dismissive: "Army officers don't make enough money to take care of their families." We have come a long way, even since the Vietnam era.

The trust of the people matters. For we are not, and have never been, a military tool for kings to apply, but a force shaped to a nation's cause. In Vietnam, a politicized, corporatist military leadership lied and betrayed a fundamental trust, yet most has been forgiven. Indeed, when those in Washington who did not serve worry that the lesson of Vietnam was that the American people will not take casualties, they are only remembering their own cowardice. With sixty thousand dead American soldiers, there were disturbances, but no revolution, and the electorate never chose a peace-at-any-cost President. The lesson of Vietnam was not that Americans will not take casualties, but that they do not want their sons' or daughters' lives wasted in European-style wars of political nuance and balance-of-power calculations. Give Americans a cause, or provoke them, and they will fight. But they want to win, and preferably win big, and they do not want to get bogged down in hopeless situations. Aroused, Americans are bloody-minded. (It is another myth that Americans don't like body counts—they *insist* on knowing the score, and it had better be in their favor.)

Our national weakness is not cowardice, but impatience. That, too, is in the American tradition, although we can fight long wars when we must. But we do not want our children viewed as tools of policy. And we want results. This is common sense of the first order, though the logic is invisible to a national elite divorced from society, the military, and a sense of reality.

WHERE DO WE GO?

In the words of a fine American author, retired Cavalryman Fred Chiaventone, the future is "a road we do not know." We must struggle to see a new century, but cannot be certain of what we will find tomorrow morning. We face innumerable challenges, many of which remain unwilling to reveal themselves, dropping only hints along our path. But a few problems are easy to articulate, if woefully difficult to solve:

—However much gritting of teeth is required, the United States must accept the reality of its global involvement. We cannot do everything everywhere but will be required to do a great deal in a great many places. We do not have a choice.

—Our forces must return to their lithe expeditionary and constabulary traditions in order to effectively and more efficiently cope with our global involvement. This means that the anomalous legacy of the Cold War must be cast off—in organizations, acquisition, and personnel policies.

—Our military must capitalize upon the high regard in which it is held by the American people to draw from a wider range of society, for the force of the future will need to be even smarter and more supple. Meanwhile, our military leaders must steel themselves to educate a governing elite that refuses to serve in uniform. The Commander-in-Chief and his paladins must understand the capabilities and limitations of military operations and the U.S. armed forces.

—We must prepare psychologically and practically for a century that will be violent and irresolute. The disruption of the world in the wake of empire, aggravated by the accelerating pace of technological, social, and economic change, will not subside into a new, more peaceful order for generations. No matter how the modalities of warfare may expand, we must remain prepared to fight at the most basic levels of combat.

These propositions take less than a page to write down. Their resolution will take much of the new century.

The Plague of Ideas

Parameters, Winter 2000–01

People sense, in these disordered times, that more has changed than words have yet expressed. Ours is a restless, unsettled age, straining between unprecedented hopes and old terrors, bounded on its shining edge by possibilities undreamed of even by our younger selves and on its darker horizon by vast, enduring misery worsened by rekindled hatreds. A world order that defined half a millennium, the age of European imperial domination, ended with the collapse of the Soviet incarnation of the Russian empire, and no unitary political system will replace it in our lifetimes.

We have entered a long, inchoate interlude, in which the concentration of wealth and military power in a minority of nations obscures the centrifugal nature of contemporary change. This is an age of breaking down, of the destruction of outgrown forms, of the devolution of power. The process of building again atop the ruins and reorganizing our societies will occupy us at least through the new century. We can be sure of little, only this: The speed of change is without precedent;

for the first time in history, change has come to the entire globe, if to differing degrees and with radically different results; and no state or society can rely solely on past forms to shape the future.

Comfortable security models and industrial-age warfare between competing powers seem as obsolete as Marxism, while, in much of the world, even the legacy of statehood left behind by the old empires is under threat. Ideological and physical control over populations crumbles relentlessly in every lagging state, and hatreds and blood ties bind where law cannot. Authority sputters, increasingly ignored, wherever humans find it inconvenient. Although the evidence had never fully disappeared, across the last decade the world's ruling and educated classes began rediscovering the primitive nature of man and his unattractive tendencies when civilized constraints are brushed aside. We, the long empowered, do not know what to do.

In these eruptive times, thoughtful men and women have voiced concerns about new or resurrected threats that ignore or exploit national boundaries, both those of robust states and borders that are little more than a pretense hoping for a bribe. Whether speaking of organized crime in its countless mutations, of terrorism, of epidemic disease, of financial manipulations, or of the assaults of digital anarchists, those who would alert us do good service. Yet, the greatest "transnational threat" is the closest kin to our brightest hopes. Of all the dangers globalization brings, none is so immediate, so destabilizing, and so irresistibly contagious as the onslaught of information— a plague of ideas, good and bad, immune to quarantine or ready cures, under whose assault those societies, states, and even civilizations without acquired resistance to informational disorders will shatter irreparably.

GLOBAL INFECTION

Several years ago—an antique age by technology's present measure—Americans enjoyed a brief infatuation with books and films about horrific diseases that, once unleashed, might ravage middle-class neighborhoods. While sober attention must be paid to even the least chance of new pandemics, whether sparked by global-man's intrusion on remote territories, or spread by adept madmen or the decay of biological warfare facilities in the former Soviet Union, the alarmists missed the epoch-defining symptoms erupting in front of their faces: For the first time in history, thanks to a dynamic constellation of communications tools, ideas can spread to the world's masses more quickly than epidemic disease.

Historically, disease outpaced data, with ideas lagging far behind. Rumors might precede the first fever in a village, but a serious plague reached more human beings far more swiftly than any abstract concept ever did. Disease moved at the speed of human travel—the same velocity as the rawest information. Ideas were, statistically, far slower. One traveling merchant or sailor, or simply a rat conveyed by ship, might infect a hundred overnight, and thousands within a week, but no saint or prophet ever persuaded men in truly epidemic numbers at epidemic speed. Concepts, to say nothing of true ideas, need explication, digestion, comparison, and practical experimentation before they find more than a transient, intoxicated acceptance. But disease did not rely on persuasion. Ideas moved at the speed of a man's feet, then of his beast of burden, next of his caravan or caravel, then of his automobile or passenger aircraft, only to arrive at rejection far more often than not. Disease did not offer choices.

Persuading people to accept a new belief, whether regarding the path to salvation or the efficacy of hygiene, required fortuitous historical timing, reserves of patience greater than any single life span, and sacrificial single-mindedness—to say nothing of the ruggedness and adaptability of the idea itself. Until the meridian of the European Renaissance, the Roman church was able to label every reform movement within its geographic sprawl a heresy and to suppress it before it could overturn anything beyond local hierarchies—since the church's enforcers could move as swiftly as any dissenting missionaries, as well as moving in considerably greater numbers. The creed riding on the back of a mule could not outpace a powerful bureaucracy.

Then the first information revolution struck, that of the book or broadside sheet printed cheaply on a movable-type printing press, fortifying the Protestant Reformation by enabling the spread of its timely ideas beyond the scope and speed of bureaucratic response. The book still moved at the speed of the human's means of transport, and it could not spread its "infection" with the vigor of the Black Death, but the equation had begun its long shift. The Reformation was the crude dress rehearsal for today's "information revolution."

Elsewhere, numerous societies, even entire civilizations, managed to seal themselves against contagious information from foreign parts. Japan, an island nation, is a classic example of a state that successfully turned its back on the world for centuries until external forces, empowered by informational synthesis, grew irresistible. China, vast and ever porous at the edges, nonetheless managed, through the power of its culture and the culture of its power, to hold the greater world at bay for thousands of years, its long introspection punctuated occasionally by invasions that were quickly digested. Self-satisfaction and perceived sufficiency, a sense of order perfected, made for a world within a world. Today's China, with its exposure to the greater world increasing hyper-geometrically, is a new entity— its evolving qualities akin to a chemical compound transferred from a vacuum chamber into the open air. Whether or not the reaction will be explosive remains to be seen.

Even in late-Renaissance Europe, Spain, the apotheosis of a Counter-Reformation regime, managed to close not only its own borders but those of its then-incomparable empire to unwanted influences and the information explosion of the early modern era—but, given its strategic integration into the European sys- tem, with destructive results. Self-deprived of the nourishing strains of Moorish and Jewish culture, and militantly opposed to northern Europe's secular innovations, Spain's vibrant culture stiffened and slowed, its economy withered (enervated by vast, annual welfare checks from the New World's silver mines), its statecraft grew impotent, its military slowly decayed, and the population lost the impetus to modernity. Theories that blame the Spanish decline on excessive military spending mistake the symptom for the disease: Spain was an early casualty of the first, primitive information revolution, as various information-resist- ing regimes are of today's deluge of data.

INFORMATION AND WEALTH FORMATION

Indeed, the fates of European states and peoples from the six- teenth century forward provide a rudimentary model for the successes and failures in today's world, when postmodern economies—not the governments lagging behind them— shape the rules of global interaction and even the United States cannot pretend to be a hermetic fortress. Consistently, those nascent European states that had the most liberal infor- mation policies dramatically outperformed those states or regions where the Counter-Reformation clamped down hard not only on religious dissent but on the sciences in their fumbling, haunted childhoods.

The most informationally liberal European state of its day, the Dutch Republic, prospered astonishingly even as it fought expensive wars to achieve and guarantee its independence. Only after a civil war permanently destroyed the darker powers of kingship and assured essential informational freedoms did more-populous, better-protected England outstrip Holland in wealth and power. Meanwhile, Italy, the cradle of the Renaissance, grew static, even backward, under the book-banning, idea-fearing, comforting and comfortable tyranny of the Counter-Reformation. Corrupt and hypocritical, somnolent and cruel, outwardly pious and privately lascivious, silver-age Italy resembled today's Iran, becoming, literally, a masked culture.

Inevitably, the greatest Western thinker about the power of information to drive change emerged in the British Isles in the guise of a political economist. Adam Smith, with his invisible hand of the marketplace, described two centuries in advance why the United States will continue to outperform mainland China, despite the astonishing energies the Chinese people bring to bear. Certainly, others have recognized the greater dimensions of Smith's revelation implicitly—most recently Thomas Friedman in his incisive book, *The Lexus and the Olive Tree*—but it needs to be stated explicitly: Adam Smith confined his observations regarding the self-correcting force of that "invisible hand" to free markets because, in his day, the economic sphere was the most liberal sphere within Britain (a situation reversed, with pathetic consequences, in the middle of the twentieth century and only put back to rights under Margaret Thatcher). Certain political and social truths could not yet be uttered, but the market increasingly was allowed to speak its mind from London to Glasgow and Edinburgh. Describing the capitalism he knew and could foresee, Smith intuited the dynamics of the information age precisely.

That invisible hand applies not only to the trader's domain, but to virtually every aspect of a healthy human society. Mature, informationally open societies, such as today's English-speaking nations of Western culture, are self-correcting, not only economically but socially, culturally, and politically. Citizens consummate change before bureaucracy can stymie it. The people vote not only with their wallets, but with each minor, mundane choice. Self-improving through dynamic trial and error, learning from the results of countless unfettered actions, these societies confound competitors with the speed with which they can innovate, seemingly defiant of physical principles equating mass with inertia.

Above all, states whose behavioral contours are determined by that invisible hand are practical. The past is preserved in museums, not in confining cultural strictures. Free societies guided by the aggregate effects of individual choices are not only the highest expression of human—and humane—attainment to date, they are far and away the most efficient. While their defense establishments, behaviorally distinct and informationally crippled, limp behind, states that do not constrain the flow of data nonetheless generate sufficient wealth to allow for a startling degree of military waste.

In these successful societies, the efficacy and worth of ideas are determined in the same way that the price of a household object is arrived at. Societal rules are not enforced from above or inherited uncritically from buried generations, but are selected and constantly refined from below by the living. The results are not only high-quality goods at low prices, but adaptive individual and collective behaviors that allow the population, statistically, to maximize its human potential.

The culturally liberal nations of the West are, in many-layered senses, marketplaces of ideas (to the dismay of intellectuals on the right and the left, with their totalitarian instincts). The citizens of such states have acquired, over generations, if not centuries, the internal compass necessary to navigate through the storms of information confronting them today. While a minority of citizens from the underclass and aberrant performers who make headlines with statistically irrelevant acts may believe that which is false or even lunatic, the average citizen makes highly effective economic, moral, and cultural calculations on a daily basis. Simply put, the good citizen has been culturally educated to pass the true-and-false tests of everyday life. He chooses what works best, then makes it work better.

This is no small thing. The most threatening aspect of today's information revolution is the power of comforting but false information to infect populations that lack the instinct for empirical reality that enables the West and key East Asian states to outperform the rest of humanity. Whether we choose as our examples the Gulf War, the economic competition of the Cold War, or the comparative successes of the two Korean states, it is absolutely clear that the side that deals with facts and freedom clobbers the side that indulges in fantasies and repression.

Instead of being self-correcting, societies deficient in the ability to discriminate between different qualities of information grow self-deluding, embracing reassuring myths—or comforting rumors—instead of adjusting to embarrassing realities. This is true not only of individuals and states, but of entire civilizations today. Serbia, the Russian Federation, and various sub-Saharan African and Middle Eastern countries offer trenchant examples. When an informationally inept population must compete with one that is informationally adept, the deficient state or region always loses.

Over the past few decades, the West often had to listen to self-adoring lectures from Asian tyrants whose informationally sluggish countries were achieving impressive growth rates. But those states were developing so quickly because they finally had entered the industrial age two centuries after it began. Meanwhile, the United States and a few like-spirited nations, derided as irresolute and faltering, took a deep breath and plunged into the post-industrial information age. The "social laxity" decried by authoritarians proud of a handful of new factories turned out to be the cultural foundation for the creation of fabulous wealth and power. Now, societies with undereducated, informationally stunted populations and a litter of smokestack industries find themselves left behind again, their national economies dwarfed by the revenues of individual Western corporations. Populations that make running shoes for populations that design computer networks have won the global economic booby prize.

CHOLERA AND THE TELEGRAPH KEY

Returning to the greatest familial establishment in economic and political history, Britain and the United States, the nineteenth century saw the beginning of the second information revolution, that which has accelerated and expanded so dramatically in our lifetimes. The first of the great cholera pandemics barely preceded the advent of the telegraph, and the latter was able to report news of later outbreaks ahead of their arrival. This was a critical step in the emancipation of information from the tyranny of physical transport. While it was an inefficient and inadequate tool for transmitting ideas, the telegraph could move limited amounts of data over great distances at a comparatively low cost.

A stunning innovation in its day, the telegraph nonetheless remained only the crudest precursor of the information dissemination devices of our time, since it was an easily controllable device, subject to governmental oversight in various forms, as well as to moral codes, physical infrastructure limitations, cost restraints, and the limited volume of data it could transmit. Better suited to deliver orders than insights, it remained a tool of the already empowered echelons of society, although its benefits increasingly reached the average citizen in the form of brief personal messages and the from-the-scene dispatches that accelerated the newspaper's phenomenal expansion in the nineteenth century. Of note, the English-speaking countries fostered the private development and use of telegraph networks, though with state backing at crucial points, while continental states favored greater governmental control—initiating a crippling monopolistic pattern in communications that still hampers Europe today, although the advent of wireless communications and international pressures are finally breaking down these antique inhibitors.

Likewise, when the telephone appeared, with its hint of anarchic possibilities, English-speaking nations were more likely to permit the private sector to exploit the technology—which the private sector did more swiftly and efficiently—while European states generally preferred state monopolies on communication, imposed as soon as each new means matured. When the radio crackled to life, both market democracies and repressive regimes saw its potential, although they read its utility differently. At one extreme, the United States adopted a liberal licensing program that diffused a large degree of communicative power to localities, while, at the other, the Soviet Union and Nazi Germany centralized control of the first broadcast medium. In the United States, the radio voice might speak *to* the government, but in the gathering European darkness the voice on the radio spoke *for* the government.

Radio marked the early adulthood of our information revolution. For the first time, *ideas* could be disseminated to the masses, along with unadorned information and entertainment (simultaneously, feature films and newsreels hinted at the power of today's media, although they reached much smaller audiences than did radio). Given our contemporary challenges, it is worth noting that the initial masters of the communication of ideas over the airwaves were men with messages of hatred, just as the internet has become a forum for hate speech, delicious delusions, and conspiracy theories today. Hitler may have been a poor strategist in the end, but he was a master of the broadcast medium.

Even in the United States, the early days of radio were marred by populist—and popular—demagogues, from racist politicians to men of the cloth who ranted against all things foreign in terms far fiercer than those used by more recent profiteers and panderers of the airwaves. It was not unlike the broadcast environment in many less-developed countries today. Only under the stress of worldwide depression, then of world war, did the voices of liberal democracy come into their own— one thinks, inevitably, of the incomparable Winston Churchill and of the savvy Franklin D. Roosevelt, whose physical disability might have marred his effectiveness in the soon-to-come day of television, but who was perfectly pitched for his fireside chats over the radio waves.

Yet, even radio was subject to laws, regulations, and, everywhere, ultimate state control. A small station in the midst of America might broadcast bigotry, as some still do today, but there are lines the disembodied voice may not cross. In wartime, underground stations might appear, or pirate broadcasts from offshore might enliven a peace, but radio is ultimately controllable, given the ease with which it can be monitored and its dependence on licensed frequencies.

In fact, the information revolution of our time has not been a straight-line march of progress. Television was, in one sense, a step backward in informational freedom, even as it increased phenomenally the amount of information it conveyed by adding the visual element pioneered by the cinema. While bringing images of a greater world to remote populations and capable of communicating sophisticated concepts through multisensory effects, television is a much more expensive endeavor than radio for those who want to originate a signal, to say nothing of offering attractive programming. With the television age came a reassertion of governmental control over broadcasting virtually everywhere, with corporate wealth a secondary filter in market democracies, and that control is only now experiencing a gradual breakdown with the advent of the cheap satellite dish.

Still, the synergy attained by all these communication means, as well as from teletypes and facsimile machines, voice and video cassettes, satellite communications, cell phones, and wireless, hand-held computers, began to reach critical mass as the twentieth century drew to a close. Increasing global prosperity, though uneven in its distribution, meant the proliferation of receivers—first radio sets, then televisions, then computers that, joined to the internet, finally give the common man a broadcast means of his own. The informational floodgates opened. Even comparatively simple devices destabilized societies, from the Soviet bloc to struggling states freed of both the colonial yoke and colonial order.

Ideas can now travel more swiftly than any human being— or disease. The global AIDS epidemic illustrates the point. An unknown sickness (admittedly slow-acting) appeared nearly simultaneously at different points on the globe, with fearsome initial results. But local infection rates and trends quickly diverged. In informationally adept, self-correcting societies, even libertine subcultures acquired the information about the disease necessary to modulate and then dramatically reduce rates of infection. In informationally deprived or self-mythologizing societies, the epidemic has raged on, devastating entire generations, states, and regions. In Africa, where idea transference remains a slow process due to both infrastructural and educational deficiencies, the disease moved classically along trade routes, its impact, scope, and nature initially unrecognized then long denied. Meanwhile the United States hyperbolized its own epidemic and waged multiple aggressive educational campaigns, resulting in transmission rate declines in those social groups that were informationally aware and responsive to fact-based arguments.

Today, we still hear heartbreaking denials of medical evidence from African leaders dumbfounded by the AIDS epidemic's implications, while, in the United States, the disease has been confined largely to micro-groups within social subgroups that are unwilling to alter self-destructive behaviors. Clearly, the ready availability of factual information correlates to low rates of infection, even adjusted for cultural proclivities and radically different levels of medical infrastructure. Today, vastly more people are aware of the causes of the disease known as AIDS than will ever contract it. Compare that to the centuries ravaged by the Black Death or, more appropriately, syphilis. It is a contemporary truism that a previously unknown disease might reach New York City at the speed of a jet aircraft. But information spans the globe at the speed of light.

THE INTERNET AND FOREIGN DEVILS

Just as those ignorant of the sources of infection are more likely to contract AIDS, societies ignorant of global realities are more likely to become victims of the plague of ideas ravishing our world. Troubled, faltering, humiliated societies—and failed individuals everywhere—are more likely to be seduced by lies or comforting myths than are the successful, and the dark side of the information revolution is that it makes a vast spectrum of very bad, stunningly false ideas and notions available to those seeking an impersonal reason for personal failure. Whether speaking of individuals or entire cultures, the successful have a healthy immunity, while the failed and failing are candidates for infection. And yet, establishing a *cordon sanitaire* is as impossible as it is, ultimately, undesirable.

With a sure grip on the past, Jacques Barzun has noted that since the appearance of the railway, mankind has been forced to learn a greater physical dexterity in everyday life to avoid harm from ever faster-moving, more powerful, and more numerous machines. But twenty-first-century men and women must add to that skill a dramatically increased intellectual suppleness to avoid being maimed by our informational juggernaut. Only a minority of the earth's population is prepared.

Certainly, the information revolution has spread many good ideas. It is historically positive in its effect, breaking the hold of tyrants and shining the light of knowledge into long-curtained worlds, while enabling phenomenal economic performances. Awareness is liberating—but the challenge is to prevent the free-but-frightened from volunteering for an even more dangerous bondage. Different cultures at different levels of development respond differently to the flood of information increasingly available in even remote corners of the planet. Cultures that perceive themselves as making progress display a better collective sense of true and false than those that feel themselves threatened or sense that they are falling behind. As with individuals, the successful are usually willing to accept criticism and learn new techniques that reinforce their success, while the faltering grow increasingly sensitive to criticism, self-doubting, defensive, and close-minded.

Over two centuries ago, Johann Gottfried Herder remarked that encounters between cultures excite self-awareness in those cultures. Today, collisions between cultures infect weaker cultures with self-doubt (loud assertions of superiority are the symptom indicating that the disease has entered a critical phase). We live in a world where the success stories are increasingly evident to all, while the fear of failure haunts the majority of the world's population. That fear may manifest itself as rabid pride and spur aggression, but we must not mistake the terrorist's or tyrant's desperation for anything other than what it is: fundamental, inarticulate terror. Spite, hatred, and fitful violence are hallmarks of decline. They are the responses of frightened men who cannot bear the image in the mirror held up by the globalization of information. They imagine, as do children, that they have a choice in their fate, that they can refuse to see what they cannot endure. But the choices confronting information-resistant societies are not really choices at all.

THE BRAND-X CHALLENGE

Consider the dilemma of Country X. Formerly the colony of a European power, its autocratic government sponsors a restrictive interpretation of the national religion, retains control of all decisions it considers significant, attempts to regulate the information to which its citizens have access, and is baffled that its recently booming economic growth has withered. Its official statements blame an unjust "neo-colonial" economic order for its weakening currency. Intelligent, but aging and increasingly out of touch, its leaders recognize with chagrin that countries they had heckled as yesterday's powers are not only resurgent, but growing wealthier and more dominant by the minute. Its citizens are split between the better-educated, who want greater personal and political freedoms, and the rest, who want a better material life but are more or less comfortable with the customary social and moral strictures. Corrupt elites and young people hungry for global culture form the statistical fringes. Younger technocrats within the government attempt to persuade the leadership that economic progress depends on more open policies, including an opening of the society to a liberalized flow of information, but the leadership is reluctant to risk the loss of any control.

The leadership of Country X imagines it faces a dilemma, but really it faces an inevitability. Better than the bright, young technocrats, the old leaders sense that once the informational floodgates are opened a crack, the pressure of the informational waters will force them open the rest of the way. They fear (rightly) that greater awareness of the world will bring with it demands for change and (wrongly) that it will bring a moral collapse. They worry (rightly) that a general availability of information will erode their monopoly on power and reveal their shortcomings, while worrying (wrongly) that the Western-dominated internet and the rest of this suspicious "information revolution" is just a return of colonialism in disguise, even a plot to dominate their country and its culture. The leaders *think* they have a choice between continuing to restrict the flow of information and opening those floodgates.

Strengthening the dikes no longer works. Faced with the global torrent of information, you either learn to swim or you drown.

The leadership's only choice, to the extent Country X has one, is between letting the economy and society go hungry for the informational nutrition it needs to have even a hope of competing globally or accepting a threatening loss of authority. And the lesson of liberalization that authoritarian regimes draw from the events of the last decade is that, once begun, the pace and scope of liberalization cannot be controlled. So the leadership argues and dithers, making cosmetic attempts at alternative reforms and reassuring themselves with state banquets. Meanwhile, the plague of ideas has already infected the population to a greater extent than the old men realize.

Except in the cases of utterly failed states, such as North Korea, the march of information is relentless. Attempts to block its progress result only in collapsing competitiveness and a delay in beginning the long, imperfect process of educating the country's citizens to tell fact from fiction. The choice isn't between prolonging an idyll and risking change, but between a belated attempt to secure a global niche and a decline into obscurantism likely to end in prolonged violence and general incapability. Leaders who convince themselves that they can preserve rigid informational hierarchies refuse to see the signs that those hierarchies are already eroding underneath them. Soon enough, they will have no credibility and no effective means to halt the disintegration of social order and the state they cherish.

And what of that charge of neo-colonialism? Is it any more than the demagogue's incitement of a restive population to blame foreign devils for local faults?

The global information revolution is explosive, insidious, irresistible, and destructive of traditional orders. It increases Western cultural and economic dominance, at least for the present. It is the enemy of all hierarchies except the hierarchy of merit. But it is not a new form of imperialism.

AN END, AND A BEGINNING

We stand at the bare beginning of the post-colonial era. Following 500 years of European colonial domination of the world, much of it involving physical occupation, we have hardly begun the process of recovery from colonialism's deformations and the digestion of its legacies, both positive and negative. The old colonial world is still in a disintegrative stage, wrestling with faulty borders agreed in distant capitals and with the inheritance of the European-model nation-state itself—which may prove to be the most fateful legacy of all. Now that the last of the great physical empires is gone, the mini-empires left behind in the colonial wake—artificial states such as Nigeria, Congo, the Russian Federation, the former Yugoslavia, Iraq, Pakistan, Indonesia, and, perhaps, India—are breaking apart or struggling to develop a sustainable political order.

We will be fortunate if the worst of the imperial legacies can be overcome by the end of the new century, and there is no doubt whatsoever that many of today's disorders may be laid at the doorstep of those vanished European empires. Yet, it grows increasingly counterproductive to blame colonialism for today's poor choices. We may blame nineteenth-century conferences in Berlin when Africa's borders provoke and exacerbate bloodshed, but no one can fault Europe (or the United States) when the leader of a state that has been independent for half a century looks the other way when his own citizens are massacred because of their religion or ethnicity, or when he stages show trials of potential rivals that alienate the greater world and its investors, or when he imagines that national ignorance is not only bliss, but economically productive.

Despite the fact that we will all wrestle with colonialism's legacies for many decades to come, there is no further utility, if there ever was any, in obsessive, paralyzing accusations. To blame is to enjoy oneself at the expense of achievement. Europe no longer has a colonial problem. Except for the occasional military intervention or embassy evacuation in a legacy state unable to function responsibly, Europe has washed its hands of any serious responsibilities left over from the colonial era, while concentrating on business (and while business practices can be devastating, they are not synonymous with imperialism). If anything, backward, protectionist elements in Europe worry about becoming the victims of a "hyper-power" America they have conjured as their own imperialist threat, forgetting that real imperialism is bloody, commanding, possessive, physically present, economically outmoded, and a very poor business model.

Imperialism is also purposeful. But the global information revolution is creatively anarchic, subject to that invisible hand, not to the hands of statesmen who can barely send an e-mail. Indeed, had the marketplace been allowed to determine the course of the European colonial adventure, many lands would never have been occupied, or would have been handed back to their occupants far sooner. There were certainly exceptions, but, overall, imperialism was about vanity more than it was about sound economics. The United States, for its part, willingly suffers no end of public humiliations as long as the business side of the relationship is good. Above all, as the Soviet Union finally realized in its death throes, old-fashioned imperialism is simply too costly. When merchants traveled the world to trade, the risks made perfect economic sense. But when armies followed, the results rarely paid a return—or did so with destructive results, as in the case of Spain's colonial bounty.

Imperialism is an expensive boot on an impoverished neck. The information revolution is a boot in the backside of those who move too slowly. The age of Western imperialism is over. But the triumph of the knowledge-based economy has barely begun.

Perhaps the best thing we in the West can wish for the many states (logical or illogical in their geographic contours), cultures, and civilizations that endured imperialist occupation or suffered its lesser attentions would be that they might gain a level of intellectual sobriety that would allow them to assess colonialism's legacies honestly, both the bad and the good. For there was much good done, as well, if some of it was incidental. Independence will be mature when former colonies can acknowledge their debt to those imperial powers that left behind an educated civil-servant class, traditions of law-based government, at least the shadow of democracy, physical infrastructure that still functions, and that ultimate enabler of the information age, the English language. After the honest weighing up, those states and peoples have to move on, to look forward and not pick eternally at yesterday's sores. But the chances are not good for such an objective evaluation: Blame is too addictive and comforting. Blame is the heroin of dying regimes.

I'LL CLOSE MY EARS, I'LL SHUT MY EYES . . .

The consequences when governments wage a hopeless struggle to restrict the flow of information to their populations may be varied, but they are all bad. The plague of ideas affects even countries such as the United States, or Germany, or England, spreading ludicrous, exculpatory beliefs among the underclass and leading to occasional acts of violence—but it does not impede progress on any front for the majority of the citizens, nor does it threaten the government. For most citizens of informationally adept states, the abundant availability of data and the access to a swift flow of ideas are every bit as empowering as television commercials sponsored by high-tech firms would have it. But in societies that, literally, believe what they want to believe because they have not developed the discriminating mechanisms that prevent self-delusion, the information explosion leads to other types of explosions, some of them bluntly physical. Only an informed population has any hope of developing successfully on any front in the new millennium.

The ignorant believe lies. This is a fundamental truth in all cultures, illustrated by the universal appeal of rumors and the alacrity with which men and women believe the worst of their neighbors. Now, much current repression—in mainland China, for example—is based upon a misreading of the fact that those denied global frames of reference will embrace local fantasies. The problem is that the informationally deprived won't necessarily believe the lies the leaders in the capital city want them to accept. Far too many heads of state and ruling cabals, worried about the durability of their regimes, have muttered along with the exhortations of religious fundamentalists in the hope of renewing their appeal to the masses. This is disastrous—for the population, for progress, for the economy, for minorities, and, more often than not, for the leadership that opened the lid on this worst of Pandora's many dreadful boxes. Playing the ethnic nationalist card is almost as bad, and occasionally more direct in its incitement to violence. When, as in Suharto-era Indonesia, the leadership panders to both nationalist and religious elements, the state is torn apart.

The collapse into obscurantism initially appeals to much of the public in underdeveloped states, as well as to their misguided, selfish leaders. Yet, the infatuation rarely lasts—witness the internal struggles in Iran today. While opening the gates wide to today's torrent of information destabilizes traditional structures if they are unsound and lack the required suppleness to adapt to contemporary needs, attempting to keep those gates shut is far, far more dangerous. An informationally naive population has a better chance of adjusting to the shock effect of informational freedom than to continued deprivation in a changing, inevitably intrusive world. The upheaval delayed is only intensified, and the time lost cannot be recovered. Iran has lost a quarter century, Burma and North Korea twice as long, and even states such as Saudi Arabia, which may appear successful to some, are brittle, hollow, and unprepared for the changes globalization will force upon them (today's oil-rich states are the postmodern equivalents to imperial Spain, stunted by their addiction to single-source "free" wealth). The populations of such states literally do not know what to believe, and, given human nature, many of their citizens are apt to believe the worst. Even Russia, which has pretended for three centuries to be Western, is a land of wild, inopportune beliefs.

As noted above, some information always seeps through. In the absence of trustworthy comparative data, it is almost always misinterpreted. Worse, comforting rumors and messages of hate have the power of an incantation where countering data is not readily at hand. The peasant or proletarian is unlikely to believe the droning messages from Beijing, but may well believe lies far more dangerous and more pleasing.

Nor must the debilitating information be outright lies— it may come as messages of faith assuring believers that all of their failures and lacks are the fault of the infidel abroad and the minority in their midst. The appeal to *believe,* to submerge yourself in the comforting promises of extreme, exclusive religion (comforting as much for the damnation promised to your enemies as for the salvation promised to you), is, of course, timeless. Indeed, the will to faith seems to exist in people everywhere. But the vigorous resurgence of the most intolerant varieties of fundamentalism—Muslim, Christian, Jewish, and Hindu—is demonstrably a product of the decades-long process of globalization and the threatening (to the less capable, the weak, the fearful) flood of information sweeping over the planet.

Extreme religious fundamentalism, like oppressive ethnic nationalism, is not an indication of a strong faith or shining conviction. On the contrary, the human being of deep, abiding faith can afford to be tolerant in thought and deed, to question and be questioned. Those who are comfortable with their deity are comfortable with their neighbors. They are also open to change, once they are convinced of its utility. Doctrinally rigid fundamentalism is always a symptom of insecure faith. This age of resurgent belief is really one of explosive doubt.

Those who feel compelled to force their vision of God upon others are trying to convince themselves, thus their ferocity. The possibility that alternative paths to salvation exist isn't an affront to their God, but a personal threat to them. We see it in the cruel cleric everywhere, and in the villager who murders the neighbor converted away from the old faith, in the unemployed American who attacks a "Godless" family-planning clinic, in the warrior who insists that God Himself denies rights to women, and in all those who insist not only that those of other faiths are doomed, but that their own more tolerant co-religionists are damned, as well.

The weak need certainty, while the strong can afford doubt (and reasonable doubts are the catalyst of all human progress). As with men, so with nations. Failing states and cultures crave beliefs as firm as iron. But iron, struck with sufficient force, shatters. The information revolution has the required force, and to spare.

WARS AND RUMORS OF WAR

The information wars have already begun. They have little to do with the Pentagon's dreams of cyber-strikes and network paralysis, although these are certainly matters worthy of judicious consideration. The information wars that will shape our time are not about what information is electronically vulnerable, but about what information is culturally permissible. The closest military organizations come to the real challenge is when they attempt, amateurishly, psychological operations campaigns or fumble with "perception management."

Certainly, the digital dimension has expanded, somewhat, the range of conventional war—but conventional war is of declining relevance. What matters is the power of information to terrify men of decayed belief. We live in a world in which the West is most willing to fight for economic causes, while the rest of the world squabbles over identity, be it religious or ethnic. Certainly, there have been plenty of rehearsals for these conflicts over blood and belief down the millennia, but the global lines have never been so sharply drawn. On one side are the Western and sympathetic states that believe in the freedom of information, while the opposition is composed of those terrified at the freedom information brings. This is not a precursor to a next world war—humankind is too disparate, and material power too lopsided at present. Rather, it portends a long, bitter, intermittent series of struggles on various fronts between those who cling to the hope that they can control their neighbor's beliefs and behaviors, and those states committed to the risks, misbehaviors, and triumphs of free societies. Barring unforeseeable cataclysms, the free societies will win. But the extent of human misery we shall see along the way is incalculable.

Consider a minor player on the world stage who has been hyped by his enemies into international stardom. Osama bin Laden is not waging war against the West's realities. He doesn't know them. He struggles against a riveting, overwhelming, wildly skewed, personal vision of the West, exemplified by an America he has conjured from shreds of information and his own deepest fears. (A startling Freudian note is that all cultures in which women are openly repressed and the males remain psychologically infantile display strong anti-American currents—Western civilization's discontents are minor compared to those crippling social relations elsewhere.) Mr. bin Laden's acolytes know little—often nothing—of the mundane West, but are galvanized by the psychologically rewarding opportunity to hate. Men of few earthly prospects, they imagine a divine mission for themselves. It is the summit of self-gratification.

The remarkable ability of men and women to deny reality is driven home by Osama bin Laden's counterparts in the United States itself: those citizens who, in the Year of Our Lord 2000, want to ban the teaching of evolution, remove "offensive" books from school shelves, limit women's choices, and glorify themselves by consigning their fellow citizens to a medieval version of Hell. It is never enough to "protect" their own children or spouses—those immoralists who do not see the light must be protected from themselves. It is an old and universal story newly supercharged by the threats the literalists of faith detect in the information age—although, like those elsewhere who reject the content, they are usually ready to employ the means of the information revolution to their own ends.

An exemplary case from the technologically distant past is the Iranian revolution of the late 1970s. The faction that ultimately seized control of the state apparatus had as its goal secession from the Western-dominated course of history. Yet even twenty years ago—light years in informational terms—it

proved impossible. The most powerful result of the Iranian revolution has been to deny Iran the chance to behave competitively for more than two decades—while killing a great many
Iranians along the way. At the risk of redundancy: There is no
real choice. You either outperform the global leaders, create a
competitive niche, or fall behind. Cultural and economic
autonomy is no longer possible.

Recently, in Indonesia, we have seen the inevitable consequences of informational underdevelopment when exacerbated by demagoguery (and by irrational borders). In East
Timor, in Aceh, the Moluccas, and elsewhere, the global
plague of ideas spurred hateful messages of nationalism and
religious fundamentalism that destroyed Indonesia's threadbare hope of being an equitable, secular state. In the absence
of trustworthy data and a framework for national understanding, rumors ignited massacres. And now it is too late to preserve the Indonesian state within its post-colonial borders
without levels of oppression the rest of the world is likely to
find intolerable. Regarding the remarks above to the effect
that the European concept of the state—with all its vanities—
may prove imperialism's most pernicious legacy, Jakarta's
reflexive unwillingness to consider a peaceful shedding of
those regions that reject its rule underscores the point.

In mainland China, the Beijing government wages multiple
counterinformational campaigns against its own population,
from utterly wrongheaded attempts to regulate the internet and
limit access to technologies to the suppression of religious sects
that likely would have found far fewer adherents in a more
informationally adept state. In India, Hindu extremists sense
that traditional advantages are undermined by any increase in
social and religious freedoms, so they murder Christian
converts and missionaries. In Kashmir, religion overlaid with

ethnicity draws endless blood on both sides. In Pakistan, a pandering leader banished English-language curricula from the school system a quarter century ago in an early nod to anti-globalization pressures. Since then, Pakistan has gone backward in virtually every sphere, and is less equipped for global competition than it was when Zulfikar ali Bhutto did more than any other man in its history to destroy the country's future.

OVERDUE UPHEAVALS

The popular struggles, terrorist acts, violent conflicts, and occasional wars ignited by the global information revolution will prove largely impossible to prevent, since few states will be willing to take the risks involved in unclenching antiquated notions of sovereignty in time for their citizens to find a comfortable place in the new global environment. The information revolution can only be locally delayed, not avoided. Unschooled populations will be exposed, haphazardly, to data they cannot digest, resulting in local tumult and transnational acts of desperation.

Yet, there is a positive transformation on the horizon, if still a distant one. The era of the common man that Marxism failed so painfully to induce is coming at last, driven by the democratization of information. For all the dangers described above, facts in the hands of men and women everywhere will ultimately displace even the sweetest falsehoods—though the latter will never disappear entirely, given human nature and even the best society's inevitable inequities. The problem is not the ultimate end, but the long, difficult transition faced by the world in our lifetimes.

Still, those of us who believe in the importance of fundamental human rights and decencies have reasons aplenty for optimism. Never before has there been such an irresistible threat to the old, unjust orders. We have entered an age when the individual's ability to comprehend data, assimilate ideas, and synthesize innovations upsets hierarchies that have apportioned unmerited rewards for centuries. This is the age not only of mass culture, but of opportunity for the masses. While much of the West has a lead of a century or two, the effects have begun to reach the remotest outposts of oppression. Already, an Untouchable may prove a far better software writer than a Brahmin; a woman may demand a voice in her own fate (still at her own risk, though); the highly talented outsider trumps the backward insider; victims tell their tales to microphones and video cameras; and people everywhere have a growing awareness, however flawed, of the possibilities that would be their birthright elsewhere. Add greed and fear on the part of those whose traditional privileges are under assault and the likelihood of violent upheavals and reactions threatens to slow, if not outpace, progress in many lagging countries. Yet, many an individual will shine, and in the end it is the genius of those individuals that will bring about the collapse of the last autocratic regimes.

The information revolution is by far the greatest transnational threat of our time. It is also man's hope. I believe, firmly, that societies that embrace informational freedom will triumph. But the victory will not come without costs.

Stability, America's Enemy

Parameters, Winter 2001–02

The diplomats and decisionmakers of the United States believe, habitually and uncritically, that stability abroad is our most important strategic objective. They may insist, with fragile sincerity, that democracy and human rights are our international priorities—although our policymakers do not seem to understand the requirements of the first and refuse to meet the requirements of the second. The United States will go to war over economic threats, as in Desert Storm. At present, we are preoccupied with a crusade against terrorism, which is as worthy as it is difficult. But the consistent, pervasive goal of Washington's foreign policy is stability. America's finest values are sacrificed to keep bad governments in place, dysfunctional borders intact, and oppressed human beings well-behaved. In one of the greatest acts of self-betrayal in history, the nation that long was the catalyst of global change and which remains the beneficiary of international upheaval has made stability its diplomatic god.

Our insistence on stability above all stands against the tides of history, and that is always a losing proposition. Nonetheless, our efforts might be understandable were they in our national interest. But they are not. Historically, instability abroad has been to America's advantage, bringing us enhanced prestige and influence, safe-haven-seeking investment, a peerless national currency, and flows of refugees that have proven to be rivers of diamonds (imagine how much poorer our lives would be, in virtually every regard, had our nation not been enriched by refugees from Europe's disturbances in the last century).

Without the instability of the declining eighteenth century, as the old European order decayed, we would not have gained the French assistance decisive to our struggle for independence. Without the instability of the twentieth century, protectionist imperial regimes might have lingered on to stymie our economic expansion. And without the turbulence that seeks to rebalance the world today, much of humanity would continue to rot under the corrupt, oppressive regimes that are falling everywhere, from the Balkans to Southeast Asia. A free world subject to popular decision is impossible without the dismantling of the obsolete governments we rush to defend. In one of history's bitterest ironies, the United States finally became, in the 1990s, the reactionary power leftists painted us during the Cold War.

Before examining in greater detail why instability abroad is often to America's long-term benefit, let us consider the foolish manner in which we have descended from being a nation that championed change and human freedom to one that squanders its wealth, power, and lives in defense of a very bad status quo.

We began well enough, applauding Latin America's struggles to liberate itself from the grip of degenerate European empires (except, of course, in the case of Haiti, whose dark-skinned freedom fighters made our own Southern slave-holders nervous). The Monroe Doctrine was not about stability, but about protecting a new and beneficial instability from reactionary

Europe. We did take an enormous bite of Mexican territory, which Mexico had inherited and could not manage, but we did not attempt to destroy or to rule Mexico. At the end of our Civil War, we were even prepared to intervene militarily on Mexico's behalf against European interlopers, had not the "Emperor" Maximilian met a fitting end at Mexican hands.

It all began to go wrong when we found ourselves with an accidental empire. Future historians, with the clarity allowed by centuries, may judge the Spanish-American War to have been America's decisive conflict, a quick fight that changed our nation's destiny and practice fundamentally. Brief, nearly bloodless, and wildly victorious, that war's importance has always been underestimated. Unlike almost all of America's other wars, it was a war that need not have been. Because it did happen, we turned outward, abandoning the convent for the streets, and could not go back. With that war, we became an imperial power, if a benign one, thus denying our heritage as the key anti-imperial power in history.

Domestically, the nation we have today is the result of our Civil War. Internationally, our fate was shaped by the Spanish-American War—more than by any of the wars that followed, despite their greater scope and striking results. Occurring at the peak of unbridled domestic capitalism, the Spanish-American War made of us an extractive power, in which the earnings of fruit companies became more important than support for freedom and democracy. Our bayonets served business, not ideals. This pattern of valuing profit above our pride—or even elementary human decency—holds true in our present relationships with states as diverse as Saudi Arabia and China (during the captivity of a U.S. military aircrew in the spring of 2001, some American businessmen went to Capitol Hill to make China's case, rather than rallying to support our service members; our diplomatic blank check written to Saudi Arabia on behalf of our oil interests has allowed behind-the-scenes Saudi support for terrorists, while Saudi intelligence services stonewall us and Saudi citizens commit unprecedented acts of violence against the United States).

Despite evidence to the contrary throughout the twentieth century, it has remained our conviction that stability abroad is good for business and, thus, for the United States—yet, the globalization of America's economic reach was enabled only by the colossal instabilities of collapsing empires. We argued that peace was good for business, no matter the human cost of an artificial peace imposed with arms, across a century when wars, revolutions, and decade after decade of instability opened markets to American goods, investors, and ideas. Were the maps of today identical to those of a century ago, with the same closed imperial systems in place, our present wealth and power would be impossible. America has always had a genius for picking up the pieces—the problems arise when we insist on putting those pieces back together exactly as they were before. I know of no significant example in history where an attempt to restore the status quo antebellum really worked. The new "old" regime always turns out to be a different beast, despite attempts to fit it with a worn-out saddle. Neither bribes nor bullets (nor clumsy, corrupting aid) can make the clock run backward.

Consider another decisive event roughly contemporary to our war with Spain, the Boxer Rebellion in China. Anxious to prove we were equal to any member of the club of great powers, we joined the punitive expedition to Peking (as it then was spelled) and fought against an indigenous movement which, despite its grim methods, hoped to free its country from outrageous foreign exploitation and humiliation. Of course, that was a time when men with yellow skins were judged by most

Americans as incapable of anything but mischief or lassitude, and I do not imagine that we might have switched sides—after all, our own legation was under siege, along with those of other, far more brutal powers. Still, imagine how much less savage the twentieth century might have been in Asia, and how much more peaceable the world today, had the Boxers won. The weakness upon which the European powers insisted frustrated any hope of internal development and left China naked in the face of Japanese aggression a generation later. Even during the greatest struggle in China's history—that against Japanese barbarism—we demonstrated our appetite for an imagined stability, creating for ourselves an image of Chiang Kai-shek that ignored his venality, callousness, cowardice, and impotence.

Our support for Chiang prefigured the behavior of the American diplomats of the eruptive 1990s, men and women who pretended that a functioning government remained wherever a single mid-level bureaucrat had a working phone in the blazing capital city. Stamp our feet in outrage as we will at Chinese intransigence today, we hardly may claim to have been China's benefactor in the past. As the nineteenth century ended and the twentieth began, we chose to collude in defending the existing world order, thereby losing a world of possibilities. Our actions may have been inevitable in the context of the times, but that does not make them wise.

The Great War began to break up the old imperial system that hindered the expansion of American trade, but we did our best to defend the old order to spite ourselves. Apart from President Wilson's hand-wringing at Versailles, our newly acquired appetite for order trumped any concern we had for human freedom and self-determination. And we paid a rarely acknowledged price for our complicity in propping up the *ancien régime* one more time. Given our preference for micro-causation and our snapshot approach to historical analysis, we may have misunderstood the true cause of the Great Depression. The "irrational exuberance" of the day served as an accelerator, but the historical force that drove so much of the developed world into the Depression was the attempt by the cartel of Great War victors to preserve the imperial trading order, with its restricted markets and an inherent stress on the metropolitan production of every type of industrial good without regard to efficiency. The imperial system, despite a bit of jerry-rigging, no longer answered the world's economic requirements. A brutally simple economic law is that only the expansion of possibilities enables the expansion of wealth, but the goal of Europe's waning empires was to restrict possibilities. Another seeming law is that developed economies cannot exist in equilibrium: When they cease to advance, they retreat. The old pre-globalization machine could not go forward anymore. The Depression marked the breakdown of a world economic system that had lingered into decrepitude.

Of note, the nations most immediately affected by the Depression were all trading nations, because those were the states the international system had failed; the more autarchic the state, the less it suffered in the short term, giving rise to the illusion that isolated Russia and sequestered Germany provided viable models for the future. We defended a static world order and ultimately reaped the most destructive war in history (one doesn't need a revisionist bent to recognize the economic logic that drove the monstrous German and Japanese regimes to attack the tottering imperial system that excluded them from dependable access to resources). Even our willingness to wink at the rise of Hitler and Mussolini was symptomatic of a preference for stability above all. Mussolini "made the trains run on time," and Hitler did seem to get the Weimar Republic under control at last. Did the Great Depression and the Second World War occur in the forms in which we experienced them simply because America voted, along with the depleted European victors at the end of the Great War, to stop the clock wherever the clock could not be turned back?

History insists. The thrust of the imperial twilight was toward breaking down antiquated structures, and World War II did just that. The single great beneficiary was the United States. Yet, we assumed our resounding success was somehow fragile and provisional; immensely powerful, we exaggerated our weaknesses. The Cold War was the last gasp of the last old empire, the Soviet incarnation of the Russian domain of the czars, over extended—fatally—into Eastern and Central Europe. And the Cold War deformed American strategic thought and our applied values beyond recognition. From the amoral defender of Europe's rotten empires, we descended to an immoral propping up of every soulless dictator who preferred our payments to those offered by Moscow. We utterly rejected our professed values, consistently struggling against genuine national liberation movements because we saw the hand of Moscow wherever a poor man reached out for food or asked for dignity. At our worst in the Middle East, we unreservedly supported—or enthroned—medieval despots who suppressed popular liberalization efforts, thus driving moderate dissidents into the arms of fanatics. From our diplomatic personnel held hostage in Iran a generation ago, to the September 11, 2001, terrorist attack on the United States, we have suffered for our support of repressive, "stable" regimes that radicalized their own impoverished citizens. In the interests of stability, we looked the other way while secret police tortured and shabby armies massacred their own people, from Iran to Guatemala. But the shah always falls.

Would that we could tattoo that on the back of every diplomat's hand: The shah *always* falls. Our age—roughly the period from 1898 through the end of the twenty-first century—is an age of devolution, of breaking down, of the casting off of old forms of government and territorial organization in favor of the popular will. Certainly, the forces of reaction can look very strong—deceptively strong—and the temptation is always to back the devil you know (and who allows you to explore for oil on his territory). But make no mistake—in one essential respect, today's America is on the same side as the most repressive voices in the Islamic world and the hard, old men in Beijing: We are trying to freeze history in place. And it cannot be done. In our ill-considered pursuit of stability (a contradiction in terms), we have raised up devils, from terrorists to dictators, who will not be easily put down.

The Cold War warped our thinking so badly that when the Soviet empire finally collapsed in 1991, we proclaimed a new world order while thoughtlessly doing our best to preserve the old one. Our diplomats and decisionmakers needed new thinking at least as badly as did the men in Moscow. Look at our track record over the last decade: It is a litany of predetermined failures that would be laughable were it not for the human suffering that resulted.

• When our greatest enemy, the Soviet empire, finally came apart, then–Secretary of State James Baker hurriedly tried to persuade the empire's components to remain together. Blessedly, the newly independent states weren't having any of that nonsense. When the American effort to keep Humpty-Dumpty up on his wall failed, we nonetheless continued, unto this day, to support the territorial integrity of a Russian Federation that remains an enfeebled, but cruel empire. No matter how many Chechens may be slaughtered, we content ourselves with a polite wag of the finger, shrug our shoulders, then concede that massacre is an internal matter.

• After a stunning battlefield victory against Iraq, we ensured that Iraq would not suffer a "power vacuum," but would remain a sovereign state within its existing borders— even though Iraq was an unnatural, constructed state, not an organic one, and the price of its continued existence was the slaughter of Shiites in the south, the continued suffering of Kurds in the north, and the deprivation of the remainder of Iraq's population to suit the vanity of a criminal dictator. Infatuated, as usual, by the mirage of a restored status quo ante bellum, we still face the same enemy we did a decade ago. Another reason for leaving Saddam in place was our fear of offending neighboring Arab monarchs and leaders, who themselves dread deposition. Our reward has been their discreet approval of the worst terrorists in history (no Arab or other Islamic state has made a serious effort to interfere with Osama bin Laden or his confederates; on the contrary, many are quietly gleeful at American suffering, even while professing their "deepest sympathies," and elements within Saudi Arabia and Pakistan have provided funding or other support for anti-American terrorism).

• In Somalia, we insisted that a collection of incessantly competing tribes was a bona fide state, and we paid for our willful illusions in blood and embarrassment (note to Washington: lines on a map do not make a functional state).

• In Haiti, our priority has not been popular well-being, but the preservation of a central state apparatus, however incapable, demeaning, and corrupt.

• In the former Yugoslavia—a miniature empire if ever there was one—the senior Bush administration and then the Clinton administration attempted to persuade the constituent parts of an ever-shrinking "state" that it was in their best interests to remain together, citing our own campus theorists who reasoned ethnic hatred out of existence and insisted that, all in all, the peoples of Yugoslavia got along just fine. Of course, the specimen populations paid insufficient heed to our professors and slaughtered each other with enthusiasm. Instead of considering the evidence of ethnic incompatibility at this point in history as displayed in blood before our eyes, we sent in our troops in the blithe expectation that corpses might be made to shake hands with one another. Today, we pretend that the Bosnian Federation is more than a hate-crippled criminal refuge and that Kosovo will someday be a happy component of Greater Serbia. As of this writing, we are making believe that a Band-Aid or two will fix whatever might be wrong with Macedonia. Our quest for stability in the Balkans has led to a false, fragile stability dependent on the presence, for decades to come, of foreign troops. To our credit, we stopped the killing, though belatedly, but we botched the peace so badly that our most enduring achievement has been to make the Balkans safe for black-marketeers.

Operation Desert Storm was our only victory of the past decade, and we threw its fruits away. We clutched the false god Stability to our bosoms, and now we are paying for our idol worship. History (for want of a better word) does have a god-like force, and we have stood against it. We have devalued our heritage, behaved as hypocrites, and succored monsters—and there is no sign that we will change our ways. From decomposing Indonesia (the questions are only of the speed of secession and the cost in blood) to the Arabian peninsula, we refuse to imagine the good that change might bring.

How did we come to this? In all other spheres, we have been the most creative, imaginative, innovative, and flexible nation in history. How is it that our diplomats and those who must rely upon them fell in love with the past, when our national triumphs have resulted from embracing the future?

Unfortunately, it can be easily explained. In times of sudden change, men look to what they know. When, after 1898, America abruptly found itself a world power with possessions offshore and across the Pacific, our diplomats relied on the existing model—the European system of collusion and apportionment designed at the Congress of Vienna by Prince Metternich, manipulated artfully in the next generation by Palmerston and his associates, and perfected, tragically, by Bismarck, whose genius led him to design a European security system that only a genius could maintain (and Bismarck's successors were not men of genius). Just on the eve of a new century that would sweep away the old order, we bought into the European system of mutual protection and guarantees (even defeated countries are not allowed to disappear; the lives of rulers, however awful their behavior, are sacrosanct; and states do not interfere in the domestic affairs of other states, etc.).

It was especially easy for our diplomats to accept the "wisdom" of the European way of organizing a strategic regime because, at that time, our diplomatic corps was dominated by the sons of "good" New England and mid-Atlantic families whose ties to and affinities toward the Old World were already out of step with those of their less decorous and more vigorous countrymen. If the Army belonged to those born in Virginia and south (and west), then the Department of State belonged to those from Virginia and north, and to the aspirants from elsewhere who emulated our Anglophiles and Europhiles most sincerely. Today, in 2001, America's diplomatic wisdom is that of Metternich and Castlereagh, brilliant reactionaries whose intent was to turn back the clock of history, then freeze the hands in place, after the Napoleonic tumult. America's international successes in the twentieth century occurred *despite* our diplomatic corps' values and beliefs.

Surely there is a middle way between supporting every failing state (usually a state that deserves to fail) and hunkering down in a bunker in Kansas while genocide prevails. The greatest immediate difficulty is that any such "middle way" would, in fact, be a number—perhaps a great number—of different ways. The classical age of diplomacy, from Metternich through Bismarck to Kissinger, is finished. In truth, a one-size-fits-all diplomatic framework never really worked, but during the Cold War we expended tremendous efforts to make it function, or at least to pretend it was working. Today, in a world that is systemically, developmentally, economically, and culturally differentiated and differentiating—despite the surface effects of globalization—our diplomacy cannot rely on easy-to-use constructs or unifying ideology (a great triumph of the twentieth century was the destruction of the historical aberration of ideology in the West; today's European "socialists" owe more to trial and error than to Marx, LaSalle, or Liebknecht, and all but the most bigoted Americans are political pragmatists in the clinch).

Our strategic approach must be situational, though shaped in each separate case by our national interests and informed by our core values. Of course, we must recognize the limits of the possible, but our greatest problem as a global power seems to be understanding what is impossible abroad, whether the impossibility is creating enduring ethnic harmony in the Balkans through armed patrols, willing a Somali state into existence through the presence of a few thousand undersupported troops, or trying to control terrorists with blustering threats and the occasional cruise-missile spanking.

The hardest thing is always to think clearly, to slash through the inherited beliefs that no one ever examines and to defy the wise men who have built careers on exorbitant failures. All people, in every culture, are captive to slogans, but Americans must strive to do a little better. We have made a slogan of democracy abroad, imagining it as a practical means when it is, in fact, the glorious end of a long and difficult road. We speak of human rights, then wink at the mundane evil of Saudi Arabia, the grotesque oppression in China, and any African massacres that don't leak to the press—because, inside our system of diplomacy, human rights are finally regarded as a soft issue. Yet, sincere and tenacious support for human rights is always good policy in the long term. The oppressor falls, whether in one year or fifty, and it is easier to do business with a nation whose freedom struggle you have supported than with one whose suffering you ignored or even abetted.

Regarding the business sector, it is the job of Wall Street to maintain short-term vigilance. But Washington must learn to counterbalance that short-term view with a longer-term perspective. Instead of a revolving door, there should be a steel wall between Wall Street and Washington. Diplomatic and military concessions to a repressive regime that allows select U.S.-headquartered corporations economic advantages today may prove a very poor investment for our country's greater interests tomorrow. We need to think across disciplines, to break the dual stranglehold of diplomatic tradition and economic immediacy. Were we only to apply our own professed ideals where it is rational and possible to do so, we would, indeed, find our way to a better, safer world in time. But we must stop trying to arrest the decomposition of empire's legacy. We are in a period of unprecedented and inevitable global change, and we must learn to accommodate and to help shape local changes constructively. But we cannot prevent the future from arriving.

Again, there is no unified field theory of diplomacy at our disposal. This is the hardest thing for Washingtonians to understand. Our responses to the world's dramas must be crafted on a case-by-case basis and founded upon nuanced knowledge of the specific situation. There is no single framework, and the rules change from continent to continent and even from week to week. Our national interest, too, evolves. Only our core values—the rule of law, the rights of the individual, and religious and ethnic tolerance—remain constant.

Democracy is a highly evolved mechanism for maintaining the society we have achieved, but it is not a tool for creating a society worth maintaining. Without good and respected laws, a commitment to essential human rights, and the willingness to honor differences of birth and confession, democracy is just a con game for bullies. Democracy as we know it also may require a certain level of popular affluence. But democracy alone will not bring affluence. Weak, new governments, or those transforming themselves, need training wheels on the bicycle of state, and we try to insist instead that every government should jump on a Harley. Far from building trust, democracy may shatter the remaining social bonds of weak or brutalized societies, dividing survivors into ethnic or religious factions. The overhasty imposition of democracy can lead directly to a degeneration in the respect for human rights. Where citizens have not learned to value their collective interests, democracy intensifies ethnic and religious polarization. Democracy must be earned and learned. It cannot be decreed from without. In a grim paradox, our insistence on instant democracy in shattered states (never in strong states or in those with which we do lucrative business, of course) is our greatest contribution to global instability. We have become strategic doctors determined to prescribe the same cure for every patient we see, before we have bothered to examine the patient's individual symptoms. Without a thought, we apply the rules of the Congress of Vienna to Somalia, Bosnia, and the West Bank, then try to graft on democracy overnight. We might as well attempt to cure cancer by the application of the best medicine of the eighteenth century.

Let us examine, briefly, just a small selection of the strategic issues facing the United States in which the quest for stability may prove antithetical to American interests.

• The *Balkans* represent the worst of all worlds: The slaughters occurred, fatally deepening the local hatreds, before any of the world's mature governments intervened, and now we are left with artificial states overlapping with de facto states, each within unsatisfactory boundaries, each with irreconcilable minorities, and each abundantly armed and criminally funded. "If only" may be pathetic words, but consider what might have been had the Euro-American community recognized, early on, that Yugoslavia was a Frankenstein's monster of a state that begged to be dismantled. There would have been no way to satisfy all, but plebiscites under international auspices—on which we had the raw power to insist—would have saved countless lives and prevented much, if not all, of the misery that benefited only criminals, bigots, and journalists.

• The *Russian Federation* gets a pass, no matter how awful or simply contrary its behavior, in the interests of stability. Having faced down and defeated the magnificently armed Soviet Union, we have talked ourselves into fearing the weak rump state that survived its ruin. In Washington, a great deal of sanctimonious cant may be heard about the danger of nuclear weapons falling into criminal hands should Russian stability fail, even though the Soviet regime was the most powerful criminal organization in history and those left behind are petty thugs by comparison, incapable of initiating a nuclear war as Moscow suffers through its new "time of troubles." A Russia in which power devolves to outlying regions or from which territories might secede would be a more promising, amenable Russia than the slimmed-down autocracy with which we are currently enamored.

Above all, though, we must demand an accountable Russia. In dealing with Moscow, the best policy is one of calm fearlessness and quiet rigor. We should accept neither lawless behavior nor tyranny in the name of law, when it is within our power to resist it (in this regard, our power lies primarily in blocking or discouraging grants, loans, or access to beneficial financial terms). Our support for human rights should be unwavering. Instead of excusing Russia's misbehaviors, we should deal with Moscow equitably (the one thing we have never tried), rewarding good behavior and punishing bad behavior—making a wide range of linkages explicit to the Kremlin. Never hand out rewards in advance in the hope that good behavior will be forthcoming from Moscow. Yes, Russia is suffering through a period of psychological dislocation that requires patience and understanding, but there is a crucial difference between understanding and indulgence. We must display the enlightened firmness of a parent dealing with an unruly child: Russia must never be allowed to throw a tantrum and have its way. Finally, even should Moscow aid us in our fight against terrorism, that will not give license to the Kremlin to terrorize its own people.

• *China's* future is unpredictable, whether the analyst sits in Washington or Beijing. One potential course would be a breakdown of central control and a return to fractious regionalism. Should such a scenario come to pass, our instinctive reaction would be to support the failing central power against insurgent or secessionist regions in the interests of stability—especially given the tens of billions of dollars U.S.–based corporations have invested, and continue to invest, in China. But we must struggle against the short-term view. A fractured, squabbling China would be less threatening to U.S. strategic interests in the region and might well emerge as a far more advantageous business partner (or partners). At present, our China policy, which drains American coffers to enrich a minority of American businesses, is captive to lobbyists and demonstrates no strategic vision beyond that of individual corporations. We pay China to become stronger and to prolong internal oppression—and if China weakens, we will prop up the vicious regime that spites us today. The ideal China would be a federalized, populist state, observant of basic human rights, that was economically open and militarily subdued. We are more likely to back a disciplined, tank-patrolled, centralized state that is economically restrictive—in the interests of stability. Faced with the slightest possibility of disorder, we will grunt and digest any number of Tiananmen massacres.

• *Africa* is slowly and agonizingly struggling to undo the deformations colonial regimes left behind. In the heart-rending tragedies of West Africa, where stability was the only Western idol (at least we are true to our monotheist heritage), we and the Europeans supported hollow men and hollow regimes for so long that the inevitable collapse has been especially horrific. Yet, even now, we will deal with the devil, if the devil will just promise to stop the massacres for the weekend. We must rethink our approach to West Africa fundamentally, and recognize our culpability. "States" such as Sierra Leone and Liberia are now so thoroughly broken that they require international mandates for reorganization under neo-colonial regimes. Borders should be redrawn—in other states as well—to reflect tribal and ethnic differences or harmonies. Elective affinities are welcome, but brotherhood cannot be enforced to suit nineteenth-century boundaries. In Africa, separatism is a natural and healthy force, until it is perverted by delay. Much of Africa has to be reduced from imperial-sized states to elemental building blocks before the construction of healthy organizational entities (perhaps called "states," but perhaps not) can begin anew on a more nat-ural and hopeful foundation.

In Central and East Africa, the process has taken a modified form, with African power groupings redrawing boundaries on their own, despite fervent denials that they are doing any such thing. In this region, outsiders simply need to keep their hands off, except when the killing threatens to become too egregious. Wherever possible, Africans need to discover African solutions, with corrective hands applied only when human rights abuses escalate intolerably. (Of course, it would be best if we could stop all human rights abuses, but we cannot. Regrettably, we must ignore Africa's misdemeanors and concentrate on the felonies, at least for now.) Any attempts to enforce the old European-designed borders indefinitely are bound to fail, while exciting ethnic tensions to an even greater degree than wrongheaded meddling did in the former Yugoslavia.

• The *Middle East* defies solution. A functional compro-mise between Israelis and Palestinians was impossible when the fanatics were merely on one side, and now they compose the decisive elements on both sides. Barring cataclysms, an Israeli born as this essay is written is likely to wade through his or her entire life in an ebb and flow of conflict. Meaning well, and behaving foolishly, we plunged into the Arab-Israeli conflict as an "honest broker," although neither side can accept the compromises required by such brokering, while our baggage as both Israel's primary supporter and the long-time backer of many of the most reprehensible Arab regimes is a debilitating handicap to mediation. We declare that stability in the Middle East is critical, no matter if it is impossible without a Carthaginian peace imposed by one side or the other.

The Israelis and the Palestinians can coexist. They already do. But their coexistence is of a different, dynamic nature that belies the meaning we attach to the term. Their struggle fulfills both sides. The Palestinians will never be satisfied, no matter how much they might regain, and the siege mentality Israelis affect to deplore may be essential to the continued vigor of their state. For both factions, struggle and the self-justification it allows may be the most fulfilling condition.

Americans assume that violent disorder is an unnatural state that must be resolved, but high levels of violence in a society or region may simply maintain a different kind of equilibrium than that to which we are accustomed. At the very least, periods of violence may be lengthy transitions that cannot be artificially foreshortened. We need not condone violence to recognize that it is not an artificial imposition upon human nature, nor will insisting that violence is unnatural make it so. We know so little about the complex origins of violence that our beliefs about it are no more than superstitions. Whether in regard to the violence of the man or the mass, our theories attempt to explain it away rather than to understand it. The Middle East may be inhumane, but it is one of the most explicitly human places on earth.

And would a peaceful resolution of the Middle East confrontation benefit the United States, after all? Hardcore terrorists would not cease and desist—no peace could ever satisfy them. And wouldn't we lose critical leverage? Israel, no longer dependent upon the United States as its ultimate defender, might prove a worrisome maverick. The Arab world might come to rely even more heavily upon the United States, but that would be one of history's great booby prizes.

Nor do the repressive, borrowed-time Arab governments in the region really want to see a successful, independent Palestinian state. The Palestinian struggle is a wonderful diversion for deprived Islamic populations elsewhere, but none of the Arab elites truthfully likes or trusts the Palestinians, who, if they achieved a viable, populist state of their own, would provide an unsettling example to the subjects of neighboring regimes. Arab rulers regard the Palestinians as too unpredictable, too obstreperous, too secular, too vigorous, and much too creative (resembling the Israelis, in fact). As it is, the rest of the Arab world is happy to fight to the last Palestinian, insisting the Palestinians maintain demands unacceptable to Israel. The struggle will go on for a long time to come. The best the United States can do at present is to inhibit the most excessive violations of human rights, while placing responsibility for the conflict on the shoulders of the participants, not on our own. We also must avoid absurd knee-jerk reactions, such as condemning legitimate efforts by Israel to strike guilty individuals, which is a far more humane and incisive policy than Palestinian suicide-bomber attacks on discos and restaurants.

By exciting false hopes of an ill-defined peace, we only inflame passions we cannot quench. Again, we have gotten into the habit of speaking loudly and laying our stick aside. We would do better with fewer press releases and more behind-the-scenes firmness—when engagement is to our advantage. And the occasional show of overwhelming force in the region works wonders.

• *Islamic terrorism* merits separate discussion now. It is not the result of creative instability, but of the atrophy of a civilization exacerbated by generations of Western support for an artificial stability in the Arab and Islamic world. While most Islamic terrorism is culturally reactionary, another aspect of it is an impulse for change perverted by hopelessness. And terrorism is, finally, a brutal annoyance, but not a threat to America's survival, despite the grim events of September 11. Osama bin Laden and his ilk may kill thousands of Americans through flamboyant terrorist acts, but their deeds reflect tormented desperation and fear, not confidence or any positive capability. Terrorists may be able to destroy, but they cannot build, either a skyscraper or a successful state. Destruction is the only thing of which they remain capable, and destruction is their true god. These men seek annihilation, not only ours, but their own. No entrances are left open to them, only the possibility of a dramatic exit. They are failed men from failed states in a failing civilization. Claiming to represent the oppressed (but enraged by the "liberal" behavior of most Palestinians), fundamentalist terrorists of so hardened a temper would not be contented, but only further inflamed, by any peace settlement that did not inaugurate their version of the Kingdom of God on earth. They are not fighting for a just peace, but for their peace—and even if they attained that peace, they would desire another. They are, in every sense, lost souls, the irredeemable. Their savagery is not a result of the failure of any peace process, but a reaction to their own personal failures and to the failures of their entire way of life.

These lines are written on the thirteenth day of September 2001, two days after the most horrendous terrorist attack in history, and America is seized by a just fury in which even the worst effects of local disasters are exaggerated. But before this essay goes to press, Americans will realize that their lives remain gloriously normal, even as the media delights in hysteria. Despite the thousands of personal tragedies and the practical disruptions that resulted from the seizure of commercial aircraft and the attacks on the World Trade Center and the Pentagon, the astonishing thing is how little permanent effect the terrorists will have had on daily life in the United States. There will be a scar, but the long-term effects of this grotesque tragedy will ultimately strengthen America. It has reminded us of who we are, and now we are rolling up our sleeves for the task ahead.

Without in any way belittling the tragedy, the fact is that the United States will emerge stronger and more united, with a sobered sense of strategic reality that will serve us well in the decades to come. In the long term, the terrorist immolations in New York, at the Pentagon, and in the Pennsylvania hills will prove to be counterproductive to the terrorists' cause, context, and ambitions. We are a phenomenally strong and resilient nation, while the societies that spawned our enemies are decaying and capable only of lashing out at the innocent.

• *Afghanistan.* If any conflict of the last three decades requires a revised assessment, it is the Soviet engagement in Afghanistan. Blinded by the brinksmanship and the reflexive opposition of the Cold War era, we failed to see that the Russians, in this peculiar instance, were the forces of civilization and progress. I do not defend their tactical behavior, but they did attempt to sustain a relatively enlightened, secular regime against backward, viciously cruel religious extremists—whom we supported, only to reap a monstrous harvest. Our backing of the most socially repressive elements within the Afghan resistance (because they were the "most effective") backfired beyond all calculation. Incredibly, blinded again by the seeming verities of the Cold War, we trusted the advice of Pakistan's Inter-Service Intelligence Agency (ISI), an inherently anti-Western organization that has since supported both the Taliban and

Osama bin Laden, as well as lesser terrorists, providing them with weapons, funds, safe havens, and free passage to the rest of the world.

Afghanistan, as we realize all too well in the autumn of 2001, has become the terrorist haven of the world, and we helped to make it so. We were determined that communism would not be allowed to destabilize the region. Now, in one of the bitter returns of history, our military forces in the skies over Afghanistan may face American-made and American-provided surface-to-air missiles. Our folly in Afghanistan should be final proof of the falsity of the dictum that "the enemy of my enemy is my friend." Sometimes, the enemy of your enemy is just practicing for the big game.

• *Cuba* may be a small problem in the geostrategic sense, but it certainly fixes America's attention. The instability likely to embarrass us in Cuba will come after Castro's disappearance, as the island's current regime weakens and dissolves. The Batista-Cubans we have harbored in South Florida, whose political influence has maintained one of the most counterproductive of American policies, will try to reclaim, purchase, and bribe their way into power in the land they or their elders exploited and then fled. The Cubans who stayed in Cuba, for better and worse, do not want their rich relatives back. And were we to be the least bit just, we would recognize that those who stayed behind have earned the right to decide how their island will be governed in the future. For all our ranting about the Castro dictatorship—which may not be admirable, but which is far more liberal and equitable than many of America's client governments (tourists clamor to go to Havana, not Riyadh)—an honest appraisal reveals that the average Cuban, though impoverished by the policies both of his own government and of the United States, enjoys a better quality of life than that of the average resident of many a "free" Caribbean state. If we intervene at some future date to protect the "rights" and the "legitimate property" of the Miami Cubans at the expense of the Cuban people themselves, we will shame ourselves inexcusably. Post-Castro Cuba, on its own, has an unusually good chance of evolving into a model democracy, but it will not do so if we sanction and support the carpetbagging of emigres who have never found American democracy fully to their tastes.

• *Indonesia* is the ultimate illogical state. Spread over thousands of islands and forcing together ethnically, culturally, and religiously different populations, this mini-empire almost certainly will continue to fragment, no matter the contours and composition of the Jakarta government. Inevitably, we will try to arrest the state's decomposition (as of this writing, we are rushing to renew our support of Indonesia's corrupt, abusive military). Just as inevitably, we will fail. If we and other interested states are not thinking about how to manage and facilitate Indonesia's breakup, we will find ourselves embarrassed by history again. Supporting what is essentially an ethnically based colonial regime against the will of powerful minorities on the periphery is bound to fail, first morally, then practically.

Devolution threatens a great range of other states, from Pakistan to Italy. The problems of each will be unique. But the common thread will be that attempts to arrest instability and to prolong the life of decayed, unnatural states, rather than to assist populations through longed-for political reorganizations, will always carry an exorbitant price and, ultimately, will fail.

At present, a portion of the armed forces of the United States is mired in stability operations that simply bide time in the hope that somehow things will come out right, while an even greater portion is focused on avenging the recent terrorist attacks against America. We may wish all of these endeavors Godspeed, yet it would be a disservice to the men and women in uniform not to ask how we have come to this pass. Self-examination in the strategic sphere has not been an American strength. Perhaps it is time to make it one.

Meanwhile, we deny causes, ignore unpleasant realities, put on our flak jackets, and hope for the best. Certainly we should not replace stability operations with "instability operations" to provoke or accelerate change beyond its local, organic pace. And we must differentiate between unpopular terrorist groups and genuine mass movements: There is a great difference between the vicious Basque terrorists of the ETA and the African National Congress that triumphed over apartheid. All dissident organizations are not equally legitimate.

But we do need to stop providing life-support to terminally ill governments, and we must be open to new, unprecedented solutions, from plebiscites that alter borders to emergent or re-emergent forms of administration in failed states, whether enlightened corporate imperialism or postmodern tribalism. If the corporation can manage more humanely than the dictator, why not give it a chance? If the tribe can govern more effectively than a thieving, oppressive government, why not let the tribe reclaim its own land?

Of late, we have heard all too much about the United States being the world's policeman. We are not, we cannot afford to be, and we couldn't bring it off if we tried—not least because policemen have to be on the beat everywhere, around the clock, and their most successful work is preventive (a concept that democracies, which are reactive in foreign policy, find anathema). Apart from our new and essential crusade against terrorism, which must pursue preemptive measures, our role should be that of a global referee, calling time out when the players hit below the belt or get too rough, and clarifying the rules of the game (no genocide, no ethnic cleansing, no mass rape, no torture, etc.). Instead of trying to stop the game, which was our approach across the past decade, we should try to facilitate it when it is played by legitimate players for legitimate stakes. In the case of terrorists, of course, we need to throw them out of the game permanently.

But what on earth is wrong with people wanting their freedom? Why shouldn't populations want the armed forces of a central government that is essentially an occupying power to leave their territory? Why are yesterday's borders more important than today's lives? Why should we support religiously intolerant regimes that virtually enslave women and persecute nonbelievers to death? How much mass suffering is it worth to keep things geostrategically tidy? How dare we send our soldiers to support bigoted monarchies that forbid our troops to worship as they choose? How stable can any government be that fears a Christmas tree? Why should we pretend that every war criminal is really a democrat waiting for his opportunity to vote? Why should we reflexively support the rich and powerful against the poor they abuse and exploit? Why must we insist that history can be made to run backward?

A new century demands new ideas. The notion that stability is the fundamental strategic virtue is not going to be one of them.

The Black Art of Intelligence

With the Atlantic Ocean separating us, my extended family's generations slipped out of synchronization. Thus, it was my cousin who served in World War II on the German side. A tactical reconnaissance NCO, or *Aufklaerer*—one of the most dangerous jobs in any army—he fought on the Eastern Front throughout the war, yet never was captured or seriously wounded. When we met at last, in the early 1980s, I encountered a vigorous, sinewy, skeptical Hessian farmer. Serving at the time as the intelligence officer in a U.S. Army infantry battalion, I asked my cousin how he had managed to survive on a battleground that consumed millions. Matter-of-factly, he told me he just "knew" where the enemy had been and where danger lay. It startled me, because I already had my own catalog of peculiar experiences, from exercises to real-world analysis, in which I, too, just seemed to know—beyond the logic of intelligence reports and indicators—what was going to happen. I could no more explain my ability to read a situation than could my cousin.

Certainly, what I frequently was able to do had no place in the careful processes devised to train intelligence analysts and

officers—although formal techniques have their value—nor did
I ever make an issue of how I "knew" things. My greatest challenge was convincing superiors who wanted proof that two and
two made five. These were good, often brave men whom the
intelligence system had failed, earlier in their careers in Vietnam and continually in the Cold War. When trusted, I could
deliver to an uncanny degree, whether delineating Soviet war
plans in Europe, locating a small special operations unit hiding
in a vast area, or, when alone in the Caucasus, sensing where I
could and could not go. Now, much of this was simply common
sense, that least valued quality in armies and governments. I
also enjoyed the lack of a good education, which put me well
ahead of officers whose vision of the world and humankind had
been distorted by fine universities. But the similarity of experience between my cousin, who survived the cruelest front of the
worst war in history, and my own chocolate-soldier peacetime
adventures still strikes me as more than coincidence. Traits do
run in families, from physical robustness, to mental acumen, to
artistic talent. Did it matter that my anthracite-mining father, in
his prime, could walk into a valley and say, "There's coal over
there," and coal would be found where he pointed? Was it relevant that my paternal grandmother could "read" certain ill-
nesses and cure them by the laying on of hands—while
repeating incantations from the Scriptures?

These things are true. But are they relevant to anything?

I believe so. I offer these bits of family lore first as a delayed
answer to all those who, over the years, have asked me, "But
how do you *know* that?" and, second, to tease those already convinced that I've long been "off the reservation." Third, and
most importantly, this tale-telling makes an extreme case for a
proposition I have argued for years: that intelligence analysis,
done well, requires not only rigorous training and much

practical experience, but innate talent, a predisposition. One need not have a mystical bent to accept that all men (and women) are not created equal when it comes to the ability to do intelligence work. We accept readily enough that specific talents are required to play major league sports, for a successful career in the arts, or even to become a great con man. (One of the problems we have with our intelligence services, by the way, is that they are run by minor con men, mere bookies.) We still hear that someone is a "born leader" as we wonder at his or her inexplicable charisma and quick grasp of necessary matters. Yet, we assume that anyone with a moderately high IQ can be trained in a few months to grasp an enemy's mentality, character, fears, intentions, hopes, beliefs, vulnerabilities, and individuality—without even speaking his language.

As a result, we have a network of intelligence services that can count bomb craters with great accuracy, but upon which we cannot count to warn us of "illogical" dangers, such as the brilliant, if ultimately counterproductive, strikes of September 11, 2001. As I have written—to the point of whining—it is a paradox of the twenty-first century that, in this age of technological wonders, the threats to our lives, wealth, and order are fundamentally, crudely human. We may diagram bunkers, bombs, and entire armies, but we falter at understanding the human soul. Nor will the human heart fit into our templates. Love, fear, and hatred, not machines, are the stuff of which wars are made, whether we speak of terrorist jihads, campaigns of ethnic cleansing, or conventional offensives (and do not underestimate the deadly power of love, whether felt toward a god, a people, a clan, a flag, or an individual).

During my bleak Washington years as an intelligence officer, no one dared to speak of the forces of love or hatred, or of any other emotion. Nor could they say anything profound about

religion or culture. The sexual devils that haunt entire civilizations, as the fear of female sexuality cripples the Islamic world,
were beyond the pale of "serious" discussions. Statistics were preferred, whether dependable or not, and intercepts or satellite
imagery were quite the thing. Intelligence products were tai-
lored to the available information, when we should have been
demanding information to support our genuine intelligence
needs. The system was at once superficially prim and intellectually slovenly. Briefings and discussions were as studiously gray as
the men and women behind the podium or around the table,
and all the human wilderness wherein past civilizations have perished—the furious, wild, destructive, often monstrous power of
the human animal itself—was banished as a topic of discussion.
More than any other figure, we all resembled T. S. Eliot's prema-
turely old paragon of timidity, J. Alfred Prufrock, who asks himself eternally, "Dare I eat a peach?" We tried to deal with the
torrid world of flesh and blood as if it were made of fitted nuts
and bolts. We understood nothing that mattered.

Without such understanding, we are reduced to the retaliatory exercise of power and expressions of regret for pre-
ventable losses. There is no lack of bravery in the ranks of our
armed forces, but bureaucratic cowardice rules in our intelligence establishment (as well as at the highest levels of military
command). Whenever my turn came up to represent the Army
Staff at the National Intelligence Council, or NIC, whose meet-
ings were held in the CIA's dull and spotless headquarters, representatives of all the intelligence players would sit around a
table, show off their knowledge of trivia, then agree, by the end
of the session, on a lowest-common-denominator position. The
intelligence produced was not bad—only mediocre. It told you
a bit about things, but not enough. There was great pressure
on all participants and their organizations not to make a fuss.
A dissenter might "take a footnote," but the practice was

discouraged. The point, you see, was not to get things right, but to avoid getting them demonstrably wrong—a critical distinction. Boldness, no matter its quality, was not wanted. And insight had to be backed up with hard data—proven beyond a doubt, which is impossible in serious intelligence work. The desired result was to make certain that we could, when faced with catastrophe, all point at one another as having agreed in the errant assessment: "This is what the entire intelligence community believed, based on the best information available." Perhaps we might inscribe that on the graves of our fellow citizens who died because of our inadequacy.

Rare was the man or woman who even cared.

My own form of cowardice was to avoid the NIC sessions whenever I could, while writing what I believed to be true in unclassified journals. Today, I stand by all that I wrote ten years ago but do not believe our intelligence community could say the same of a fraction of the drivel it produced. Of course, by the time the over-classified reports and studies are made available to researchers, those who drafted and approved them will be long retired (after many promotions) or dead. But our habit of stamping high classifications on low-quality work to dignify it is yet another subject.

Theoretically, we petty creatures who came together to discuss the strategic future were the best and the brightest; in fact, we were dreary bureaucrats, far less than the sum of our parts. But, then, our intelligence community is, above all, a massive bureaucracy—and bureaucracies discourage risk-taking or excellence that does not match the models of the past. The motto of our vast intelligence establishment is "Play it safe." The mindset may protect careers but does little for our country.

Nor do I underestimate the technological wonders at our disposal, for I have seen what these near-miraculous machines can do, but I know too well that my countrymen overestimate those same seductive devices. It is always safer, bureaucratically, to rely on what the machine tells you, whether or not it is appropriate, than on the fallible human being who begs you to believe him. No one is ever fired for showing the boss satellite photos, but it is a rare man or woman who will back a subordinate based on the analyst's personal experience of foreign people and parts. Trust the machine, and you will prosper, even as your country's needs go unsatisfied.

Understanding, understanding, understanding! Get at the human beings, and the rest falls into line. Understanding your enemy is the most effective weapon of all, but a weapon we rarely wield.

We have tried—clumsily, if earnestly—to make intelligence into a science, when it is an art. Certainly, science plays a mighty role within the larger boundaries of the art, from those fabulous collection systems, to communications, to computer analysis of technical data. Nor will we ever have an intelligence community composed solely of virtuosos—not everyone should be expected to be a soloist or even the first violin. Someone has to raise the curtain, turn the pages, and work on the acoustics in the hall—but, in the world of intelligence, the stagehands have taken over the performance.

The last clarinetist in a quality orchestra has to have a dependable level of competence, or the sound of the entire orchestra suffers. But diplomas alone do not make musicians, and they do not make intelligence analysts. At present, we pretend that anyone with a college degree can play in the intelligence world (in the military, the degree is not even required). Try that at the New York Philharmonic ("Oh, you just graduated from Julliard? Thank God, we've been looking for a replacement for Maestro Masur . . ."). For those logic lovers out there, does it make sense for our premier intelligence organizations to have lower standards than a third-rate orchestra somewhere in the Midwest? Pretending that intelligence analysis is, if not fully quantifiable, at least subject to methodical processes has left us skilled at predicting the arrival time of a tank within range of our weapons, but helpless at seeing into the mind, heart, and soul of the enemy leader who commands, perhaps, five thousand tanks—or five thousand terrorists. We lack a natural sense of pitch, of human harmonies and discords. And we play the same tune over and over again.

As for science, the one thing we have not even tried to do with it is to use it to select potential analysts for their counter-scientific skills, for talents that would augment, even fulfill, the technological array we can bring to bear upon our enemies. But that, of course, would lie in the future, well beyond the numbing tests the military and government now use to guarantee the standardization of mediocrity ("Mark your choice with a number two pencil and erase any errors completely . . ."). I do not think we need a horde of mystics and cabalists in Pentagon cubicles or gathering in covens in the cafeteria at the Defense Intelligence Agency. But we need to try to understand that a good analyst's mind is wired a bit differently—he or she need not go into a trance and speak in tongues but had better have a richer, cannier vision of the world than that possessed by the average Washingtonian bureaucrat. Sometimes, in the phantasmagoria of human hatred and violence, two and two not only make five, but ultimately add up to twenty-seven . . . or to collapsed skyscrapers.

We view analysts as parts of the intelligence machine—and interchangeable parts, at that. But good analysts—the truly good ones—are rare and, sometimes, irreplaceable. That, too, is anathema to a bureaucracy and to a military that still has an industrial-age, draft-era mentality within its personnel system.

We must find ways to attract, identify, develop, and retain analysts who have special potential. In far too many intelligence organizations, someone becomes a specialist simply by virtue of assignment or duty position (Brazilian navy desk last week, terrorism expert today). We neglect intelligence—not because it isn't vitally necessary, but because it is very hard to do well (and, in the military, because it's geek stuff—real men don't think). Were we a weaker power, we would pay far more attention to intelligence, since it is a great equalizer. Instead, we rely on strength and wealth to get us through. But poor intelligence forces even a superpower to be reactive, when it should be leading, preventing, and shaping.

Much has been made of September 11, 2001, as an intelligence failure. Well, it was and it wasn't. Not even the finest intelligence organization, with highly developed cadres not only in the analytical field but in the other vital, difficult field of Human Intelligence, would be able to predict and prevent every event. The world is too complex and too vast, and humanity too ingenious. No intelligence structure will ever be perfect—at least, not in our lifetimes. But we can do a great deal better than we have done up to now.

The status quo is perverse. We will spend tens of billions of dollars on a network of satellites, then pay the young man or woman analyzing the data a salary far below that of a plumber. In my own career, I repeatedly was encouraged to take jobs that had nothing to do with intelligence but which were considered the premier Military Intelligence positions. Friends at the National Security Agency or Central Intelligence Agency routinely found themselves required to leave the analytical fields in which they were skilled and go into management in order to gain the promotions they needed to care for growing families. Analysis was the bottom rung, an entry-level job—and even the best analysts saw their work so neutered as it filtered up through the bureaucracy that the insights of greatest value often disappeared long before the paper or study reached the National Command Authority. No one in the management chain wanted to risk being asked a question by his boss for which there was no documented answer. Intelligence work became a poor cousin of academic research—with all "new" products relying on the wisdom of that which had been published (safely) in the past. It was especially laughable when a general or senior executive would say, "Now, I want you to think out of the box on this." What he meant was that he wanted to hear fresh justifications for his existing beliefs. The only innovations the system valued were those that saved money on office supplies.

Of course, when things go wrong we immediately hear cries from Congress and the pundits for intelligence reform. Now, let me tell you what intelligence reform means to the Hill: more money for the contractors who build the systems whose data we lack the manpower to analyze. There is always a constituency to buy expensive hardware, but there is no enduring constituency for the skilled human beings we sorely lack. In the military sphere, the cost of one F-22 fighter—an utterly unnecessary, irrelevant system—could fund about 2,000 more analysts for five years . . . or train about 2,500 more linguists in the nation's best language programs. (Foreign language ability is another human skill in chronically short supply in our intelligence community, and, personally, I believe analysts should speak the language or languages of their target region.)

Our intelligence machinery does produce wonders upon occasion. But that machinery simply has limits that only human beings can extend. The recent conflict in Afghanistan made this abundantly clear. Despite the hundreds of billions of dollars worth of intelligence surveillance equipment available to us, our bombing remained largely ineffectual until special operations teams hit the ground, drew information from the local combatants, spotted targets with their own eyes, and directed the airstrikes. We could have bombed Afghanistan for a year and had less effect than that produced by a few weeks of bombing guided by skilled human beings on the ground. Similarly, the literally immeasurable amounts of data generated by our technical systems have little meaning—or can actually deceive us—if we do not have skilled analysts with good instincts honed by experience to help us understand what it all means; or, to be more accurate, to tell us what the few pertinent drops in the vast flood of information mean.

Good instincts? That's a quality that never shows up on report cards. Yet, I've known plenty of well-educated, knowledgeable, dedicated, brutally hard-working intelligence officers who were worthless when it came to serious intelligence analysis. They could make the office look good in a bureaucratic environment; they could brief; they could do research—but they could not understand that, sometimes, the world refuses to behave as they were taught it should behave. They plotted out the templates, scratched their heads, and got on a kicked-puppy look when the bad guys failed to behave as the Intelligence School at Fort Huachuca said they must.

In one tactical assignment, I had a subordinate officer who was superb in every respect that mattered to the institutional Army—but his instincts actually tipped into the negative column and he got even simple analytical calls whoppingly wrong. (Fortunately, this was in peacetime, at Fort Hood, where nothing much matters.) In the same organization, I had an officer who looked more than a little rough around the edges, who couldn't keep a smirk off his face when the leadership came around barking platitudes, and who had a gut instinct for battlefields, psychology, and plain old human nastiness that no training course could ever instill. He was the one I would have relied on in wartime. Despite my best efforts, guess which one the Army promoted, and which one was passed over and forced out of uniform?

Ultimately, intelligence work comes down to dealing with humanity. After all the calls are intercepted and the missiles counted, the bank accounts monitored and the nerve gas canisters located, we still need to look inside the minds, hearts, and souls of other human beings. And, unlike the mechanical and electronic things of which we are so fond, human beings are not fully predictable or understandable—even to themselves. Contrary to the wisdom of Washington and the academic world, human beings are not rational creatures. Laws, customs, and enlightened self-interest may drive men and women to behave predictably some of the time—in daylight, on a peaceful street—but in the dark night of the soul, or in the stunning midnight of atrocity, the rational man dissolves into the feral, instinctive, vividly mad descendant of Cain.

Perhaps, one day, satellites will be able to locate every single one of our opponents. But I doubt that they will ever be able to see into the human interior to tell us what our nemeses intend, or hope, or fear. What will X do tomorrow? The truth is that X himself does not know for certain. The deed yet undone contains myriad alternatives. A good analyst, enraptured by his work, may actually have a better grasp of what X will do than X does himself. To many, this will sound impossible. But it is only impossible for those who rely upon technology to cope with humanity.

This is hardly a new tug-of-war. Those who insist that all things are knowable and that men and women act rationally have been on one side of the stadium of mankind for centuries, while the opposing bleachers have been filled by those who insist that even the light of reason casts dark shadows, and that man's nature is never fully knowable. In our technologically advanced culture, the power of systems easily seduces the multitude to believe that machines are, or soon will be, omnipotent—an enduring myth. But at the most elementary, unshakable level, we have barely begun to understand the complexities, motivations, and patterns of human behavior. The frightened cling to the tangible, and the worried demand simple answers. But an effective intelligence system must learn to deal with the ineffable and dauntingly complex. As Shakespeare put it four centuries ago, "There are more things in heaven and earth, Horatio, than are dreamt of in your philosophy." Words to live by for the Director of Central Intelligence.

Of course, we will never have an intelligence system composed purely of virtuoso analysts and linguistic geniuses. But, with an intelligence budget above thirty billion dollars a year, we certainly can do better than we are doing now. A little more money—just a tiny fraction of the budget lavished on technology—redirected to Human Intelligence operatives, to analysts, and to linguists could make an enormous difference. But personnel policies would have to be reformed at the same time—and in the absence of additional money for analysts, linguists, and Humint specialists, personnel system reform becomes even more important. Once within the system, the basic question is simple to articulate, if difficult to answer: How can we exploit the gifted, instead of rewarding the conformist? We are always readier to embrace the individual who commits himself slavishly to the system as it exists than the one who devotes himself to improving the system—with the inevitable pain change brings. We make far too much of loyalty, and far too little of integrity, despite our wanton use of the latter word.

Talented people are difficult, from start to finish. They require special care and feeding—not consistently, but often unexpectedly. Brilliant analysts may be a chronic annoyance in the otherwise collegial staff meeting; they're often priggishly self-righteous and sometimes obsessive: Arcane in their interests, they are, as the English used to put it, "not the club-able sort." They may occasionally look like model soldiers or fashionistas (not hard, by Washington standards)—but they also may look like they need help dressing themselves. And they don't play golf. My point is that intelligence personnel, above all, cannot be judged by externals—but that is how our system likes to judge people, since it's the easiest way. If only shiny boots indicated intellect, we would have the most brilliant military in history. It's no accident that the one thing we're good at in intelligence is "reading externals," milking the value from surface data, whether targeting information or communications webs. But, in the end, it is the internals that matter.

How might we best go about building a better cadre of intelligence analysts and related personnel? In the long term, we might be able to develop sophisticated testing to identify certain deep traits. But, for now, the required steps are easy to list, but much harder to implement.

First, analysts need to be valued, with the most talented identified, protected, and groomed. This is surprisingly tough, since most of the managers in our intelligence system are bureaucrats who truly cannot tell the difference between compiled information and valuable intelligence—and all managers, in uniform or not, tend to promote in their own image.

Second, especially in the military, supervisors need to recognize that the most-talented young people tend to make more mistakes. They're at least trying things out, instead of waiting cautiously for orders. In the "zero-defects" military our generals and admirals continue to insist doesn't exist—although it shaped their every step—promising young analysts (and other soldiers) see their careers ended for minor infractions by commanders or other bosses afraid that, if unpunished, the incidents might damage their own future prospects. When young, the smartest people often do the dumbest things. Some survive by luck within organizations (almost invariably, because of a far-sighted superior). Most don't make it past the first cut.

Third, analysts have to be rewarded. In the military, this means appropriate promotions—yet, in the Army's Military Intelligence branch, the quickest way to the top is to avoid actual intelligence jobs and build a career in management (disingenuously called "leadership"). In the rest of the intelligence community, it means respect but, frankly, it also means money. Intelligence work may sound seductive to a recent college graduate, but to a husband or wife in the mid-thirties, with a mortgage on a townhouse in Springfield, Virginia, and two kids who are going to need college money in no time at all, life as a GS-11 with little prospect of serious advancement doesn't look quite so romantic. In a capitalist society, you don't always get what you pay for—but you rarely get what you don't pay for. If the government wants superior analysts and agents who speak multiple foreign languages and are willing to work overseas for years in particularly unpleasant circumstances, or to serve in that Heart of Darkness known as the Greater Washington Area, they should be paid at least as well as accountants by mid-career. And they should be defended, not hung out to dry, when they do get things wrong.

We want to do intelligence cleanly, without embarrassment. That's another losing proposition. Clandestine and covert intelligence work, if it is to be successful, often has to engage in practices unthinkable within America's borders. But that is yet another issue that wants discussion at another time. This brief essay is concerned with the art of intelligence analysis—a field in which we insist that our product dare not be offensive to other religions, cultures, minorities, or to either political party, just in case a White House staffer leaks it. The most wrongheaded words a manager in the intelligence world can mouth are, "You can't say that." We live in a world where every unpleasant truth must be spoken, before it becomes far more unpleasant.

I offer no formula for analysis itself, beyond hard work, open eyes, and dedication—without which even a great talent is meaningless. I have always been skeptical of those prescribed by-the-numbers processes taught in our intelligence schools. Past a certain point, they only blind us. And perhaps all that I have written about the need for special abilities is nonsense. Perhaps all that is required is the willingness to see things as they truly are. But that is a rare enough quality by itself.

I am convinced that talent matters profoundly. We never would pretend that we could take people with no gift for music—no matter how great their raw intelligence—and turn them into fine pianists. Is it such a stretch to imagine that an art form whose ultimate task it is to intuit the deep secrets of an enemy's mind—or soul, as I prefer to put it—might also require special talent? Certainly, talent isn't everything. No matter how much innate talent he or she might possess, a musician needs training, practice, experience, and time to develop to his or her full potential. A maturation process is always required—even for a Mozart (of course, his talent was fairly mature by age six, so we have to be flexible). But the talent has to be there to begin with, whether we speak of artists or of analysts, and talent is as little understood as love or hope or the aching for God—or the indelible will to violence.

Henry Ford did wonders for the American economy of his day, but his model of the workplace has done terrible and enduring damage to the American government and, especially, to our military. The business of protecting our nation with the best possible intelligence cannot be done with faceless workers who function as interchangeable parts, no matter the current management fad inflicted upon them. We Americans pride ourselves on our individualism. Recognition of the indispensable contribution of talented individuals to our intelligence system is long overdue. Machines may decipher a world of technical data, but only a gifted analyst can read the heart and soul of another human being.

The Rejection of the West

This essay was written in 1994, as a personal initiative, while I was assigned to the Army Staff in the Pentagon. In the early years of the Clinton administration, Washington was a fantasyland of optimism about the state of the world, and when I converted the essay to a series of military briefings, they were deemed too pessimistic by far, since irregular forces, terrorists, and the like were but a minor annoyance soon to disappear in the triumph of democracy, free markets, and peace in our time. The services made a devil's bargain that substituted consumerism for strategy, and the Clinton-era defense budgets were, quite literally, hush money. Strategic thought withered within the Department of Defense, just as the world entered a phase of upheaval and metamorphosis unlikely to end in our lifetimes. It was a bleak time to be an officer, especially in an Army stunned by the end of the Cold War and desperate to insist that, really, nothing had changed. One kindly general, summing up the Army's attitude as nicely as he could, told me, "All that stuff about culture and religion is fine, Ralph, but I just don't see these bad guys of yours as a serious threat."

We have entered the second and final phase of the rejection of the West by noncompetitive cultures. The first phase of this rejection began in earnest in the wake of the First World War. Colonial subjects who had received Western educations founded national liberation movements that aimed to remove the Western presence from their homelands while retaining Western-style institutions and values, either democratic or socialist, grafted to the indigenous culture. This phase culminated in the post–Second World War collapse of empires. From Africa through Asia, newly free states, while distancing themselves rhetorically from Western examples, sought to become European with a native face. Even as many of these states drifted into authoritarian or even totalitarian rule, they retained the formal structures and economic ambitions of the West—while clinging to their European-drawn borders. The most pernicious legacy of colonialism was the example—and physical dimensions—of the nation-state, which no emerging country could transcend.

Today, what appears to Western eyes as a tumult of religious fundamentalism, nationalism, tribalism, and dissolution of social order is, in fact, an understandable, though not pre-ventable, response to the failure of Western governmental, philosophical, social, and economic systems to flourish in the soil of other cultures. It signals an impending revision of bor-ders on a massive scale and a process of redefining statehood while breaking the bonds of "legitimate" governmental struc-tures. Hybrid forms of traditional modes of social organization are emerging, slowly and painfully, and relationships between those governing and those governed increasingly refuse the Western model. Democracy as we preach it has reached its high watermark, and collective welfare—indigenously defined—increasingly takes precedence over human rights. Where elec-tions are held in the noncompetitive world, "democracy" is used to legitimize the tyranny of the largest tribe or dominant inter-est group. Those who purvey democracy to an unprepared cul-ture aggravate ethnic and religious divisions to the point of violence—and even find themselves the unwitting sponsors of genocide.

Having failed miserably in competition on our terms, oth-erwise disparate populations in Africa, Asia, and the European borderlands are attempting to develop or reconstruct their own terms of political, social, and economic organization. This is not a conscious or rational process, but an instinctive fight for survival. For all of the pan-African or pan-Arab rhetoric about third paths and alternative models of development, resi-dents of the third world tacitly viewed the West as the standard by which they needed to measure themselves. They struggled to become those whom they reviled, and failed. Now, inarticu-lately enraged by the evidence of that failure, these broken states are attempting to do no less than to detach themselves from our history. The sole concession they are willing to make is to accept those Western material items to which they are addicted and with which they cannot supply themselves, such as armaments and videocassette recorders. Otherwise, these states, from Algeria to Zaire, from Iran to Serbia, are plunging willfully backward into the embrace of the old familiar, be it the penitentiary of religion, an opiate vision of a lost golden age, or simply the primal fury of the have-not.

This dual-phase model of the "other" world's rejection of the Euro-American vision does not signal any apocalyptic decline of the West. The West is immeasurable in its relative power and has even expanded to include key nations that are "Eastern" on maps. In hospitable cultural environments, the adaptive nation-state is enduringly viable and efficient. From the Western perspective, this rejection by noncompetitive states does little more than limit potential vacation spots and increase the risk to certain investments. The "apocalypse" is occurring in the rejectionist states themselves, where demagogic leaders, mass movements, and criminal gangs impoverish their lands and peoples—perhaps irremediably. In the name of cultural integrity, states such as Iran commit structural suicide. The challenge for the West is to salvage the essential, while avoiding commitments that can lead to nothing but blood, expense, and policy failure.

For the failed states themselves there is one slim hope. It is that their passage through anarchy will not excite Western interference, allowing these regions to enter a synthetic phase in which they fashion organic structures of control and efficient geographic parameters for their home areas and regions—a process interrupted by the rise of the West. In the noncompetitive world, apparent chaos is seeking equilibrium. Outside influences only prevent the achievement of that equilibrium, as we have done most recently in Somalia and the former Yugoslavia.

Africa, over which the well-intentioned wring their hands, can wish for nothing better than abandonment until it finds its own path. The process will appear gruesome to outside observers, but intervention will only prolong the present misery. The Arab-Persian Islamic world, on the other hand, is so entangled with the West that all the fervent mullahs in the world may not be able to return its cultural integrity and chart a divorced course. But this passage to resolution is a next, hypothetical stage, and all that we in the West can know is that much of our planet has entered a period of breaking states, resurgent nations, dissolving boundaries, and bloodshed which we cannot prevent, ameliorate, or even fully understand.

ON COLLECTIVE KNOWING

If we are to achieve any useful understanding of the sense of "senseless violence" and the logic of what so often appears to us to be illogically destructive behavior in the noncompetitive world, we must strive to cleanse ourselves of the received prejudices current in the Western-thinking world. We must seek an "extraterrestrial" view—one that looks at this planet as an entity from an intellectual remove. This is, of course, not wholly possible. But so many of our most beloved paradigms, from the universal efficacy of democracy to the inherent morality of the human animal, are proving wrong that we need to seek as neutral a vantage point as we can achieve. Our understanding of human social and political behavior is on the verge of a breakthrough—perhaps a series of breakthroughs—which are only delayed by our unwillingness to apply laws that are accepted in the world of physics, biology, or environmental studies to humankind. Our fear of discovering that which we may not like has an impact equivalent to the Roman Church's sixteenth-century fear of science: crippling. We have reached the point where complexity studies are far more apt to explain mass behavior than are traditional works of political philosophy, but we cannot bear the notion that we might, beyond our cherished individual roles in the world, be slaves of a collective determinism that manifests itself as Hutus and Tutsis butchering each other a hundred thousand at a time, as Serbs mass-raping Muslim women, or as merciless criminal organizations filling voids left by Russian non-government. Yet, when pressed for an explanation as to why such things occur, diplomats, vicars, and social scientists have no meaningful answers.

The interdisciplinary study of complexity, mass behavior, and cultural determinism is going to be a growth field, no matter how many Galileos are called up before the Inquisition. Naturally, the accepted tools for interpreting the world around us have powerful defenders who will resist any truth that threatens what they have published or taught, or around which they have organized their careers and personal belief systems. To move to another analogy, anyone who attacks the supremacy of the individual, the universal applicability of democracy, and the sanctity of the nation-state is in the position of those nineteenth-century doctors who developed the germ theory of disease and had to win over a highly respected, well-paid, socially dominant collegium of doctors whose life-works had been devoted to inflicting mistaken, often deadly, ideas on the suffering.

Just as individuals cannot adequately explain why they love their particular beloved (often "beyond reason"), so collectives, such as clans, tribes, and nationalities, do not always act in full consciousness of the motivations of their behavior. While facile explanations abound, the Germans still cannot logically explain the Holocaust any more than the Azeris of Sumgait can tell why they suddenly began torturing and massacring the Armenian population of their city—beside whom they had lived for a century or more. In retrospect, historians believe they can explain the ascendancy of Christianity in the waning centuries of the Western Roman Empire, but who at the time would have believed it possible that an esoteric cult risen from the Palestinian dust would digest the highest regional civilization? In books, vast tribal migrations and wars of cultural resolution now appear logical and neat, but it is unlikely that the actual participants one day woke up and said, "Well, it's time to change the cultural equilibrium in Eurasia. Saddle up."

We are all parts of greater entities. We can accept this when the evidence is tangible. We are webbed into corporations, social clubs, armies, unions, political parties, governments, credit unions, and so forth. These organizations often take on a "life of their own." But we resist the notion that ethnic or cultural groupings might have an organic life of their own, with inarticulate collective impulses that are just as savage, uncompromising, and virulent as the individual drive to love.

The point is that the murderous children in Liberian rebel Charles Taylor's Small Boy's Unit or the renegade warriors in Russia's lost dominions may be rejecting failed models and striving toward new forms of social, political, and moral organization without the least personal knowledge of the greater consequences of their actions. The mass senses and the mass acts. Sometimes it acts functionally and the result is "progress." At other times, mass instincts are dysfunctional—just as the individual's choice of lover or spouse may be flawed. The mass intoxicated by pogroms and the lover intoxicated by desire cannot coherently explain their sudden "aberrant" behavior. Statistically, however, collective choices are apt to equal survival choices.

The clans, tribes, belief groups, and peoples who are in the process of attempting to reject the West are not fully cognizant of what they are doing. For radical Islamic fundamentalists, the West is a clearer target than it is for the African rebel at a road-block, yet neither could identify the full range of stimuli and impulses behind their behavior. But, if the practitioners of rejection do not entirely understand what they are up to as they act on collective inspiration, we in the West have got our analysis of events almost entirely wrong.

THE GRAND ILLUSION

The West missed the essence of the first phase of its rejection by cultures it had overwhelmed because we interpreted events through the lens of fear. With the rise of Bolshevism in Russia, we sank into a dualistic interpretation of the world. Movements striving for liberation from colonialism and newly independent states were either (at least nominally) democratic-market in nature and thus "Western bloc" in their orientation, or communist-socialist and therefore "Eastern bloc." Bluntly repressive states that did not mouth leftist slogans were quietly accepted into the Western camp. We focused on the manners and missed the soul of events. Both democracy and socialism (two worldviews that shape political, economic, and social poli-cies) are Western creations, the first refined in North America, the second largely defined at Europe's eastern extreme. Both democracy and socialism embodied "Western" aspirations and possibilities. The first was the eccentric harvest of an isolated island where it had been nurtured for centuries by elites work-ing in a hothouse environment until it was ripe enough to make international market inroads in an era, known as "the Age of Reason," when part of Europe rejected nonquantifiable paths to knowledge. The second solidified within a worldview compacted by continental oppression then exposed to the twin storms of Romanticism and nationalism—both of which brewed up in the "other Europe" in reaction to the limitations the Enlightenment implied for existing and emerging elites. The differences between democracy and socialism are best embodied by the opposed tonalities of "We, the People," versus *das Volk,* but, in any case, both schools of political philosophy developed in the cultural soil of the West, and, should any last proof be wanted of socialism's ineradicable Westerness, one need only turn to the case of Russia, the eternal half-breed.

Russia was never more Western than between October 1917 and October 1993, and may never be so Western again. Before the Bolshevik coup, only Russia's elites had a Western mantle, which they wore self-consciously, if extravagantly. The peasants lived in circumstances of poverty, filth, and remarkable ignorance that had no like in Europe after the Black Death pandemic of the fourteenth century, whose elimination of surplus labor resources began the long processes of labor-class empowerment and social self-knowledge. Russia's pre-revolutionary industrial workers huddled in nightmarish slums and factory barracks where they enjoyed few rights and fewer prospects. Under a veneer of law, Westward-peering Russia remained a khanate, and even the Great Reforms did not change its slave-culture mindset (Soviet Russia's adoption of the legacy of Spartacus was especially appropriate, since the Russian "Civil War" had so many characteristics of a slave revolt—especially its merciless destruction of the ruling class along with its totems, as well as its corollary obsession with social leveling). The subject of Russia's identity crisis, of Slavophiles versus Westernizers, needs no further development here, except to note that the issue was decisively resolved for the Communist duration. Although Lenin, Stalin, and their pale successors never tired of reporting Russia's besieged uniqueness, their behavior was consistently that of the most desperate Westernizer, making Peter the Great appear no more than a tinkerer in comparison. Precursor to other "third world" states, Communist Russia aped the West with more vigor than insight, planting the soil with vast "Western" factories, militantly educating the masses, sanctifying the hard sciences, expanding the role of the female citizen, developing the structures of government into a secular church, and organizing, organizing, organizing. No other state tried so hard or so willingly paid so high a price in its attempt to compete with—and, ultimately, join—the West.

Yet, in the end, Marx was right—Russia was not ready for his European system. And Russia in its Soviet incarnation failed. Today, the old voices sound again in Moscow, stressing Russia's separate destiny and rejecting Western solutions to the present calamity. And, at least in this, the Zhirinovskis and Rutskois may be right—while the West itself has not failed Russia (we had neither the interest nor the resources nor the chance), Western ideas have failed Russia miserably. Now Russia will find its own path to misery. A European system—socialism in its Soviet variant—could not be transplanted even onto a hybrid, neighboring culture.

Is it any wonder that socialism has failed farther afield?

The bad news, of course, is that democracy is equally bound to fail in those regions where it does not adequately coincide with preexisting cultural dispositions and economic circumstances.

WHY DEMOCRACY DOESN'T WORK IN BUJUMBURA

Enlightened Euro-Americans would not dream of descending upon an African or Asian country with an ultimatum to the effect that all government-to-government and trade relations will depend on the immediate adoption of Western dress. We think nothing, however, of attempting to inflict upon other peoples forms of government ill-tailored to their needs. The Western crusade—and it is nothing less—to make democracy fit the body of every state is nothing more than evolved imperialism.

Democracy cannot function as we wish it to in any country where the population is in daily competition for survival resources. Democracy is a luxury whose maintenance requires the ready availability to the general population of surplus, or enhancement, resources; otherwise, the electorate votes not wisely but hungrily. The less developed the economy, the greater the tendency to block vote along tribal, ethnic, or religious lines. After the election, the majority grouping uses democractic legitimization to oppress the minority group or groups who lost, depriving them of any "fair share" in the state's resource pool. At the extreme, this leads to man-induced famines, internal blockades, water deprivation, exclusion from state organizations, and the use of state instruments of power to oppress . . . or kill. Once in power, majority-backed or power-base leaders too often declare that their democratic mandate means the people have spoken—once and for all; alternatively, the victorious party adjusts state structures to insure its continued success at the polls. No voting block is inclined toward compromise if compromise means its own constituents perish. Only states "rich" enough to routinize non-confrontational resource swapping at the level of individual citizens can hope to make democratic forms of government work—and even then cultural restraints more often than not prevent democracy from functioning in the Western style.

We expect impoverished Russia, ruined Zaire, or disappointed Algeria to perform at the level of political tolerance and cooperative participation of the British or United States systems, and when the hungry, the disemployed, and the outraged vote for Vladimir Zhirinovski or an Islamic fundamentalist party promising to begin its rule by dismantling democracy, we in the West are all thoroughly surprised. Yet, even in the United States, newly enfranchised groups have a history of block voting. In the second half of the nineteenth century, urban Irish immigrant populations gained political control of cities such as Boston, and Irish block voting has only begun to break down in the last generation. Minority Americans continue to vote in blocks for one party over another. What saves the United States from the majority tyranny of noncompetitive states is not only our Constitution but ethnic dilution that allows no single group to dominate; further, the prosperity of the United States continually provided for upward socioeconomic mobility, and the higher the class status, the more diversity of opinion emerges, no matter the ethnic background—as long as the attained socioeconomic status is perceived as secure. When the most successful members of a society believe in their own continued upward mobility, they enjoy the luxury of voting with the relative have-nots on noncritical issues. In a benign political environment, prosperity fractures ethnicity; however, the speed of assimilation depends on the degree of cultural matching between prevailing norms and values in the receptor society and those of the immigrant group (this also applies to internal migrations from agricultural to urban settings or from poor to more prosperous regions, in which adaptive ability is crucial to socioeconomic success).

In the diaspora that followed the European revolutions of 1848 and in the wake of the concurrent Irish Potato Famine, the United States rapidly moved from relative ethnic and confessional homogeneity to a melting-pot diversity that diffused power among so many groups that political parties needed to generalize their appeal in order to gain majorities, and popular interests became sufficiently dynamic and fluid to prevent stasis. At the same time, forced social norm and language integration fractured ethnic identities within a generation—and no immigrant group had to make war for survival resources—although they may have had to struggle for enhancement resources and social recognition. Even among first-generation immigrants, there soon were rich and poor German-Americans, rich and poor Jewish-Americans, and rich and poor Italian-Americans (despite a great deal of well-intentioned rhetoric, contemporary African-Americans are not struggling for survival resources; rather, the contest is for a greater share of enhancement resources—equitable luxury attainment). Although ethnic or religious groups in the United States may retain a vestigial bias in favor of one party or the other, ultimately the individual decides. There are WASP Democrats and African-American Republicans, and the trend throughout American history has been for greater interparty mobility as individual socioeconomic interests evolve.

Interestingly, the very Americans who champion individual human rights and democracy abroad are now much more apt to protect perceived group rights against the effects of democracy in the West. Calls for multiculturalism are perhaps the greatest threat to democracy in the United States since the Civil War, amounting to the tyranny of often-arcane minorities. The United States is a unified culture with multiple roots and cannot function as a democracy otherwise. When voters and citizens begin again to perceive themselves as Tibetans or Animists first, the melting-pot process that has served democracy so well reverses itself and a centrifugal effect comes into play. Democracy works in the United States because we had the material resources to break apart immigrant "tribes" using an accreted system of rewards. Proponents of multiculturalism and linguistic relativism in the West are unwittingly supporting re-tribalization. Although apt to picture themselves as the true champions of democracy, they are its mortal enemies.

Democracy along ethnic lines brings you Yugoslavia. Democracy amid religious confrontation brings you Nigeria. Democracy in a collapsing economy brings you Algeria. Democracy under all three conditions brings you to the clot of states that spilled from the former Soviet Union.

BUT PEOPLE LIKE DEMOCRACY . . . DON'T THEY?

Yes. Promises of empowerment have a universal appeal. Virtually anyone can be inspired by the prospect of more control over his or her environment. But, beyond the golden notion, there are crippling practical problems. As noted above, electorates in noncompetitive states vote along clan, ethnic, and religious lines. Majorities, enthroned, persecute rather than share (deprivation democracy). Also, such electorates lose interest in elections very quickly when the results fail to bring swift, positive change, and economic crises polarize the population until democracy becomes dysfunctional. Democracy has been oversold as a wonder drug for ailing societies and cultures. Present-day Russia is exemplary. Voter participation diminishes, and those who do vote use democracy to emplace nondemocratic figures. In the end, democracy is not a utopian state of being, but simply a tool that is applicable in some circumstances but not in others. It is also a tool that can be savagely misused. When leaders or dissidents in the noncompetitive world call for democracy, we must be more critical, asking ourselves how they understand democracy and how they really mean to employ it. Jonas Savimbi espoused democracy until UNITA lost an election. Suddenly, the West's democratic darling looked a bit bloody around the mouth. Tribal conflict remained tribal conflict. We in the West have become vulnerable to manipulation by anyone in the noncompetitive world clever enough to pronounce the word "democracy." Perhaps it is time to judge men by their deeds and not their words.

WHAT DO WE REALLY WANT?

In marginally competitive states, such as Turkey or Pakistan, where democracy can claim partial success, there has been a recurring requirement for correctives—usually military intervention to put the ship of state back on a course that avoids fatal shoals. Whenever this happens, the West reacts reflexively, damning those who interfere with electoral results. Yet, anyone who knew Turkey before the last military intervention in the affairs of state and who witnessed the results of that action a decade later, would have to admit that the Turkish military saved democracy—the Turkish General Staff took over a country wracked by terrorism and economic failure and repaired it to the point where democracy could resume. Pakistan has a similar experience. Euro-Americans have learned a blinding anti-militarism that prevents them from understanding that, in some states, the military is the most consistently responsible element— and, paradoxically, the only institution capable of preserving democracy in the long term. It appears that we would rather see a country collapse into disgovernment and misery than see it rescued by means we find unflattering to our system of prejudices. Instead of howling for democracy at any cost, we might do better to evaluate each state and region on its own terms, trying to grasp where democracy can and cannot work, what hybrid forms democracy must take—and when democracy is merely a guise for repression of those not numerous or influential enough to protect themselves from the tyranny of the majority.

Democracy, partial democracy, and aspirant democracy each exist with numerous variations and, where they are viable and beneficial to the population as a whole, deserve the support of the West. When we insist, however, that democracy is always the only answer, we risk harming those whom we seek to help. Given the proper conditions, democracy remains by far the most attractive form of government. Under the wrong circumstances, democracy can be the wrong system at the wrong place at the wrong time—and with utterly wrong results. We in the West need to get beyond the talismanic effect of the word "democracy" and examine the real conditions under which foreign populations suffer. Then we must ask ourselves what we really want to achieve. If our only response to socioeconomic illness in the noncompetitive world is to attempt to enforce democracy and free markets without intelligent discrimination, we are equivalent to a doctor who prescribes the same drug for every patient without taking into account the individual symptoms.

In the right cultural and economic environment, democracy is an inexhaustible treasure; in an unprepared environment, it is Pandora's box.

EVERYBODY'S RIGHT!

A basic flaw in the argument over whether command-distribution or market-economy systems more efficiently utilize resources is that the arguers generally assume a neutral state of development. Since the Soviet Union and its deformed offspring states failed, we in the West (and elsewhere) assume that proof positive now exists that the market always knows best. This is a dangerous error that can badly damage if not destroy states in the noncompetitive world.

These two opposite systems of resource management are each appropriate at different levels of poverty or prosperity.

While local considerations make for myriad exceptions, generally, command-distribution (authoritarian or even totalitarian)
systems are not only more efficient but usually fairer under the
circumstances of poverty (defined as insufficient or barely sufficient survival resources). As a state or society transitions to
prosperity (fully sufficient survival resources and increasingly
available enhancement resources), the market gains in relative
efficiency—and fairness. Market systems under conditions of
poverty disproportionately concentrate available resources;
conversely, command systems are soon overwhelmed by the
volume of resource management requirements under the conditions of prosperity. The mercilessness of the market so often
cited by Marxists genuinely exists in poverty structures, and
grows more brutal as poverty intensifies. In prosperous structures, however, market systems undergo a remarkable transformation and begin to demonstrate inclusive generosity—the
market needs consumers able to consume.

Poverty means not only fewer resources but fewer alloca-
tional decisions, allowing centralized management. As prosperity increases and resource-exploitation webs complicate
exponentially, however, decisionmaking must be diffused to be
timely and effective. This is evident in the case of the former
Soviet Union. Following the Russian Civil War's devastation of
an already underdeveloped economic infrastructure, the
poverty inherited by the Red victors was perfectly suited to
command management and planning. The macro-economy
operated on so simple and needy a level, that the centralized
mobilization of resources achieved levels of (admittedly
roughshod) development the speed and scope of which astonished and frightened the West. The great Soviet mistake was
the failure to recognize the point of development at which a
rigid command system becomes counterproductive and only

the plasticity of market mechanisms can accommodate further progress. Five-year plans were terrific, if harsh, tools during the Soviet Union's first forty years or so, and resource distribution, despite the eccentric horrors of Stalinism, was statistically far more equitable than it had been under the czarist regime. But, as the Soviet economy grew in complexity, even the metastasizing Moscow planning bureaucracies could not adequately forecast critical interactions—and could not respond flexibly to problems even as their existence became clear. The plan giveth, and the plan taketh away. The rise and fall of the Soviet economic system also became a story of technological progress. Command methods are suitable to building a traditional industrial base, a highly structured endeavor; they are not appropriate for post-industrial development, which depends on unpredictable numbers of informal interactions that play chicken with chaos. The acceleration of the post–World War II technological revolution meant that economies had to react ever more quickly, and under conditions of ever greater complexity. Micro-economic decisionmaking must occur locally, and those decisions help shape macro-economic policy in healthy post-industrial states. The Soviets had it just the opposite: Macro-economic policy, directed by bureaucrats in the capital, drove micro-economic decisions about milk production in distant provinces. This is also the dilemma faced by the late Soviet and current Russian military—a rigid, hierarchical system served them well in the Great Patriotic War and became institutionalized. Contemporary techno-war requires an unnerving amount of decentralized decisionmaking. As in their economy, today's Russian military is stuck with yesterday's system and fierce bureaucratic loyalties to it, and transforming that system is far easier in the realm of theory than in the realm of the regiment.

State economies worldwide that have made the greatest
progress in the last generation, from the East Asian "tigers" to
Chile and Mexico, recognized the roles central planning and
market mechanisms play at different levels of development. The
majority of these states also have either become more democratic or are struggling to control democratic impulses among
their populations. The lesson seems to be that if you really want
democracy to have a chance in a country, the best initial step is
to sponsor economic development—and not to demand fully
free market systems from insufficiently developed states.

Successful economic development does not guarantee an
eventual transition to democracy, since cultural factors also
play a role. But it comes close. It is hard to find a truly prosperous state where the political role of the general population is
not increasing. Obvious exceptions, such as Saudi Arabia and
various Persian Gulf states, do not track because they have not
undergone a process of balanced, participatory economic
development. They are not economies, they are banks. Their
wealth fell from the heavens (or rose from under the earth's
surface, anyway), and, were oil resources to lose their value
tomorrow, most such states would have few productive alternatives to which they could resort. They would be the geopolitical
equivalent of spinsters living off of yesterday's investments, with
nothing to offer a world passing them by.

KRISHNA AND COMPANY

Our national desire to uniformly apply democracy without taking account of the local environment is indicative of how far
we have come from basic survival concerns. Our societal organization, our evolved religion, even our way of making war are
predicated upon material surplus. While our ancestors worked
hard, we have also been very lucky. Other societies have been

less fortunate and have been faced with structural decisions utterly alien to Euro-Americans. Generally, the organizational choices most foreign to us have been made by peoples either too rich demographically, too poor in material resources, or both.

Consider India. The Indian caste system evolved as a system of resource distribution. This system was so crucial to elite survival that it was codified by an overlay of religion. India (and China, which also evolved into a highly structured society) faced the burden of too many people and too few resources for as long as records or even legends exist. Much as a besieged city apportioned its most generous rations to the soldiers defending its walls, India had to insure the survival of its most essential subpopulations—its genetic defenders. Thus Indians fashioned a religious system functionally suited to their predicament. This is not meant to belittle man's religious impulse, but to acknowledge the often unrecognized role religious structures can play in resource allocation within a society. China, faced with similar dilemmas, made religious choices that appear quite different at first, but also served to condition surplus population to acceptance of resource inadequacy.

Islam came from the opposite corner of the ring, originating in a desert region where the actual numbers of the population were relatively small, resources were genuinely and not just relatively scarce, and violence was an acceptable solution to resource competition (violence does not settle resource apportionment in demographically dense environments, but only inspires retributory violence—as in Kashmir today; on the other hand, violent solutions work where populations are small enough to allow the extermination of competitors, a Middle Eastern tradition dating at least to the military states of ancient Mesopotamia). Where both Hinduism and Buddhism have deep strains of passive acceptance, Islam is aggressive. Just as Indian and Chinese societies have great capacities for cultural absorption, Arab-Persian and, to a markedly lesser extent, Turkic cultures have a very low tolerance for foreign cultural penetration. Hindu and Buddhist/Buddhist-derivative cultures are resilient; Islam has the strength—and brittleness—of iron. Ultimately, the stories of the decline and collapse of the Arab, Ottoman, and Mameluke empires are a single tale of the inability to fully internalize foreign technologies and organizational methodologies. That which is distinctly foreign is also distinctly threatening to the Islamic world—and the more successful the foreign mechanism, the more threatening (and fascinating) it becomes. Historically, attempts to open Islamic societies to technological progress have resulted in social cataclysms such as those recently experienced by Iran and currently under way in Algeria.

While the Ottoman elite initially drew great strength from its exploitation of cultures it conquered or contacted, employing Armenian architects, Slavic elite troops, and hired Venetian cannoneers, its core members never developed the technical skills relevant to modernity. Within the Ottoman Empire, a division of labor prevailed that effectively excluded Turks from progressive fields until it was too late. A victim of elite exclusiveness, the Ottoman Empire perished. Cultures such as those of Japan and China, on the other hand, have demonstrated remarkable capacities for digesting foreign means without compromising cultural integrity. Such cases bring us beyond simple models of economic development to the more painful study of culture.

THE UNSPEAKABLE MR. DARWIN

What if that rough contemporary of Marx, Charles Darwin, was dead right but too humble in his scope? What if entire cultures, like species, can become noncompetitive and doomed? History offers plenty of dinosaur cultures for inspection, but, in our current intellectual environment, the likes of Mr. Darwin are not invited to the happy multicultural party. Just as we instinctively assume that the world order to which we have become accustomed in our adult lives is the only possible order (and all aberrations must be either righted or rationalized away), we place ourselves above history. The Babylonians and Aztecs might be gone, but we refuse to contemplate the notion that any extant culture might perish. Unwilling to accept that cultures may have life cycles, which extend or contract depending on their ability to interact with or assert themselves over other cultures, we pity the Inca and scorn the cruelty of the Spaniard. To the contemporary Westerner, other cultures are to be respected and preserved (an attitude that makes us unique).

We may be in the midst of the most epochal phase of cultural competition since the destruction of the Byzantine world by the Ottoman Turks and the roughly contemporary Iberian expansion into the Americas. Not the later stages of European colonialism, nor the Mughal embrace of India's upper torso, nor the Russian conquest of Central Asia had a like impact, since the Byzantine and pre-Columbian cultures were so vitiated as to be utterly noncompetitive, while nearly all of the latter subject cultures possessed the strength to survive in a recognizable condition. In dealing with today's sub-Saharan Africa or the Islamic world, we may again be colliding with cultures as relatively fragile as those of end-game Constantinople or Tenochtitlan. Our "opponents" in this conflict of cultures are struggling for their last shreds of identity. We are so musclebound that we are insensitive to their desperation.

THE GOLDEN PROMISE

It was impossible for us to grasp what was really happening in the post-colonial era. First, we would have had to see past the internecine Western squabble over democracy versus socialism. Next, we would have had to look beyond the rhetoric of third world leaders, theorists, and revolutionaries to their actions, but such dispassionate analysis is not part of human nature. When Franz Fanon damned us, when Nkrumah briefly drowned us out, and Dr. Mossadegh seemed poised to betray our interests, we weighed their words on Western scales and failed to discern their deeper intentions—intentions these impressive figures could not themselves fully understand, so imprisoned were they in webs of culture. They and thousands of their peers had been hopelessly seduced by Western ideas. For all their regionalist or particularist trappings, such men dreamed of the moral amenities described by Jefferson and Marx. They burned to sweep away the colonizers, real or imagined, but they had been fatally infected by political visions acquired in English, French, American—or Soviet Russian—universities, in colonial schools, or while wearing the uniforms of colonial regiments. Post-colonial doers, such as Nasser, who sent us packing, and Nehru the nonaligned, had only Western models to emulate, and their crucial vocabulary was that of Western political science. Even Gandhi, the Christ of anti-colonialism, could not transcend the Western framework of statehood. Contemporary critics in the non-Western world decry the omnipresence of Western pop media. But Western ideas of statehood, government, and the inviolability of borders got there first, and were at least as pervasive—and every bit as impossible to replicate.

The idea of the nation-state was so enchanting that colonial borders—each a guarantee of discord—were embraced by most newly independent states. Would-be nations, such as Nigeria and Zaire, fought horrid civil wars to preserve unions that had no internal logic.

Stripped of revolutionary or devolutionary rhetoric, the goal of the Western-educated elites who led Europe's colonies and mandates to independence was to transplant the best of the West with an effectiveness that would astonish the erstwhile colonial masters. Even the more brutal military cliques who so often and so quickly replaced those nationalist leaders with the Oxbridge accents nursed a Western vision for their countries. Unfortunately, this was the vision of the barracks, not of the debating society. When their rejection of the West seemed at its fiercest, it was only that their frustration had grown so terribly. For neither the earnest doctors of philosophy nor the heel-cracking ex-NCOs proved able to turn Lagos into London. Even the most vehemently nativist programs were about dressing up in costumes while aspiring to compete with Shell or Chevron.

THE MOVING GOALPOST

Entire books have been and will be written about the failure of post-colonial states to compete politically or economically. Depending on the bias of the author or professorial collective, past and current developmental disasters are blamed upon CIA plots or the malevolence of multinational corporations, on the International Monetary Fund, incorrect investment decisions, or the proxy wars of the Cold War. Rather harder to find in print is the possibility that some cultures simply may not be able to compete by the rules of other cultures.

This idea need not imply any bigotry about racial inferiority. North Americans and Europeans have had a devilish time competing in the Japanese market, and, although laws and tariffs play their roles, it's clear to all that foreign business strategists simply did not (and largely do not) understand Japan's business or social culture. In that context, *our* culture has been noncompetitive. This is the stuff of which acceptable parlor talk is made. But to suggest that Nigeria is a mess or the Shah's Iran collapsed because they tried to become another culture in crucial respects might only be whispered in the hushed tones once reserved for the discussion of venereal disease. The operative maxim for Westerners is that the only culture whose failure can be acknowledged is our own.

Race genuinely does not matter. Culture does. When transplanted from a noncompetitive culture to the West, some individuals succeed beyond Western societal norms, while others languish. The difference appears to come from the willingness of the individual immigrant to embrace the values and totems of the Western society by which he or she is received, as well as on individual traits, such as skill, intelligence, and ambition. Some source cultures, such as the Islamic closed-universe culture, hinder attempts at integration more than do others, but, even so, achievement ultimately depends on the individual. Cultures with values congruent to Western values, such as those of much of East Asia, give the immigrant an initial advantage, since he or she does not have to break out of a hermetic worldview. This also applies at the macro-level of competition, as will be discussed below.

The competitive plight of third world states has been complicated by their lack of a static target. At no point could a president or economic planner state that, when such-and-such had been achieved, his government would be an equal partner for the West. The West (and its real competitors in East Asia) continued to develop, raising the bar ever higher. Even in periods of recession and stagflation, so evocative of doom to Western analysts who never saw a real slum, the West and its Far Eastern adjuncts continued to lunge ahead in both real and relative terms. Soviet Russia, despite its enormous resources and agonizingly acquired industrial base, failed because formal long-term planning could not keep pace with the ever more complex technological integration of the West. How much real competitive possibility did that leave for Zaire?

CULTURE, CULTURE, CULTURE . . .

While individual state failures might be blamed upon a lack of oil resources or transportation infrastructure, on collapsed ore prices and overpopulation, the unifying denominator in the inability to compete with the West governmentally, militarily, economically, and socially is culture. The noncompetitiveness of some cultures, such as the Arab-Persian Islamic or sub-Saharan African cultures, is highlighted by the success of other cultures in taking charge of their destinies—despite a near-total lack of resources, the ravages of war, and a slow start out of the gate. The economic powerhouses of East Asia—Japan, Singapore, Taiwan, upstart South Korea, and, perhaps, gigantic China with its gigantic problems—have each come from behind with sufficient force to make the traditional West, of which they are becoming an effective part, very nervous.

Liberal critics will object that the "failed" cultures of Africa and Asia were victims of colonialism. Yet no African and no Islamic countries were colonized for so long or so harshly by Europe as was Korea by Japan. Singapore exists *because* it was a colony. And Iran, although its shahs were sometimes made or unmade by foreign powers, was never a colony. Colonialism was responsible for many ills, but it ultimately falls short as an explanation for chronic underdevelopment. China was as sullied by foreign interlopers as was Egypt, and Japan suffered a military defeat in living memory that inflicted more human and material damage in real terms than did any colonial regime since the Spanish conquest of southerly America. In contrast, the more enlightened colonial regimes left functioning infrastructures and educated elites to manage them.

Although all generalities can be driven to an extreme where they founder on particulars, it appears clear that there existed a felicitous consonance between the existing cultures of much (though not all) of East Asia and the demands of Western techno-industrial modernity, while the social structures had sufficient strength to absorb the impact of Western ideas of government and nationhood, selecting those that rhymed and discarding those that did not. The successful East Asian states had the cultural robustness to go shopping in the Western arcade without running into excessive ideological or moral debt. Less self-disciplining cultures tried to buy all of the toys at once and ended unable to afford any of them. Perhaps the crucial cultural quality of the East Asian (nation-) states that allowed them to succeed was, paradoxically, their capacity for humility as well as pride.

NO SECOND CHANCES

The noncompetitive world is entering the second, genuine phase of its rejection of the West at an accelerating pace. The fundamental consequence of the renewed ascent of the West in the "post-industrial" age has been the establishment of an even greater, ever more unbridgeable gulf between the failed states and the West. Fanon's wretched-of-the-earth no longer merely need to learn to write in order to stride toward competitiveness, they now need to learn to write in computer languages. The response of the have-nots—or know-nots—is illiterate, inarticulate, and ultimately physical rage that hastens their own destruction.

In the modern age, the history of competition between cultures (civilizations) has been largely a tale of technological

progress (although that progress is only a surface manifestation of deeper cultural proclivities). In the premodern
era, organizational progress could overcome a competitor's
incremental technological improvements, but today technology drives organization to an extent that makes technology the
sine qua non of progress. Increasingly, unless a child is
immersed in the total cultural environment of the West, he or
she cannot catch up and compete at a later date. This is a
nascent trend that will extrapolate almost vertically. The infrastructure of progress has become so complex, webbed, and
interdependent that it cannot be absorbed piecemeal. The real
lesson of Desert Storm was that you cannot buy bits of a system,
no matter how high the quality of those fragments, and hope
for a return equal to that received when the subsystem is used
in its synergistic context. The coalition victory was the triumph
of the U.S. military's integration of the means of knowing with
the means of doing. Modern weapons—and computers and
hospital appliances—are less than the sum of their parts unless
they are employed in the overarching framework for which
they were designed and where they must perform competitively in order to survive.

There is nothing more overtly Darwinian than the struggle
for "life" of applied technologies in the Western system. The
ruthlessness of the market ensures the survival only of the
fittest. Were we to apply our protective standards for human
rights to "product" rights—something planned economies,
such as the Soviet, have done—our progress would largely disappear. The Western cultural receptivity to change—although
very imperfect—is greater than that of any other extant culture. It is a weapon so secret we don't realize its power ourselves. We, in the West, don't really suffer from future
shock—only from occasional indigestion. The debilitating
shocks strike traditionalist cultures.

The constant flux of techno-progress is impossible for traditionalist cultures, such as the Arab-Persian, to bear. The ideal state for traditional cultures is obtained when the clock stands still. In Iran, Algeria, Egypt, Sudan, and elsewhere, religious activists struggle to turn back the clock. It argues against their long-term survival, unless they can seclude themselves from external influences to an extent no modern state has managed to sustain. This inability to finally shut out the rest of the world is a source of constant frustration for Iran's clerics, for whom hanging smugglers and citizens in possession of the wrong foreign goods has become a Persian form of import tax.

If there was some hope in the past for other countries to pull abreast of the West in terms of socioeconomic achievement, that hope has now vanished for all but a handful of East Asian and, perhaps, those Latin American states (see below) which are already substantially developed. The window of opportunity has closed. Starting from scratch, as many African states must do, or from a deficit of incorrect developmental decisions, as Russia must do, not a single state will catch up with the West. The interval has become too great. Both trade and diplomacy will be conducted at an increasing disadvantage by these states. The best outcome that any failed state can now hope for is to find an internal equilibrium that placates the most dynamic elements of its own social order.

The tragedy lies in those states that tried the hardest to match the West on its own terms, however veiled that attempt may have been by local rhetoric. Dr. Brzezinski's incisive arc of crisis is only a focused condensation of a much broader belt of failure. Although the number runs well into the dozens of states which have sought, on the wings of democracy, socialism, military rule, and economic competition, to rise to Western heights of governance, influence, social welfare, and wealth, five superficially diverse examples must serve here to illustrate the irresistible pattern of failure and rejection. These cases cover past, present, and impending secessions from Western models of development.

LA VIE EN ROSE

Algeria won its independence from the French government in 1962, but it did not win its "independence" from France. Algeria rid itself of the French but not of French ideas. Far from being a rejection of the West, Algerian socialism was a common-law child of French universities, of French philosophers whose understanding of language far exceeded their understanding of the human race, and of the harsher school provided to Algerians by the French military, from the Western Front to Dien Bien Phu. Underneath the socialist tinsel, the administration of Algeria remained French in its mechanics, and its international economic relations relied upon the devices of capitalism. By the immediately measurable standards, Algeria should have succeeded in its efforts at self-development. The population had a fund of revolutionary energy. The French left a sound, if austere, infrastructure and an educated native elite (although some key revolutionaries were not formally educated). Oil provided the funds for development. Nor were practical ties severed with France, which provided jobs in the metropolitan that served as an escape valve for young Algerians, as well as a wide variety of tutelary relations.

After an initial flurry of infrastructural development, Algeria began to decline. As elsewhere, oil moneys deformed the state. Corruption spread. The government became addicted to its export income and made the classic mistake of linear extrapolation of commodities values: Since oil prices were rising in the 1970s, they must continue to rise. Ambitious development schemes were based on loans which were, in turn, calculated against anticipated future income. But oil prices did not rise consistently. They fell. Investment funds went into classically wrong projects when they did not go into individual or organizational pockets. The National Liberation Front, the FLN, found that peaceful development was far more difficult than insurrection against a galvanizing oppressor.

Today, three decades after Algeria's first, false rejection of the West, the second and real rejection is held at bay only by desperate and increasingly ineffective military rule. The FLN is utterly discredited, and the halo it once wore as champion of the downtrodden has passed to a radical opposition, the Islamic Salvation Front (FIS). The FIS, which rejects all that is both Western and inconvenient, would win any nationwide election—using a Western tool to end the colonialism of Western ideas. The FIS is the Algerian variant of militant Islamic organizations throughout the Arab-Persian world. It does not discuss, but dictates. It knows no compromise. It is exclusive of all behavior that is not in accord with its severe interpretation of Islam. Above all, it wants a reckoning with anyone who admires or emulates the West.

CAN'T BUY ME LOVE . . .

Long bullied, even occupied in fitful bites, but not colonized, Iran did not pass through a classic initial phase of rejecting the West by ejecting a European administration. Instead, there was a long tension between the extremely strong Persian sense of identity and the threat posed to that identity by the superiority of Western tools and organizational means. Russian military forces came and went in the northwest, the British mucked about on the Gulf, and Protestant missionaries and teachers from the United States sponsored Persian rebellions against Persian authorities. Foreign oil companies bought fortunes, and foreign governments bought influence. But Iran never suffered the indignities of orderly government by colonial officers or the cultural humiliation of a Western-style liberal education for the masses. Iranian elites slowly acquired the material symptoms of Westernness, but the social integrity of the masses was never corrupted by examples of alternative models of interpersonal relations. Despite his self-fulfilling accusations of Western control of Iranian affairs, Dr. Mossadegh's brief tenure in power was in reality an attempt to accelerate the Westernization of Iranian society and government. The Shah represented a "medieval" organization of Iran, in which a small number of powerful families exercised hereditary rights over feudal domains (although the Shah himself was the offspring of an upstart family). Mossadegh's objection to Western behavior was that the West propped up an un-Western system. Mossadegh stood for those quaint panaceas of postwar revolutionaries, modernization, democratization, and nationalization. Iran was never colonized by bayonets or foreign office clerks—it was colonized by ideas.

The great sin committed by the United States in Iran was to press the Shah to modernize and liberalize. The closest Iran came to experiencing colonialism was the blind American push for ever more reform. America's uncontrollable urge to fix problems in foreign lands ultimately proved ruinous to America's interests, created a multilayered crisis in Iranian society, and did not prove particularly helpful to the Shah. The Shah's complicity in his own downfall lay in his embrace of the manifestations of modernity he saw in the West without asking why things worked as they did in North America or Europe. Vain to a uniquely Persian extreme, the Shah assumed he could purchase the infrastructure of a modern state and overlay it on a culture that had neither earned nor learned it. The result, for the average Iranian, was bewilderment, social disorientation, and ultimate humiliation. Machines and mechanisms that worked in Chicago did not work in Shiraz. A flagrant and nontraditional maldistribution of wealth polarized a society whose abiding values were under assault. Although material conditions improved for many, progress never matched promise. Western educations highlighted the cultural inferiority of the recipients, and Iran found that its newly purchased tools enslaved it to the foreigners who alone could make those tools go or repair them when they broke. The ultimate fluid Western hands-on culture, that of the United States, collided with an oriental rigidly hierarchical hands-off culture. By the late 1970s the lure of the West lost out to the pull of traditional cultural values. The bedrock and refuge of that culture was religion.

The Iranian revolution was not made only by the mullahs and their legions of the dispossessed. The merchant class had grown disenchanted with many of the Shah's policies as well. But the element that pushed home the initial victory against the Shah was composed of members of the intellectual elite. Many of those who owed their educations and well-being to the Peacock Throne had become diseased with Western political philosophy, of either the democratic or socialist school. They ascribed their country's pathetic inability to assimilate the means of modernity to the Shah's oppression and the corruption it engendered. Those revolutionaries, students, bureaucrats, and men of wealth did not line up against the Shah because they expected to impose a strict religious regime on their native land—they imagined that the mullahs could be managed, much as conservative Germans once imagined that Hitler could be kept on a leash. The Iranians who now form so much of the Persian diaspora were every bit as shocked—perhaps even more so—by the swift triumph of the Ayatollah Khomeini as was anyone in Washington. These elites, fatally Westernized, had lost the pulse of their own people.

In a sense, the brief victory and swift downfall of the liberal revolutionaries in Teheran marked the first, classic phase of the rejection of the West. They sought to sweep away or at least better control American meddling and its consequence, the Shah, so that Iran could fulfill the neo-Western potential they imagined for it. The advent of the clerical dictatorship embodied a swift transition to the second, implacable phase of the rejection of the West. Anyone who wants a preview of what is in store throughout the Arab-Persian and African worlds as more and more countries enter this second phase need only study the aftermath of the Iranian revolution. The educated, Westernized elites will be eliminated, and the frustrated, uneducated, brutal particles of the mass will turn against the shimmering, disappointing, threatening foreignnesses they cannot master.

THE MIDNIGHT HOUR

Nigeria's struggle to crystallize as a nation-state within its European-drawn boundaries has been priced in blood and petrodollars. With sub-Saharan Africa's largest population, Nigeria is divided between an Islamic north and a Christian-Animist south that is further subdivided into discordant ethnic groups (or, to use the T-word, tribes). Nigeria has accomplished a small miracle in surviving so long as a single entity. That miracle was facilitated by money and the military. When the Biafran secession threatened to tear the newborn state into pieces, the military brutally put down the rebellion then behaved with remarkable postwar magnanimity. The attraction of petrodollars cemented the north to the resource-endowed south. But attempts to emulate the example of British democracy each ended in stalemate, recrimination, and the imposition of military rule. The military, with its Sandhurst manners and indigenous morals, came to view itself, and to be viewed by much of the population, as the guardian of Nigerianness. The effort to construct an economically viable state on oil wealth foundered on corruption and a great deal of wishful thinking, much as Algeria's attempt failed. And neither the glowing promises offered in the first pure heat of independence or the ever less inspiring struggle to build a pervasive sense of Nigerian identity came to much. Much as in Russia and elsewhere in the failed regions of the world, the military is the only institution that functions with any degree of dependability (worldwide, the most resilient legacy left by the colonial example is the technique of military organization). Overpopulated, well-armed relative to its neighbors, short of money, and with its expensive overlay of modernity crumbling, today's Nigeria is tomorrow's disaster.

Nigeria is only flirting with the second, thorough phase of the rejection of the West at present, but the consummation is coming. The urban underclass, renewed ethnic and religious rivalries for power, and a regional atmosphere of breakdown all point toward bloody conflict and a rejection of failed Western forms of government and commercial relationships. This conflict may still lie years in the future, and may be postponed by the device of Nigeria's own possible imperial expansion into neighborhood power vacuums, but it is nonetheless inevitable. Once a model of stability in Africa, the West African littoral has fallen into "second-phase" multisided violence so primitive in its details that the West has resolutely turned its eyes away. As in the wreckage of the Soviet empire, African states, such as Liberia and the Gambia, are using merciless, multisided violence to forge new, indigenous (but internationally unsatisfactory) means of government. Nigeria's turn is coming.

In Africa as a whole, a generational change is under way. The "great men" who led their countries to independence are dead or aged. The likes of Julius Nyerere and Kenneth Kaunda are fading from the scene—those inspiring orators of African freedom whose vision of the future was far more Western than ever they realized. The Western-educated elites who were to lead their continent into a vibrant tomorrow have proved ephemeral, and they are being replaced by men who have no vision beyond personal aggrandizement, or, at most, the welfare of their ethnic kin, and who have no experience of the example of colonial government, which for all its deficiencies, provided a model of order, service, relative honesty, and sometimes even justice. In some countries, such as Angola, the new generation of leadership has no experience of anything but the gun. The national framework increasingly serves only the vanity of the ruler, giving him and his power base an internationally sanctioned excuse to butcher those of other bloodlines into submission, so long as those others have the misfortune to live within boundaries drawn in nineteenth-century Berlin. The new strongmen, of whom Joseph Mobutu was a prototype and who are exemplified by Jonas Savimbi and Charles Taylor, have no compunction about shedding blood and no values that transcend blood's traditional loyalties. Despite the habit of political speech, they are not governed by ideologies. They are opportunists whose viciousness throws the greatness of the earlier generation of African leaders into stark relief. Above this rising tide of sergeants, captains, "doctors," and chiefs, one lone representative of the older, morally informed generation remains—perhaps the greatest of them all—Nelson Mandela.

THE GATES OF EDEN
Nelson Mandela and the early incarnation of the African National Congress (ANC) represented the classic first phase of rejection—the movement to eliminate "colonial" rule, with the intention of retaining a nativized Western form of government and a distinctly European humanistic philosophy as its moral substructure. Given the peculiar conditions of South Africa, the white colonizers were not expected to sail for long-lost homes, but they were to join the rest of the indigenous

population on more equal terms. The tragedy of South Africa that will become evident to future historians is that Mandela's terms might have worked, had Pretoria put him in parliament instead of in prison early on. South Africa might have been the one sub-Saharan African country to "make it." But the chance passed a quarter of a century ago, and died with the end of African idealism. The South Africa over which Nelson Mandela will preside will be one of excited, implacable, and inextinguishable hatred, black-black violence, and white-black violence. As a state it may not last in its present form, and the men who rule the rump with Mandela's passing will be no better or worse than their regional peers.

The second phase of the rejection of the West has already begun. The generation(s) that grew to chronological maturity in the shantytowns and homelands while Mandela aged in prison knows nothing of his ideals. The young are led by a different breed of strong, charismatic, ethnically determined men whose loyalty is not and will not be to a state in the Western sense but to tribal and tribal alliance bases of power. Violence is their only collective outlet, the only validation of their existence. Among elements of the white population, especially those from the Boer tribe who again fly the *Vierkleur* above their armed ranks, we will also see a rejection of Western norms of behavior, even though they will cling to the organizational means of the Western state for as long as possible.

Of deadly consequence for sub-Saharan Africa, the second phase of rejection of the West, with its discarding of the model of the nation-state, rings the death knell of the concept of inter-ethnic unity. The belief that different ethnic groups can get on peaceably and equitably is a utopian Western notion, with no empirical foundation. The oft-cited example of the United States does not apply because, for centuries, diverse immigrant groups were forced to subscribe to a core of nationally accepted values and norms of behavior that preexisted their arrival. So long as immigrants came from a European cultural environment, they could be broken to the bit, but even the United States has yet to fully assimilate a single non-European immigrant group, although some groups have made distinctly more progress than others.

The inability of diverse interest groups to cooperate over the long term where one unifying set of values and behavioral norms does not dominate unassailably is readily evident within the West, whether in Northern Ireland or Canada. The former Yugoslavia, quasi-Western, is only an extreme example. In Africa, idealists, Western or formed by the West, believed that, despite ill-drawn borders, states encompassing diverse and often fragmented peoples could amalgamate in a happy carnival of unity. That fantasy survives only on the life-support system provided by Western interference in African affairs and in the regimes of aging autocrats who do not believe in the human unity of their states but are loath to discharge territory. The rejection of Western values evident Africa-wide in the behavior of the current and rising generations includes a wholehearted return to the tribe as the essential and exclusive unity. Until Africa's borders are redrawn along homogenous ethnic lines, the level of violence will continue to increase.

The final gasp of apartheid will not be accompanied by a sudden rain of rewards on the black population of South Africa, the most volatile members of which have an utterly unrealistic and dysfunctional vision of what majority rule will mean. Their leaders have made promises that cannot be fulfilled and will soon need scapegoats. They will blame each other, then the West, both in its immediate white presence and in its distant, imagined omnipotence. There will be years of violence, at least sporadic, possibly continuous. There is no imaginable compromise other than division that could bring all parties into an enduring peace. The only thing that prevents South Africa from an immediate collapse into vast intramural violence is the expectation that tomorrow will bring a miracle.

SYMPATHY FOR THE DEVIL

The second, meaningful phase of Russia's rejection of the West is under way. The first, false rejection occurred in 1917 and in the years immediately thereafter, as the "native" population expelled its "colonial" aristocratic and merchant-class masters. True to the model, liberated Russia then embraced a Western-designed form of political and social organization—socialism *en route* to communism—to the best of its gigantic abilities. No state has ever sacrificed so much in its struggle to attain Western-style modernity, and the manifestations of progress it produced in its prime were sufficient to alarm its Western competitors. Ultimately, however, Russia was not sufficiently Western in its cultural predispositions to compete. So long as hierarchy, muscle, and sacrifice could answer the requirements of modernization, Russia had a chance. A population could be driven to establish vast steel mills in the wilderness or to fortify high dams with their bones. But postmodern societal and economic organization relies on the diffusion of power and on voluntarism rooted in enlightened self-interest. As Russia's failure to compete successfully became apparent, communism (or the late-Soviet deformity thereof) was discarded. Influential Russians reflexively espoused the alternative Western formula—democracy, with capitalism as its engine. But capitalism foundered quickly, except at the traditional level of the bazaar, and Russian-style democracy shows no signs of the Western ability to synthesize consensus. Two cultural deficiencies central to this type of failure worldwide will be discussed below, but there is one immediate and uniquely Russian cause for Moscow's inability to take a deep breath and leap from communism and a planned economy to democracy and the market:

Exhaustion. Russia is worn out. Her people are as ruined as her soil, enervated by the massive efforts and concomitant deprivations they endured in this century. Her culture has withered. This is immediately evident in the arts, where Russia, which stunned the world with its creativity in the last century, has offered nothing nonderivative or even remotely appealing for half a century. In the field of the arts, as in the field of industrial production, Soviet Russia became a pathetic and inept mimic. There is not even the energy left for a good civil war (for which we may all be grateful in this nuclear world), but there are already a number of nasty little ones on the periphery, and these will flare and fade indefinitely. In between occasional gulps of local violence, and perhaps a late lunch of Ukrainian territory, Russia will drowse in a haze of undernourishment. It is impossible to move her people in any positive direction. They have been ruined by the Western philosophy of a German. Stalin and his heirs—aping the political thinkers they murdered—replaced old folk superstitions with modern political ones that hamper change. All failure was the fault of Russia's enemies, within and without. The day's sacrifices would be redeemed by a future resembling paradise on earth. And the West would collapse (an event still predicted, in spittle-drenched prose, by Vladimir Zhirinovsky). Well, none of it happened that way. And now the Russian national gesture is a listless shrug of the shoulders.

Russia, despite childlike promises of reform, has turned away from the West systemically and morally. She rages at her misfortune, blames all but herself, and seeks refuge in past glories, real or imagined. Russia will lurch forward, hungover with its Soviet economic legacy, blindly seeking its own path to the future, a way that is not communism, not capitalism, but Russian. The "Slavophiles" have finally won. The rejection of the Western cultural and intellectual legacy is now and real.

ODD MAN OUT

There has been only one passing mention of Latin America in this text. Ibero-America, which overwhelmingly dominates Latin America, is sufficiently of the West to make complete rejection of Western systems impossible. Over the past several decades, again hampered by our bipolar view of the world, we misread many events in Latin America, confusing the greater number of intracultural civil wars with the far fewer genuine attempts at intercultural revolution. Even the now-tuckered-out tendency to blame the United States every time the plumbing broke down signaled only the resentment of a stalled branch of Western culture toward another branch in ostentatious bloom. "Yankee go home" protests may have looked a lot like demonstrations elsewhere in the world, but they were different in essence. They rarely represented alternative possibilities for the dispossessed; rather, attacks on the U.S. were temper tantrums by Ibero-American elites worried about the preservation of their traditional sources of wealth. The masses were pawns— how many Latin American "revolutions" resulted in the installation of a head of state from the *favelas* or the oxygen-starved villages of the Andean Ridge?

Like the North American "revolution" that led to the formation of the United States, most of the Latin American "revolutions" that detached country after country from Spanish or Portuguese rule were not revolutions at all, but civil wars that happened to occur across international boundaries. In both North and South America, local elites fought to seize power from metropolitan elites whom they mirrored in culture, class, and blood. Real revolutions—cultural cataclysms, such as that which occurred in Haiti—were rare in the Western Hemisphere of the last century and continue to be so to this day. Especially in South America, there was rarely even an evolutionary change in the social order.

In our time, most of the conflicts in Latin America that so alarmed Washington were not revolutions but civil wars fought over which Western political variant would prevail, a local hybrid of democracy, a local hybrid of socialism, or traditional Ibero-American authoritarianism. Some "revolutions" were simply about which families were going to be in charge. There was never a danger of any key country genuinely rejecting the West.

The only worrisome situations occurred in countries with the densest indigenous or ethnically non-European populations, since only they were in a serious position to reject the West—and, generally, only they had serious grievances. Usually, however, even "native" revolts were illusory, involving the attempt by one Ibero-American faction to enlist the indigenous masses against another Ibero-American faction. This was what happened in Nicaragua, where the Sandinistas never took Indian welfare seriously. Even Peru's Sendero Luminoso relies at least partly on Ibero-American leadership, although this organization is petulant about rejecting the West and its brand of ideology is Maoist with an Inca face. Only in rare, inhospitable spots, such as Yucatan, where Ibero-American penetration remained urban and superficial, did genuine peasant revolts occur.

Overall, Mexico has experienced a disproportionate number of indigenous risings that continue down to this day. But, even in Mexico, an Ibero-American elite continues to rule. Once threatened by a civil war that got out of hand and turned into a series of revolutions before it was resolved on civil-war terms, the Mexican elite learned enough of a lesson to remain on top for good. Recent events in Chiapas and the assassination of the man who had been "tapped" to be Mexico's president will not change that.

Che Guevara's greatest disappointment was his inability to inspire the Indians of Bolivia to rise against the country's government. Their apathy bewildered him. But Che's experience in Cuba, which had no Native American population, gave him no insight into the inhabitants of the Bolivian countryside. A Westerner gone a bit delinquent, Che armed himself with French commentaries on revolution and set off to spark fire in the minds of men who could not even read. He believed his struggle was with a political system. In reality, he was ground to death between two cultures.

The indigenous peoples of the Americas have never made a successful revolution against those who colonized their lands. Their cultures were no more structured to withstand assault than were their immune systems, and, compounding the shock, the Europeans came to kill. When their sword arms tired, disease did the rest. The survivors were enslaved or driven onto lands of little value. They have never recovered. The political culture of most of Latin America was and will be decided by men and women of European extraction. This is a harsh reality that no campus good intentions will ever change.

Why, then, if it is Western and populated by elites of European extraction, has Ibero-America failed to take off economically or mature politically? Despite progress, the situation remains unsatisfactory.

Most regional experts concur that the mentality of the Spanish conquerors was corrupted and enervated by the easy wealth provided by Andean silver or slave labor, but these factors were only accelerators. The *conquistadores* arrived in a corrupt state. The Spanish mentality of the 1500s had been strongly shaped by contact with the Moors, who were only driven back into North Africa in 1492. From their Moorish overlords and adversaries, the Spanish nobility and warrior class developed a series of prejudices against manual labor and commercial enterprise that still give members of the Latin American elite a great deal in common with the elites of the Arab-Persian world. To the Spanish gentleman or would-be gentleman, the only acceptable tool was the sword. Other Europeans had a touch of this, but grew out of it, while, caught in the long twilight of their hermetic empire, the Spanish-American worldview atrophied. For the North European, especially, life centers around labor, the ideal result of which is achievement that allows labor to continue on a higher plane. To the Ibero-American, the ideal result of labor is the attainment of leisure. The operative vision is of a rich man whose life is physically luxurious—one who need not work ever again. This is a very different worldview from that of the telephone lineman who wins the lottery only to report back to work Monday morning.

The Iberian-American ruling classes also brought a codex of loyalty owed only to God, the ruler, and the self (also a Moorish socio-political framework), thus putting a low premium on any collective or civic responsibility. This Iberian legacy has enough non-Western qualities to brake Latin America's development, even while the same legacy is sufficiently Western to allow most countries in the region to outperform Third World states where none of the sons or daughters of Europe is permanently at home.

KEY CULTURAL DEFICIENCIES

In all of the failed or threatened countries discussed above, there are two salient cultural deficiencies. There is little or no sense of responsibility for individual or collective actions, and there is no tradition of political compromise.

If you want a clear contrast between Western and Arab-Persian culture, for instance, consider what happens when

something goes terribly wrong in a state. Contemporary Westerners blame themselves collectively and bawl over their deficiencies—we're slackers on the job or we've allowed our school
systems to play intellectual hooky, we've done a bad job of raising our kids or our culture is a vampiric domain of Dead White
Males. When things fall apart in Teheran or Tripoli, the country's inhabitants, from the top down, blame the West, or at least
a convenient neighbor. The West has evolved into a mea culpa
culture, and we have likely allowed our taste for self-flagellation
to reach an unhealthy extreme. But it is this willingness to find
fault with ourselves which, when kept within the bounds of social
sanity, spurs us to accomplishment. "It's time to roll up our
sleeves . . . We'll do better next time." And so on. In cultures
where all cause is external (Inshallah), the individual and his
collective "know" that there is nothing to be done, since any
human effort to improve things will soon be undone by the
Great Satan, or his dark angel, the CIA, or by Mickey Mouse. It is
a very comforting and utterly debilitating way to view the world.

Even if this is the stuff of nineteenth-century primers, it
nonetheless bears out in historical and living examples. Cultures
that do not have a mature sense of responsibility cannot compete with those that do. The East Asian states that are so power-
fully competitive with the historical West each stand on a culture
that fixes responsibility. In Russia, on the other hand, there are
two enduring questions posed by men of the nineteenth
century: "What is to be done?" and "Who is to blame?" The first
is never answered definitively, and the second always is. The
answer is never "I am" or "We are."

Political compromise is essential to both democracy and
nontotalitarian socialism. The Western countries that developed
and perfected democracy as we value it each have developed traditions which encourage compromise in the political, economic,
and social spheres. In the European border states where

democracy remains problematic, and in the failed cultures of the world, compromise is regarded as weakness, except where specific survival-essential compromises have been codified by tradition. Life is seen as a zero-sum game, and the leader who compromises implies that he is too weak to do anything else. Compromise is seen as a capitulation of manhood, as the gesture of a fool. This cripples democracy in Russia and attempts at dialog with the Islamic opposition in Egypt; it prevents tribal harmony in South Africa and promotes intolerance in Iran.

Odd, somehow, to think that the jewels of Western culture may be so mundane: a sense of responsibility and the ability to compromise.

BRINGING IT ALL BACK HOME

The new barbarians who have no interest in government or society beyond what they can seize from it are the human apotheosis of the second phase of the rejection of the West. They are violent. For many of them, violence has become a cause in itself. They may shout political or merely apocryphal slogans, but these have no moral content. The rejection of everything Western—values, forms of government, laws, modes of social interaction—is complete, with the sole exception of material goods. The warriors of this great rejection are inspired by an inchoate hatred, one that is so primal it cannot be controlled by well-intentioned aid programs or even prisons. This is violence of the failure, by the failure, and for the failure. Its practitioners gladly kill real or imaged oppressors, but always lapse back into killing their own kind. This violence embraces hopelessness. It knows neither mercy nor conventional ambition. It is violence as the ultimate expression of existence, a scream of "I am" that is more powerful than sex or religious belief. It is simultaneously suicidal. It is anarchic in a sense that Europe's gentleman-anarchists never imagined.

PERFECTING THE SUNDIAL

Western governments have twin obsessions with the inviolability of borders and the primacy of other governments that rival the most doctrinaire religious conviction in intensity—while the world has entered a period in which borders have already changed dramatically and will continue to change for decades, and in which many governments often have little or no control over the behavior of those they pretend to represent.

If there is one certainty about the geopolitical situation it is that international borders are dramatically in flux. We react as if this is an abomination and a historical anomaly. But borders have always changed. The notion that they can now be fixed forever by virtue of our modern wisdom is folly. Even the collapse of the Soviet Union was institutionally unwelcome in some Western bureaucracies where it disrupted the order of business. Yet, consider the border changes this century has already seen: the collapse of empire during and following the Great War; endless mucking about in Asia Minor by the Great Powers and their clients; the compacting of Germany and the creation of dozens of new states in the wake of the Second World War; and then the long decades of local damage-control which saw the birth of additional states, such as Bangladesh, and the unification of others, such as Vietnam. Western bureaucracies have short memories and prize stasis above all. But the coming decades are going to include massive realignments of borders and an extra-Western redefinition of the shape, means, and limits of government—including the reemergence of old and the evolution of new forms of population organization that will not resemble current governments at all.

These next changes are long overdue, considering how disastrously inappropriate are the current borders in Africa, Central Asia, and elsewhere. Serbs, Croats, Bosnians, Tajiks, ethnic

Uzbeks and Pathans, Armenians, Ossetians, Abkhazians, and Russians beyond Russia's boundaries are all presently engaged in altering borders, whether we like it or not. The next wave of border changes may be vast, redrawing the maps of Central Asia and sub-Saharan Africa. Sleepwalkers among us dream that this should and can be prevented. This is like walking down a superhighway with your eyes closed.

We must recognize that borders must, can, and will be altered. Managed change is better than explosive change. This is not to suggest that the United States or the West overall should be in the business of cavalierly moving borders about (we've done enough of that in the past), rather it is intended as a warning not to waste energy—and, ultimately, the lives of our citizens—in bilious attempts to prevent history from occurring. We may not profit from all of these impending changes, but, by looking ahead with open eyes, we may be able to minimize the damage to ourselves, our allies, and our clients.

A key aspect of changing borders, and the one that most electrifies Western publics, is ethnic cleansing. Ethnic cleansing is ugly. But it is often very effective and has a long tradition. Within living memory, the expulsion of ethnic Germans from Eastern Europe had a tremendously positive effect on the ability of indigenous populations to coalesce into integral states. It was also, ultimately, a very good *Schlankheitskur* for Germany, resulting in a curbed appetite for the lands that once separated ethnic German enclaves littered about Central and Eastern Europe.

Ethnic cleansing is happening right now in Asia, Africa, and on the fringes of Europe. It is likely to happen on an even more widespread basis, accelerating as the aftershocks of the Soviet collapse continue to ripple through Eurasia and as African states further disintegrate. It can either happen under the eyes of international monitors, or it can happen the way the Iraqis approached the problem in the Kurdish villages they gassed, or the way it currently takes place in African states such as Rwanda and Burundi, where recent massacres whose death toll ran into the hundreds of thousands drew little more than a voyeuristic shudder from the West. Instead of scolding rapists in perfectly formatted demarches, the West might more profitably study how to manage ethnic cleansing in as humane a manner as possible.

The West's obsession with government-to-government relations is also far too exclusive. Our governments are masterful when it comes to the arcane rituals employed in speaking to other governments, but we find ourselves helpless when there is no formal government with which to deal. We know how to talk to the functionaries in the ministries of foreign affairs or trade, and even how to listen to the odd dissenting intellectual, to civic-action committees for environmental affairs, or to minority-rights representatives. Our governments do not, however, know how to talk to men with guns. Yet it is precisely the armed and violent who control the fates of collapsing states around the world.

Our reaction to the dissolution of states is to cling to beleaguered capital cities, pretending that the last remaining particles of government comprise a fit and fitting interlocutor as long as there is one *apparatchik* in one office with one telephone (in a pinch, a pen will do). Then we are astonished when our embassy is surrounded.

THE MAN WHO SAW THROUGH HEAVEN

Earlier in this century, a fine, forgotten American writer, Wilbur Daniel Steele, produced a story entitled, "The Man Who Saw Through Heaven." It told of an unremarkable minister who was quite satisfied with his life and church until he visited an astronomical observatory. Looking through the telescope and realizing the physical impossibility of his concept of Heaven, on which all the complexities of his belief rested, he suffered a collapse. He lost his faith and set out wandering in search of alternatives to replace it. Finally, after many failures, he wound up in Africa. In mud-coated, primeval rituals, in a faith unencumbered by the ornate overlay of civilization, he found his way to God again. Perhaps that is what will happen in the failed countries of the world.

Perhaps the second, virulent phase of the rejection of the West will bring about some good. Perhaps, when all of the bloodshed has passed and the worst Western-drawn borders have been erased, and Western forms of government and political philosophy have been cast off like ill-fitting foreign clothes, perhaps then the interdicted histories of the non-Western states will resume along their own paths.

Much argues against this. The world economy is ever more interconnected. Events reverberate ever more loudly in a world shrunken by telecommunications and jumbo jets. The citizens of failed countries often have a weakness for Western comforts and ornaments that cripples effective behavior. The West is accustomed to meddling. There is no truly alternative model. . . .

But humanity has a way of muddling through. Just as a few decades ago no one could envision the impact of computers on our world, perhaps we are collectively blind to a true new world order that is already emerging to make the next century a better one than this has been. In the meantime, we in the West, rich and secure, need to do our best to avoid adding to the misery of the transition.

PART II

And Rumors of War

The Seeker and the Sage

This essay originally appeared as the introduction to The Book of War, *published by Modern Library, a division of Random House, Inc., in 2000. It is reprinted by the gracious permission of Modern Library and Random House.*

This book allies humankind's two most powerful works on warfare. Distant in time, space, and culture, Carl von Clausewitz and Sun Tzu offer dueling visions, with the Prussian appalled by fantasies of bloodless war and the Chinese crying that bloodless victory is the acme of generalship, and with Clausewitz anxious to increase military effectiveness, while Sun Tzu pleads, cleverly, for military restraint. Such discord assures their relevance to our time.

There is also plentiful agreement between Clausewitz's *On War* and Sun Tzu's *Art of War,* from their mutual vilification of heads of state who attempt to micro-manage distant battles to their similar emphasis on the key role of the commander. In the end—and I speak as a soldier, after decades of consideration—these two books complete each other, like a perfect couple formed of opposites. Between them, the two texts cover myriad aspects of the human experience of war—as well as reflecting the temperaments of their divergent civilizations. Clausewitz, the Western man, sought the grail of knowledge and found the pursuit endless, bottomless, and obsessive, while

the Eastern sage who wrote down the sayings attributed to Sun
Tzu polished what he knew until it shone. Each attained the
universal, transcending personality and the particularity of
experience. In the study of warfare, they have no peers, and
these works remain the brightest lanterns we have to light our
darkest endeavor.

The Western text embraces war's necessity, while the Eastern one despairs of its inevitability, but they are united by the
recognition that the human remains at the heart of each combat encounter and every campaign. Each holds a flank in our
approach to war: Clausewitz is the apostle of the relentless will,
convinced there is no substitute for victory, while Sun Tzu
seems a closet pacifist, wary of victory's hollowness. The first
sought to sharpen the sword, the second to restrain it. The
Prussian saw the power of the armed mass, while the Chinese
pitied the suffering of the common man. Sun Tzu believed that
the outcome of a campaign was predictable, but Clausewitz
insisted that, although the odds can be improved, risk is inherent in warfare. This debate across millennia continues today,
and placing these two works together highlights the strengths
and weaknesses—and the inestimable value—of each book.

Each must be read. No cram notes will do, and summaries
badly serve their genius. Clausewitz appears difficult, only to
yield a hard, thrilling clarity, while Sun Tzu, a quick swallow,
takes a lifetime to digest. One text is long, the other appeal-
ingly short. Both are inexhaustible.

Had I the skill, I would rescue Carl von Clausewitz from the
admirers who have made of him a dry and reasoned thing. He
was a man of fire, but acolytes have reduced him to ashes. His
image is of the diligent staff officer: coldly avid, narrowly
expert, and, for all his brilliance, a bit short of life. In reality,

he was a courageous, driven man, struggling to contain his passions within Prussia's turgid hierarchies. His commitments were wholehearted, his abilities immense, and his sense of duty exemplary. Born on the doubtful fringes of the nobility, he experienced war at every level, found friends among the best men of his age, won the approval of a royal court—until he enraged its king—wrote love poetry and married a higher-born woman after a courtship worthy of a nineteenth-century novel. When appeasement was the fashion, he ruined his career out of patriotism. He enjoyed a remarkably happy marriage and wrote a work so rich it may never be surpassed, yet he suffered disappointment and feared himself a failure. Above all, Clausewitz was a man of his times, and his times were the Romantic era in Germany.

Born in 1780 into a family clinging to threadbare claims of aristocracy, a relative arranged for his regimental apprenticeship to begin at age twelve. At thirteen, Clausewitz was a combat veteran. He participated in the frontier campaign against revolutionary France and the siege of Mainz (finely reported by Goethe, who was born a generation before Clausewitz and would outlive his fellow genius by a year). After the excitements of the field came garrison years, during which Clausewitz made the barracks his school. He read hungrily, with an appetite for a variety of intellectual dishes, and all his life he savored learning as only the autodidact can. Along with the current texts on military matters, he read philosophy, natural science, mathematics, and literature, developing an early fondness for Schiller, whose plays and histories, so vigorous and seductively written, exalted military valor and northern, Protestant virtue.

His superiors recognized his exceptional abilities and at twenty Clausewitz was chosen to attend the *Allgemeine Kriegsschule,* Prussia's military college, in Berlin. By age twenty-three, his talent had won him a mentor and fatherly friend in Germany's greatest soldier of the age, Gerhard von Scharnhorst, and a place at court as adjutant to Prince August. He also met the woman he would marry, Countess Marie von Brühl, a favorite of Queen Luise, who valued depth and intellect in those around her.

Prussia was in ferment then, ruled by a bold, shining queen and a dullard king fitted for survival but not greatness. The revolution across the Rhine and Napoleon's dynamism had charged the atmosphere even where French policy found no approval. In Germany, philosophy, drama, and the applied arts had found their footing a generation before and now were on the march, while the new Romantic literature conquered the educated imagination. As with all disturbed ages, it was a period of explosive creativity. The classical tastes of the Enlightenment persisted among the old, but were subverted by the young. Literary giants were the idols of the day—Clausewitz's wife-to-be favored Goethe over her suitor's beloved Schiller, eventually winning her Carl over to the creator of Faust, Werther, and Wilhelm Meister. It is always a fine thing to be young, popular, and in love, but to be so in Berlin at the beginning of the new century must have been bedazzling.

The idyll ended in 1806. Napoleon's strategic vigor and speed shattered Prussia's brittle forces in the Jena-Auerstadt campaign, scattering the Prussian army with an ease that shocked Europe. The fighting ended for Clausewitz as he stood beside Prince August, surrounded in a swamp and covered in mud, with his battalion's last reserves of powder soaked through. As the French lined up their cannon on the high ground for the kill, the prince surrendered. In wretched, ruined uniforms, the prince and his adjutant were shunted from one French commander to another as trophies until they arrived in occupied Berlin and learned they would be prisoners in France.

For the prince and his subordinate, the terms of captivity proved gentle. Quartered not far from Paris, they had the liberty to visit on occasion, although Clausewitz sulked at the glories of Europe's new capital. Pride scalded, Clausewitz detested the French. Yet he made the most of the opportunity to observe the world around him, writing compulsively in his attempt to understand how this coarse, self-obsessed nation could achieve such splendid victories (all his life, he used the act of writing to force himself to a deeper understanding). And he wrote a wealth of letters to his beloved, whose mother remained years away from consenting to the socially lopsided match. Devoted, the letters were a mix of heat and patience, of tenderness and intelligence. The lovers wrote of politics and longings, of important news and old friends, of books and dreams. Clausewitz described his efforts to appreciate painting as much as Marie did (he remained, all his life, a man whose tastes ran to ink on paper, not paint on canvas), and she wrote to soothe him in his anger and humiliation.

After a year, Prussia signed a degrading treaty and the prisoners began a slow journey homeward. En route, the prince took them on a detour to Schloss Coppet in Switzerland, to visit Madame de Staël, lioness of literary salons and author of romances unreadable today. Clausewitz liked her books, especially the sentimental novel *Corrine ou l'Italie,* liked the woman, and enjoyed the "artsy" environment so much one wonders what he might have done with his life had he not been consigned to the parade ground as a boy. While the prince flirted with another visitor, the couchable Madame Récamier, Clausewitz enjoyed long conversations with his hostess and her consort, Wilhelm Schlegel, the German Romantic writer and philosopher, as well as with yet another guest, Johann Heinrich Pestalozzi, the educational theorist. Most revealing, Clausewitz was a hit in this exclusive milieu. Surrounded by the Alps—mountains were a passion new to the Romantic era—he wrote rhapsodic letters to his wife. For the first time in over a year, glints of joy shone through his penmanship.

But, back in Prussia, the gaiety was gone. A chastised nation and the broken remains of an army lacked bearings as much as they lacked prospects. Napoleon's victories had mounted—smashing the Austrians, crushing the Russians—until he seemed invincible, almost a cosmic force. The size of Prussia's army was restricted, and the French closely monitored government and military appointments through a web of spies and collaborators. Nonetheless, Scharnhorst—a genius of maneuver at court as on the battlefield—began to rebuild the Prussian military in the shadows. The great reformer's hour had come, and Clausewitz became his primary assistant. Although still only a captain, Clausewitz had long since earned the older man's trust. Scharnhorst once stated that he had only to speak a few words and the younger man could complete the thought and capture it on paper. Scharnhorst also wrote that, except for his own children, no one had been as close to him as Clausewitz.

Never in robust health, Clausewitz exhausted himself over his desk—there is far more ink than gunpowder in an officer's life, and in defeat ink must stand in for blood. He was determined that Prussia would rise again. His conception of war had begun to mature, and the quality of thought in those early writings is remarkable for an officer not yet thirty. Clausewitz had the gift that comes to few men of seeing clearly, and then drawing universal conclusions from the partiality of experience. Intuitively, he spotted relationships where others saw only disparate events and sensed the constants underlying the disruptions of his age. If his personal experience undeniably shaped his later work, it never deformed it. Among Scharnhorst's many virtues, the ability to spot an even greater talent than his own and to utilize it without jealousy was not the least important. He gave us Clausewitz.

King Friedrich Wilhelm III, who made an art of indecision, hedged between those subordinates who wished revenge and those who believed that Prussia's future lay with France. Meanwhile, Napoleon looked to the territories he had subjugated for fresh blood to lubricate new conquests. Bending to necessity, Friedrich Wilhelm appeased the French time and again. Then Napoleon began to prepare for the invasion of Russia, a campaign in which Prussian troops were to fight under the control of the *Grande Armée*.

It was too much for the newly promoted Major Clausewitz (and for dozens of other Prussian officers as well). Leaving behind his adored Marie, whom he had married at last, he took off the blue *Königsrock* and accepted a commission from the czar as a lieutenant colonel. The defeat of Napoleon had become the central purpose of his life. But Clausewitz's yearning to contribute to the full extent of his abilities was stymied by his inability to speak Russian. For months he was shifted from staff to field unit to yet another staff, unable to find a position where his talents could emerge. It was a period of enormous frustration for the soldier who knew his talents were underutilized, but the variety of experiences proved beneficial to the military theorist. Those leaps from one post to another took him from the imperial staff down to brutal cossack raids, from rearguard cavalry actions to personal heroism on the field of Borodino. He witnessed the final destruction of the French army on the Beresina—a scene of utter savagery—and then his turn came at last. Clausewitz proved the pivotal man in

negotiations with the Prussian General Yorck, whose formation
was covering the French retreat. The Convention of Tauroggen
withdrew Yorck's Prussians from the campaign—without the
king's approval. It left the French with an open flank and
Clausewitz in lasting disfavor at the Prussian court.

The king never forgave him. Although Prussia soon turned
against Napoleon and took the field beside its Russian and Aus-
trian allies, Friedrich Wilhelm felt that Clausewitz had betrayed
him, first by putting on a Russian uniform, then through the
impertinence of undercutting his policy. Clausewitz begged to
be allowed to return to Prussian service, and his friends did
what they could to help him trade his Russian green for Prussian blue again, but the king was adamant to the point of spite.
He insisted that Clausewitz would have to prove himself, mightily, on the field of battle to have any hope of regaining a Prussian officer's patent.

Clausewitz did prove himself. Still in Russian uniform, he
served as a liaison officer (but really as a deputy) to Scharnhorst
on campaign. As Prussia rose again, the orders, directives, and
assessments that flowed from Clausewitz's pen harnessed the
power of a people in arms. This was a new world, in which regu-
lar military formations were reinforced by reserves drawn from
a patriotic citizenry. A passion for nationhood that no Prussian
king—not even Frederick the Great—had excited arose in
response to French tyranny. It was a people's war on both sides
now, and Scharnhorst and Clausewitz had been among the first
outside of France to grasp the implications of the changing
times. Even as Napoleon and his subordinates continued to win
victories, the national cause strengthened, and the Prussian
military exhibited the resilience and determination that had
been so lacking in the previous decade.

But all war brings tragedy. At the battle of Grossgörschen,
in a desperate moment, the staff of Prussia's Army of Silesia

plunged into the battle in an attempt to stave off defeat. Prussia's finest officers rode into the melee with sabers drawn— Blücher, Scharnhorst, Gneisenau, and Clausewitz. A bullet winged Blücher, Clausewitz received a flesh wound behind the ear from a French bayonet, and Scharnhorst was shot in the leg. One well-fired volley might have wiped out Prussia's military reformers. As it was, Scharnhorst refused to give his wound time to heal. He was a man whose sense of duty obliterated the self. And the general, reformer, and great soul, risen from the peasantry of Hannover, died of infection. When the king, warily, accepted Clausewitz back into Prussian service, it was a bittersweet return. Although Gneisenau—jovial, bright, and brave—assumed the role of mentor and friend to Clausewitz, their mutual affection could never fully replace the loss of Scharnhorst for the younger man. Clausewitz was the sort who does not need the applause of the masses, but who craves the approval of a hero. Germany never produced a worthier hero in uniform than Scharnhorst.

With the blue coat came a disappointing assignment. Clausewitz was dispatched to a secondary theater in the north. He learned a great deal about economy of force operations and applied himself fully—as he always did—but he longed to be part of the great campaign that culminated in the Battle of Leipzig. From then on, Clausewitz remained on the edges of the battle-fields whose names live in history. He served well in the Waterloo campaign—but not on the crucial fields of Ligny or La Belle Alliance—and his laurels were fewer than those of lesser men. His repeated requests to serve on the line denied, he was confined to the staff work that he could do better than anyone else, and that kept him out of sight of his rancorous king. Now forgotten, two of his brothers served with greater reknown on the battlefields of the day than did the Clausewitz sibling we revere.

It is, finally, to the King of Prussia's credit that he allowed Clausewitz to serve on after the war's end, even promoting him

to major general, but it is to his discredit that Friedrich
Wilhelm so distrusted his subordinate that he "exiled" the
brightest officer of the day to the Prussian military academy—
not as director of the curriculum and trainer of officers, but
restricted to administrative and disciplinary matters. The com-
mandant's job, by tradition, was used to sideline generals fallen
out of favor, and new, potentially subversive ideas were
no longer wanted. Confounding all the reformers of the
period, a repressive twilight settled over the continent they
had done so much to save. Clausewitz, the man of fire, was
reduced to tending embers.

He felt his share of bitterness, but never surrendered his
will. Only thirty-eight when he became head of the *Allgemeine
Kriegsschule,* but with twenty-five years of military service behind
him, he turned to his writing with renewed intensity. His duties
were such that he could accomplish them in a few hours in the
morning and he spent the long afternoons on the papers that
eventually would become *On War.* His greatest aide and friend
was his wife, who not only copied his manuscripts, but had the
intellect to critique his work. Like the now-dead queen she had
served in her youth, Marie von Clausewitz had more fire and
intelligence than the mass of men given pride of place before
her. Her husband's lifework is her work, too.

Clausewitz remained at his dreary post for more than a
decade, grappling with ideas as single-mindedly as he had once
struggled against Napoleon. He possessed what might be the
most important virtue in a military man, the will to persist, to
outlast the enemy. It has saved giants such as Frederick, Washington, and Giap, and although it could not prevent his bouts
of depression, it kept Clausewitz from despair. For a dozen
years, he fought to capture the complexity of warfare on the
written page—an impossibility—and never brought his work to

a conclusion. That he achieved as much success as he did is a monument to the human will.

Unexpectedly, his career underwent a late resurrection. He was assigned to an important post as inspector of artillery in Silesia, and he and his wife threw themselves into the provincial life of the Breslau garrison. Then, as Poland rose against its Russian oppressor, he was sent to serve as chief of staff to his old friend Gneisenau in the army of observation on the border of the czar's empire. The Russians drowned the rebellion in blood, and the Prussians never had to fire a shot.

But a fiercer enemy had crossed the frontier: cholera.

In the first of the great cholera epidemics that swept the world in the nineteenth century, Gneisenau, a living legend, died ignominiously. At first it seemed that Clausewitz would be spared, and his splendid work in the field regained him favor at court, with praise even from old enemies. Depressed at the loss of his great friend, but with a brighter future before him, Clausewitz returned from the headquarters in Posen to his post in Breslau.

On a bare November day not long after his return, he sickened and died in the space of eight hours, leaving his book unfinished. With bitter symmetry, Germany's other great philosopher of the age, Hegel, died in the same epidemic.

Marie arranged for the publication of *On War* in its unfinished state. It has been the most fatally misunderstood book of the last two hundred years.

So much is known. But it seems to me there is more. Even the best biographies of Clausewitz have concentrated on the military man in his professional milieu, or sometimes in his political context. But he was, indelibly, a man of his culture as well—of the yearning, morbid atmosphere of German

Romanticism. Placing the man in the intellectual context of his age reveals a new complexity in the writer and brings greater clarity to the work. This soldier was far more than his uniform.

The only philosopher referenced in most studies of Clausewitz is Kant, and then only to wonder whether Clausewitz actually read him or received his ideas watered down through a disciple who lectured in Berlin. Yet Kant—no Romantic—had at most a negligible influence upon Clausewitz, whose nature instinctively rejected Kant's belief that the essense of a thing is unknowable, embracing, rather, Hegel's conviction that human intelligence can penetrate to the essence. While Clausewitz would have been interested in Kant's theories on education, he would have dismissed Kant's political idealism as absurd. Their interests diverged as widely as did their conclusions. A range of thinkers and writers influenced Clausewitz—some directly and others by shaping the intellectual environment—but not Kant. These two Prussians shared only the regularity of habit that keeps the irregular mind from the abyss.

Clausewitz had plentiful opportunities to hear the great thinkers of his day in person—men such as Fichte, Hegel, Schelling, and the elder Schlegel (with whom he spoke at length in Switzerland). Their lectures were social occasions for the intelligentsia, of which Clausewitz was an enthusiastic member. Of even greater importance, his reading was broad and voracious. He was a man addicted to learning, and philosophy was the headiest drug. Nor could he have held his own in the court of Queen Luise—where he gained an early welcome—unless able to discuss the philosophy of the day, as well as poetry, fiction, and history, all of which blurred together in the Romantic era.

Even had Clausewitz been a blockheaded martinet—which this most thoughtful of soldiers was not—no man escapes the temper of his times. Just as today's military men are rendered inchoate by the march of technology, so Clausewitz, too, was a prisoner of his environment, if a more articulate one. Romantic thought and literature gave form to his ideas, just as his experience of war provided the content. For skeptics, there are concrete examples of the influence of Germany's Frederician and Romantic-era philosophers on Clausewitz's writing. That they have gone unexplored says more about the narrowness of his biographers than about the man himself.

First, Clausewitz's concept of the trinity that decides the success or failure of policy—which we may crudely summarize as the relationship between the state, the army, and the population (reason, chance, and passion)—is fundamentally Romantic. Trinities pervade the thought of the period, with the trinity of *Geist, Seele, und Leib*—mind, soul, and body—encapsulating the Romantic view of Man and fundamental to the movement's philosophy, sciences, and literature. Here, Clausewitz appropriated an intellectual construct common to the intelligentsia of his day. He developed it wonderfully, but did not invent his trinity from thin air.

The Romantic era was also fascinated by dualities and opposites—male and female; day and night; good and evil; the *Doppelgänger* who pervade the popular ghost stories of the time—and reading German Romantic literature one starts to sense that the world is nothing but a series of bipolarities. Hence Clausewitz's identification of dualities in warfare: the relative strengths of the attack and the defense; war as a contest of opposing wills; the contrast between limited and absolute war; his juxtaposition of ends and means in war; and his insistence on the gulf between theory and practice. Again, he used the intellectual tools his age thrust upon him to build something new—but he did not create these tools.

Even his elaboration of the "center of gravity," or *Schwerpunkt*, concept owes less to Prussian military tradition than to Herder, the eve-of-the-Romantic-era philosopher whose discussion of the "center of gravity" of cultures clearly inspired the richness with which Clausewitz imbued the term. (Now unread, Herder is stunningly relevant to today's international dilemmas.)

The Romantic era also created the cult of genius (perhaps its most damaging legacy). The titan of superhuman talents, ambitions, will, and achievements enraptured the chattering classes of the day, whether the colossus was Napoleon bathing in oceans of blood or the doomed poet Novalis yearning after the blue flower, the impossible, the infinite. Clausewitz's ambition was to be a genius on the terms of his age, to take up an impossible challenge. (*Don Quixote* was an especially popular book among the Romantics, who viewed its hero as nobly tragic more than comical.) His attempt to capture the essence of war upon the page, to explain the complexity his own description of friction *(Friktion)* in war reveals as boundless, was nothing less than heroic—and Clausewitz saw it as such. Novalis's statement, "What I want to do, I can do . . . Nothing is impossible for mankind," might have served as the motto to Clausewitz's endeavor.

From *Faust* onward, the Promethean theme resounds through the literature—and behavior—of the day. Defiance and resistance set the tone. The Romantics sought to strive with gods, expecting their rewards from the effort itself rather than from ultimate success. All his life, Clausewitz was the man who reached for knowledge. His last, greatest effort, his struggle to contain war in words, was patently impossible.

I believe he knew it.

Perhaps he began in the belief that the task he set himself might be accomplished. On the surface, his work is rational and ordered—not unlike the persona he learned to offer the world around him. Like Goethe, Clausewitz was torn between the Classical, Enlightenment impulse and the stormy drives of the Romantic, between the scientific and the artistic. His was a split personality, riven between the noonday clarity of the drill field and the dark night of the soul, and demons lurked within the fitted uniform. Goethe defied the trend of his age, fleeing the Romantic wilderness for the safe Classical garden in his later years, but Clausewitz went the other way, beginning with the Enlightenment impulse to explain, only to be captured by the Romantic urge to understand. To borrow a line from Tennyson, an English Romantic of a later generation, Clausewitz sought "to follow knowledge like a sinking star, beyond the utmost bounds of human thought." Along the way, he saw that the mission he had set for himself was impossible. War could never be fully explained. It was the perfect subject for the Romantic age.

Clausewitz avoided finishing his work, sinking into his thoughts until they consumed him. Behind the disciplined exterior, he may have felt close to madness at times. To complete the book—to see it in print—would have been to lay his life's work open to criticism. But an unfinished work can only be criticized so far before we must ask if the author might not have altered this or clarified that, had the time been allotted him. Many a writer has failed to complete his masterwork—it is a disease of overweaning ambition aggravated by cowardice. I believe that Clausewitz, the brave soldier, was afraid to finish his book and see it judged.

Even in leaving his book incomplete, Clausewitz was a child of his time. For the Romantics, the gorgeous fragment, not the finely rounded work, was the ultimate form in art. *Das Unvollendete,* the uncompleted, whether poem, symphony, or philosophy of war, was a true Romantic achievement.

Although his career had taken a late turn for the better, those who saw Clausewitz toward the end of his life described

him as despondent and enervated. He loved his wife enduringly, but even the deepest mortal love could not sustain him.
He had asked too much of himself and of the world. I believe
his death by cholera, at age fifty-one, was a relief to him.

By placing Clausewitz among the high Romantics, we do
not belittle his achievement. On the contrary, his work may be
the most enduring text of the era, save only for Goethe's *Faust*.
While he likely would have scoffed if called a Romantic to his
face, Clausewitz was, thoroughly, a creature of his times. And
he might have been secretly pleased at the epithet. We cannot
know with certainty. But we do know that no man sees himself
objectively, and only history can place us. Despite ourselves, we
are as the times are. Indeed, the central character in *Faust* is
timeless in his appeal because he is the intellectual's Everyman,
blind to himself and desperate to escape the confines of mor-
tality. He deals with the devil without to avoid the devil within.
He seeks knowledge of the world to escape self-knowledge, and
confuses excess with infinity. He must *act*, because *being* is terri-
fying. In the beginning, Clausewitz wrote to change an army; in
the end, he wrote as devils chewed his soul.

No happy man thinks deeply or writes well.

Less is known of Sun Tzu. His life is the stuff of fables, not
grounded by a single biographical fact. Said to be a general during China's "Warring States" period (453–221 B.C.) or earlier,
Sun Tzu, or Sun Wu, has spurred more debate as to his existence
as a historical figure than on the content of his thought. The single consistent story told about him, a nonsense about training
court concubines for a military demonstration, does not ring true
to anyone who has served either in a military or in a government.
Even if he did exist, he did not write down the work we know as
Sun Tzu's *Art of War*. His pronouncements on campaigning,

passed down, were recorded by other hands. The texts we have are laden with internal contradictions. Yet "his" thought endures.

Sun Tzu pierces to the heart of warfare—and to the heart of man at war. He deals not only with the mass, but with the man, with psychology and instinct. He rightly sees human failings as the cause of most defeats and gives a sense of sweat and death and truth. If Clausewitz wrote to understand, the man who first spoke the wisdom of Sun Tzu clearly knew more than he said. Here, knowledge is boiled down to its essence. I suspect this is not simply a matter of Chinese forms and conventions; rather, the speaker and the later chronicler of his speech, though separated by centuries, each understood enduring truths about rulers and generals: Their time is always short, and their attention spans often limited. Sun Tzu was the original master of the sound bite, and he still quotes well today.

I do not read or speak Chinese, and cannot place Sun Tzu in the culture of his time as confidently as with Clausewitz. I can only approach him as a former soldier—and as an officer who was occasionally sentenced to work within a government. Still, some things seem obvious. Begin with what is known:

The Warring States period was long, brutal, and destructive. Like the tumultuous Romantic era more than two millennia later, it bloomed with creativity—nothing inspires the arts to greatness more than a sense of the blown-glass fragility of human life. Plague and slaughter spur the pen and brush. The times were prosperous for many states—war has always been good business. Yet by the end, the destruction outweighed the progress, and the moral men of the day recoiled in horror. As in the Peloponnesian Wars of Greece, states were doomed or gutted.

The cost to the population, in famine, disease, dislocation, and slaughter, was high, and though a richer merchant class emerged, the lot of the common man or woman was bitter.

Social order was maintained by savagery, but even vicious punishments could not keep states from decline. Earlier conventions of warfare were upset by burgeoning state ambitions and by innovations in the mechanics of warfare. As in the twentieth century, military capability carried within it the inevitability of use. The old order faltered and died, and warfare became total war. To those who loved tradition, who glorified a more pacific past, barbarism seemed the rule.

Undoubtedly, such a period produced talented commanders, some of whom were successful enough to command attention when they spoke and have their words passed on by their disciples. Perhaps Sun Tzu was one of these, or perhaps he was an idealization of them all, a distillation. In the end, it hardly matters: We have the work.

Yet speculation is tempting. In the intelligence world, you develop a tactile feel for things, a honing of instincts, that allows you to construct models to fill in the gaps in what is known. Sometimes you are wrong. Still it seems to me there is a "likeliest" scenario for how this *Art of War* emerged from the chaos of the Warring States.

Although archaeological finds have brought us closer to the original text, we may never know whether or not Sun Tzu lived. Does it matter? In the end, the chronicler may be the more interesting figure.

Toward the end of the Warring States period, in a landscape desolate here and newly prosperous there (not unlike northern Europe after the Thirty Years' War), a ruler probably turned to a trusted minister and asked him to gather and record the wisdom circulating in Sun Tzu's name for use in formulating strategy and conducting campaigns. Perhaps the minister himself, despairing of his times, undertook the project on his own, to urge the ruler to better his performance. He would have queried scholars and military experts, sending scribes to interview them, if the budget of the court allowed (the minister probably did not serve in a rich court, since there is so much stress on costs and economies in the text of the *Art of War*). Gathering the many sayings that had appeared over the centuries, he would have pared them down to those he thought genuine—and then discarded those he felt might lead his ruler down dangerous paths. For no minister of state ever passes the entire truth to his superior. Perhaps the courtier was tasked only to gather the general military wisdom of the past for a young ruler anxious to make his mark on the world. Perhaps, to that end, he "discovered" Sun Tzu, a wise ancient—perfect for a culture that revered old wisdom above contemporary insight. Whatever the details, a close reading of the text convinces one that the chronicler was not content with what he had gathered: Before placing the work in the hands of his ruler, he tempered the military prescriptions and proscriptions with forged maxims that advanced his own view of the world.

The man who wrote this knowledge down was in despair. That much seems evident. The book speaks in two distinct voices (with other echoes, of which more later). Most of the chronicler's interpolations come early on, although there is some intermingling throughout the text. The muscle of the book is, of course, the advice on how to exploit terrain, or how to deceive an enemy, or when to attack or defend. This is the real Sun Tzu, the soldier. The minister of court, seeking to guide the ruler, appears when the head of state is warned of the terrible expense of making war, or admonished to minimize costs and suffering by employing spies in place of battalions, or, most famously, advised that "the highest excellence is to subdue the enemy's army without fighting at all." This is the chronicler and courtier speaking, the man who has seen enough of war in his lifetime to be sickened by it, and who, while recognizing how deeply the warrior impulse infects the human condition, longs for peace.

I find the higher greatness in the chronicler, although he often seems to me a fool. While we might long for a world in which "the expert in using the military subdues the enemy's forces without going into battle, takes the enemy's walled cities without launching an attack, and crushes the enemy's state without a protracted war," this rarely happens in reality. Warfare was, is, and will remain bloody and destructive. When the chronicler speaks, we may admire his virtue, but wonder if his state perished because of his tomfoolery. Such chaste ploys are especially appealing and dangerous in our time, when heads of state no longer serve in uniform and long to believe in the myth of bloodless war. But if history suggests any pattern, it is that those who wait too long to raise their swords pay a greater price in blood and suffering than those given to timely and judicious action. And yet . . . the chronicler's repeated pleas for a more humane approach to warfare, for the sparing of lives and crops and cities whenever possible, must be heard by the generals who imagine that they might, finally, achieve Clausewitz's ideal of total war. Warfare that is excessive and indiscriminate in its violence only dissipates power, while inspiring resistance.

Likewise, the chronicler gives good advice when he tells the ruler or general to "provide for the captured soldiers and treat them well," but he lies when he insists that "there has never been a state that has benefited from an extended war." He was writing in an age when powerful states had expanded profitably over decades and centuries of warfare. Small states, with limited resources, may perish as a result of extended wars, and economically hollow states may decline, but throughout history a variety of states prospered as a result of lengthy conflicts. We are dealing, ultimately, with a brilliant work of propaganda that aimed to lead a prince to wisdom.

The most difficult portions of the text to credit definitively to either the general or the minister are those dealing with intelligence and espionage, since both men would have known the value of those arts. Here the minister probably supplemented observations culled from the general's legacy. The repeated insistence on the importance of knowing the enemy, of gathering information, and of deception and subversion is superior to Clausewitz's appreciation of intelligence affairs. In the end, Clausewitz is a philosopher, but a fighter: He wants to punch and even his defense is "a shield of blows." Once we have labored through its quaintness of expression, the *Art of War* offers the better advice on intelligence and operations in the shadows. While Clausewitz, in his most famous line, states that "war is a simple continuation of policy through other means," Sun Tzu's *Art of War* is closer to the American position that warfare means that policy has failed. Clausewitz wants to win wars, while the chronicler of Sun Tzu wants to avoid them whenever possible, but to win them if they must be fought. Sun Tzu and his scribe would rather bribe than march, assassinate rather than bomb. They would have grasped the utility of the CIA immediately, while Clausewitz would have retained a measure of skepticism.

The blood-red core of the *Art of War* clearly belongs to Sun Tzu the general—or to the various generals whose wisdom was collected by the chronicler. This is where we get the enduring wisdom of the man at arms. He stresses morale, here called the *tao*, or way, counsels the commander "in joining battle, seek the quick victory," and, like his fellow soldier Clausewitz, stresses that the defense is inherently the stronger form of warfare. (If *Blitzkrieg* or the technologies of our contemporary "Revolution in Military Affairs" appear to upset this maxim, recall that the German *Blitzkrieg* won campaigns but not wars and that postmodern Western militaries have yet to annihilate a single opponent.) The military man describes much that is tactical and mechanical, from the role of fixing and flanking attacks—the "straightforward" and the "surprise"—to how to manage approach marches, but he also underscores the importance of avoiding too strict an adherence to formula. He addresses the need for concentration of effort and economy-of-force operations, stating that "to be prepared everywhere is to be weak everywhere." In essential advice for our times, he demands that victory not be compromised through political irresolution: "to be victorious in battle and win the spoils, and yet fail to exploit your achievement, is disastrous." This is the lieutenant's handbook, and also the general's and the president's.

There was, unfortunately, a third hand—actually a series of hands—that adulterated the *Art of War* we have received. Soon after the wisdom of Sun Tzu was recorded, revisions began. Various scholars and men of court inserted positions they wanted to dignify, or subtracted sections with which their recommended policies disagreed. The text has been heavily corrupted—the evidence is in the contradictions that arise from page to page. We are warned that the commander must share information with his subordinates, but then the general is cautioned "to blinker the ears and eyes of his officers and men, and to keep people ignorant." At one point, the commander is admonished not to throw his troops into hopeless situations, only to be told elsewhere that doing so will bring out the ferocity and will to survive in those he commands. He is advised to care for his men "as if they were his own beloved sons" shortly after he has been warned that "if he loves his people, he can be easily troubled and upset," because too much concern for the lives of his troops can "prove disastrous." (In fact, neither extreme is practical and the truth lies in the middle: The commander must cherish his men and protect them when he can, but he must be willing to send them to their deaths without hesitation when necessary.) Likely, these passages are all corruptions of sounder military insights in the original lost to us.

It takes extraordinary power for a work to survive such bastardization as the *Art of War* suffered over the centuries. The Bible is the supreme example of such a work, followed by Homer. That the work attributed to Sun Tzu, who may or may not have walked the earth, remains so relevant and immediate in so many of its parts is little short of miraculous. As the reader of this edition goes through the pages, he or she will likely do as I did, noting that a passage perfectly captures Napoleon or Stonewall Jackson, or Forrest, Montgomery, or MacArthur, and so on. It is intellectually breathtaking how many varieties of battle, how many command personalities, are captured in this small book. What could be more relevant for the digital age of warfare than the observation that "war is such that the supreme consideration is speed"? Or more vital to the asymmetrical, crudely barbaric conflicts that currently drain America's military resources and challenge our national will than the maxim that "the basic patterns of the human character must all be thoroughly investigated"? This small book is so encompassing that it almost seems to predict the emergence of air and space power when it says, metaphorically, that "the expert on the attack strikes from out of the highest reaches of the heavens."

Although it deals with mankind's monstrous failings, the *Art of War* is finally poetic—not in its subject matter, or in the music of its language, or even in its striking imagery, but in its economy and depth. As with poetry, it may be enjoyed at first reading, but to be appreciated it must be read more than once. And, like the greatest poems, it may be revisited for a lifetime, acquiring greater depth with each encounter.

This is a beautiful work on killing.

Will Clausewitz survive as long as Sun Tzu? He is the West's sole contender for such immortality in this field of study. And it is unlikely that we will see another entry in the race. In our time, Clausewitz is most often faulted for his failure to foresee the explosion of military technologies that would begin to revolutionize warfare only a generation after his death. The "missing technology" charge might be leveled at Sun Tzu as well. And to do so would be as foolish as in the case of Clausewitz. Both men were blessed to live in ages where the human factor remained the obvious key to understanding warfare. While even Sun Tzu's age saw the impact of new military technologies, neither writer was blinded by the dazzle of machinery—as our contemporary military theorists tend to be. The authors of the *Art of War* and *On War* worked in a timeless laboratory of death, in which the factors of knowledge, morale, mass, and will were the primary chemicals. What might Sun Tzu have made of nuclear or precision-guided weapons? His chronicler—stunningly contemporary in his prejudices—might have rued the first and embraced the latter. But would he have seen through the ornaments to the essence of war? Likewise, had Clausewitz had the misfortune to survive into the age of the telegraph, repeating rifles, the railroad, and steam-driven ironclads, he might have missed the forest for the trees.

In this volume, we meet the two military minds who were not distracted by the transitory and ephemeral. If their souls were lesser, their works possess the timelessness of

Shakespeare's—and both texts have been more influential, for better and worse, than any play. If, like Shakespeare, they are often quoted out of context or misquoted, that is the fate of genius. If their thought has been misused, it is our fault and not theirs.

The Casualty Myth

Proceedings, May 1998

There are three great myths in contemporary America: Elvis is alive; the average citizen is worse off than in some lost golden age; and the American people will not tolerate casualties in military operations. Of these three, the myth of the eternal Elvis is the most credible. The second is the most understandable, because in all civilizations, human beings have equated even the most positive change with loss. The last myth, that of American cowardice, simply reflects the views of an elite divorced from its fellow citizens, from our unifying traditions, and from any experience requiring selflessness, courage, or faith.

Utterly unjustified by empirical evidence, the conviction of our governing elite that Americans are unwilling to countenance death for any cause tells us far more about that elite than it does about our citizens in general. The myth that all casualties are intolerable is merely absolution and comfort for those committed to their own personal welfare above all.

No sane man or woman wants to die, and no parent yearns to sacrifice his or her child for any cause, but casualties are not about enthusiasm. They are about an ultimate willingness, about reluctance overcome and the self transcended. Since the 1960s, a governing and informational elite has arisen whose formative experience was the avoidance of personal participation in our Indochina wars. With Orwellian genius, their books, films, and poses redefined cowardice as heroism and reduced the traditional hero to a bloody-handed ape. The most privileged young Americans grabbed Vietnam as an excuse to escape, once and for all, from their responsibility to share physical danger with the rest of the citizenry.

Our Indochina wars were ill conceived, ineptly executed, and too long governed by a fatal combination of inertia and political vanity. We supported grotesque foreign governments, with inappropriate means and strategies that ignored human nature. Yet, after a decade of conflict and sixty thousand dead—and despite the public tantrums that briefly aroused our campuses—there was no second American revolution, nor even a student movement approaching the seriousness of the eruptions of 1968 in Europe. The defining motive of American dissent was selfishness, not ideology. Despite broad disillusion with our inchoate efforts in Vietnam, draft resistance never became more than a romanticized anomaly, and the electorate, in the final years of those wars, voted Republican.

Still, the American people did not like those Indochina fights for the simple reason that they have more common sense than any professor will grant them. They knew a losing proposition when they saw one. The message of Vietnam is not that Americans will not take casualties; it is that the American people do not want the lives of their sons and daughters wasted.

The truth is that Americans are fighters. In fact, they are capable of a savagery when provoked that our contemporary elite simply cannot accept. But they want the fight to make sense—and they want to win, win big, and get it over with. It would be easier for Americans to accept two thousand friendly casualties in a two-month effort that killed a hundred thousand of the enemy and achieved decisive results than it would be for them to accept two hundred casualties over two years in an operation with no foreseeable conclusion.

We expect to fight for measurable ends, not delicate modulations in an obscure alliance. Our national "weakness" is not cowardice, but impatience. And perhaps that isn't a weakness at all. Perhaps that impatience with political Hamlets and an endless hemorrhage of lives is fully in consonance with our national character—pragmatic, aggressive, yet mindful of the value of each citizen.

In the nondescript 1990s, we have experienced two profound and costly disconnects between leadership perceptions and the psychology of our citizens. First, at the premature end of Desert Storm, Washington elites—including military leaders—collapsed in panic at media images of the "Highway of Death," the instant junkyard we created from Iraqi formations fleeing Kuwait City with their loot. Part of the concern had to do with worries about the perceptions of our Arab allies (who certainly have never worried much about us), but the primary cause for alarm was the notion that the electorate would be repelled by the images of carnage inflicted on the enemy. In fact, the American people were pleased with the success of their forces and weapons. After two decades of listening to pundits assure them that their kids couldn't fight and their weapons didn't work, the ladies and gentlemen in front of the television sets were proud.

In fact, if there is a dark side to our scrappy national character, it is how little reality enemy lives have for us—especially when our enemies are loud, provocative, and culturally dissimilar. Nobody I know bought the baby-milk factory ruse, and the bunker strike that killed the family members of the Iraqi elite and led to a suspension of strikes on Baghdad was accepted among our population as an inevitable cost of war. We were proud of Desert Storm, and very proud of our troops. The governing elite's rush to stop the violence did not put an end to casualties, just a temporary halt. The elite panicked, and the dilemmas of Mesopotamia remain unresolved. We will go back, and we will pay a higher price next time.

In Somalia, the disconnect was even greater. Somalia was a fickle, confused effort that was executed in willful ignorance. All warnings of that nation's internal complexity and contradictions were ignored. On the ground, the U.S. armed forces did their best—and their best was very good. Laboring under paralyzing restrictions and political constraints designed to protect Somalis from Americans—a stunning example of the relative concerns of our elite—our military was frustrated but dutifully compliant.

When the environment inevitably collapsed into combat, our forces did a splendid job, despite being denied the appropriate tools for an urban fight. We broke the back of our opponent's organization and finally were in a position to redefine the local political environment. But the response of our elite was, again, to panic at the loss of life and the perceived popular reaction and quit.

At the same time, the mood at home was vengeful. The American people were ready to support any possible effort against the murderers who dragged the naked, mutilated body of one of our soldiers through those foreign streets. Instead, our national leaders sent an explicit message to warlords and thugs around the world: Kill American soldiers and the Americans go home. This perception, already registered in the wake of the Beirut Marine barracks bombing, will cost the lives of many of our service members in the future. Fear is the best deterrent, but we have done our best to assure potential enemies that our quarter-of-a-trillion-dollar-a-year military is nothing to be afraid of.

It is difficult to rationalize our presence in Somalia, but the manner of our exit amounted to cowardice deepened by folly. In quitting, we broke one of the oldest taboos common to human cultures—we dishonored our warrior dead. In the process, we did more harm than good to a broken country. Now we are told that the message of Somalia is that the American people will not accept casualties.

Of course, it is much the fashion to complain of the self-centered nature of our governing elite, but fashion rarely is a matter of spontaneous generation. Something is deeply wrong. Members of our national elite mouth high ideals, but the test of any ideal is its sponsor's willingness to sacrifice for it. If service in uniform is a measure of sacrifice—and I believe it is fundamentally so—then our elite fails the test. You can go for years in Washington, D.C., without meeting a single person whose son or daughter—or niece or nephew—serves in our military. Far from risking their lives for their country, members of our elite will not even risk their children in public schools. They cannot imagine their sons or daughters in combat and, therefore, convince themselves that all Americans are as privileged and selfish as they have become.

Americans—those outside the Beltway, whose kids go to public schools—will fight ferociously for a good cause, and they still see our country as the ultimate good cause. They do not and will not welcome casualties, but they understand and accept them. All they want in return is responsible leadership, a just cause, and the assurance that their children's lives will not be squandered. They do not even demand fairness; they will fight without a senator's son by their sides. But they believe that the senator should demonstrate courage on Capitol Hill in return for the courage they and their kin demonstrate on our nation's battlefields.

We have the greatest military in the world—and it is all-volunteer. Instead of mass desertions, Desert Storm saw our service members struggling to get in on the fight—and their families and communities were solidly behind them. The concept of duty is alive and well outside the Beltway.

Even Elvis served his country in uniform, although he could have weaseled out of it. His was a decision our contemporary leaders would not understand.

Hard Target

Washington Post, Outlook, August 30, 1998

As an American citizen, I was pleased when our president showed the strength of will to strike back at terrorists by attacking targets in Afghanistan and Sudan. As a former military man, however, I recognized the weaknesses inherent in those strikes. The targets were minor and our attack was timid.

This was a media event, not policy. Isolated attacks on broken states that cannot retaliate do not constitute a war, despite the power of the Clinton administration's rhetoric. We enjoyed a momentary thrill, but unless we follow through with further actions, all of the sound and fury will have signified nothing.

In the struggle against international terrorism, the United States has suffered from three cardinal deficiencies. We have lacked the relentless determination essential to the pursuit of terrorists. Our military system is ill-matched to the threats emerging from the ruptured world around us. And we have crippled ourselves by a strict observance of laws and precedents that our opponents ignore or turn against us.

At present, we are like a police department that ventures out of the station house every four or five years to combat crime for a day. Then, after a bath of rhetoric about no quarter for offenders, we go back inside and shut the door until the criminals again do something so heinous we have to put down our coffee and doughnuts and go back to work.

The fight against terrorism requires a long-term and unwavering commitment. Our current approach is to surrender the initiative to the terrorist, then react. It is true that the nature of terrorism and the limitations of even the best intelligence system favor the bomber's or assassin's seizure and retention of the initiative. His signature is slight and his range of potential targets vast; he is elusive and mobile where we are ponderous and constrained; his cause is his life's consuming purpose, while he is only an intermittent concern to us.

Yet it is not enough to insist that acting preemptively is practically and legally too hard to do (the administration did claim that the recent strikes were preemptive, but they were clearly retaliatory attacks against targets of opportunity).

This truly is a war. At present it is being waged against us, but not by us. Until we, too, regard it as a war, our vulnerability will not decrease. It is also a war in which there will be no final victory, and that concept is difficult for Americans to accept. But a serious national commitment would make an enormous difference in the safety, prosperity, and convenience of our citizens, at home and abroad.

Unfortunately, we are poorly prepared for this war. The asymmetry between our armed forces and our new enemies—the terrorists, transnational criminals, and genocidal warlords—is severe and growing. We have the most powerful military in history, but its power is designed to defeat conventional threats. When the enemy does not "fight fair" and deploy tanks, ships, and aircraft, we find ourselves punching thin air. We have prepared to fight machines. But the enemy is belief (or simply greed or hatred). Whether that belief lies in religion misinterpreted or in ethnic fanaticism, it commonly rejects our rules of warfare, as surely as it does the rule of law.

The systems on which American taxpayers will spend nearly a trillion dollars over the next few decades will have only limited utility against unconventional threats armed with conviction and rage. Worse, we are, and will continue to be, unwilling to use most of those systems in any crisis short of conventional war. We continue to build a military to fight an enemy that no longer exists, while ignoring the enemies at our door.

Our seventy-nine cruise missile attack appeared stunning as presented by government spokespersons and covered by the media. And it was, undoubtedly, briefly stunning to those on the receiving end. But consider what actually happened. Although the complete ramifications of our action and the extent of the damage we inflicted remain unknown (and we may never know precisely what we accomplished), our very expensive, high-tech attack was less effective than the cheap, low-tech terrorism that triggered our response.

We spent about seventy million dollars on the Tomahawk cruise missiles we used in the attacks on Sudan and Afghanistan. Those missiles were launched from networks of ships costing billions of dollars, backed by an intelligence infrastructure that cost tens of billions of dollars. Our efforts resulted in the destruction of a pharmaceutical plant in Khartoum (with only tenuous ties to Osama bin Laden, the villain of the piece) and in damage to a cluster of primitive training camps in Afghanistan. The best reports to date indicate that we killed about fifty terrorist trainees and support personnel. (Vietnam gave body counts a bad name, but in counterterrorism they are a crucial indicator of success, because the terrorist who survives often feels renewed determination.) In other words, the price tag for each dead terrorist trainee or supporter may have been perhaps a little over one million dollars in direct costs, not counting the costs of the infrastructure behind the effort.

Bin Laden's alleged attacks on our embassies in Africa probably cost in the low hundreds of thousands of dollars, if not less. If he masterminded the attacks, bin Laden is responsible for the deaths of a dozen Americans and more than two hundred local civilians, and the wounding of five thousand others. The terrorist chief embarrassed America and sent a global message of resistance against U.S. hegemony to his sympathizers. On his terms, his operation was a triumph (we fail to grasp that such atrocities appear heroic to hundreds of millions of people who resent or hate or fear us). Our efforts, which appear so powerful at the moment, likely only provoked our nemesis to further atrocities, while expanding his recruiting base. There is nothing wrong with spending money to kill terrorists, but our government's present military approach is inefficient and only marginally effective.

We did not deliver an overwhelming blow. Part of the reason goes to the heart of our weakness in fighting terrorism. In order to avoid risk, we used not the best, but the safest weapons. While cruise missiles were ideal for the Khartoum attack, with a fixed physical target and the requirement for precision, they were a not very effective way to strike terrorist training camps and facilities spread over tens of square miles.

A truly determined attack on those camps would have been a joint effort, involving a limited number of cruise missile strikes on point targets followed immediately by long-range bombers delivering heavy loads of old-fashioned bombs. A fully coordinated effort would also have included special operations personnel on the ground to designate targets for additional precision strikes and to exploit success (to be fair, the operation may have been more complex than the Department of Defense admits).

A serious attack would have involved risk to pilots and aircraft, and Washington wants to conduct military operations on the cheap, at least politically. During a past interview, bin Laden pointed to our precipitate withdrawal from Somalia after we won a street battle and suffered a handful of casualties. He claimed Americans are cowards who retreat as soon as they are bloodied. He is wrong about our troops, but right about our government.

The administration's timidity in the employment of the world's most expensive military becomes grotesque when we, the people, are told that we need three new types of fighter aircraft that will cost more than 350 billion dollars, not counting long-term infrastructure cost. These outrageously expensive aircraft are narrow in purpose, lack an enemy, and will be too precious to use. In our strike on Afghanistan, old-fashioned B-52s (or the air shows–only B-2s) would have been ideal weapons. But both the president and the Defense Department did not want to risk pilots or embarrassment. If cruise missiles really are America's weapon of choice, we could, at mass production rates, buy enough of them to mount ten thousand strikes the size of those we launched against Afghanistan and Khartoum for the price of the Pentagon's three new fighters.

Or, if we do not intend to use most of our military, we could save a great deal of money.

A long-term effort against terrorism will require the use of a wide range of military assets, from special operations forces to, yes, cruise missiles. We will continue to need a strong military—but not one that cannot be taken out of the display case. At times, we will need to deploy ground troops. And we will face opponents willing to sacrifice themselves with an avidity incomprehensible to Western elites. The struggle against terrorism will not be a bloodless endeavor. We need to be honest about these issues now.

We have been crippled by our past reluctance to violate the sovereignty of states that either sponsor or condone terrorism, or that barely exist in any real sense of governance. The core purpose of the terrorist is to violate and ultimately negate our sovereignty. When it makes sense, and when there are no serious alternatives, we must be prepared to fight back. At present, we are so obsessed with international law, narrowly interpreted, that we handcuff ourselves, while allowing the terrorist to turn borders and legalisms against us.

But laws lose their validity when they no longer protect those who adhere to them. We must not be afraid to change in a changing world. When a foreign state or region either cannot or will not curb terrorists or international criminals operating from its territory, we have a moral, practical, and legal right to act. In an age of innovation, we cling to a nineteenth-century model of international relations. The greatest refuge of the terrorist isn't Afghanistan, it is our own fear.

The president's decision to attack one terrorist's infrastructure in Afghanistan and a bonus target in Sudan was an enormous step in the right direction. It was, however, a flawed and limited step. We need a serious, long-term policy that acts preemptively (and when necessary, vengefully) against terrorists, employing the best, not just the easiest, weapons in our arsenal. We must recognize that terrorist attacks are acts of war, not merely of criminality. When we cannot kill or capture an attacker who has struck at our citizens or at our national or religious symbols, we must ultimately be willing to strike his supporters and his cherished symbols. Terrorists must face disproportionate costs for their actions, not merely tit-for-tat exchanges. Above all, American efforts must be bipartisan efforts, elevated above electoral bickering, as any threat to our national security must be.

The strongest message we can send to terrorists around the globe is the demonstration of a relentless national will (our national will is, after all, the terrorists' real target). If the strikes on Afghanistan and Sudan marked the beginning of a new, more aggressive policy, we can make a powerful difference in the struggle against terrorism. If they turn out to have been just another of our tantrums, they will have been a waste of expensive ordnance.

The Human Terrain
of Urban Operations

Parameters, Spring 2000

Tasked with urban operations, soldiers think of buildings. The initial mental image is of physical forms—skyscrapers or huts, airports and harbors, size, construction density, streets, sewers, and so on. Planners certainly are interested in the population's attitudes and allegiances, but cities are more likely to be classified by their differences in construction than by the variety of their populations. This focus on "terrain" leads to the assumption that military operations would be more challenging in a Munich than in a Mogadishu. But the latter "primitive" city brutally foiled an international intervention launched with humanitarian intent, while "complex" Munich whimpered into submission at the end of the fiercest war in history. The difference lay not in the level of physical development, but in the human architecture.

While the physical characteristics of the assaulted or occupied city are of great importance, the key variable is the population. At its most obvious, the issue is simply whether the citizenry is hostile, indifferent, or welcoming. Too often, the evaluation of the flesh-and-blood terrain, of the human high-ground, ends there. Yet few populations are ever exclusively hostile, or truly indifferent, or unreservedly welcoming. Man's complexity is richer than any architectural detail. It is, finally, the people, armed and dangerous, watching for exploitable opportunities, or begging to be protected, who will determine the success or failure of the intervention.

TYPES OF CITIES

Analyzing the "human architecture" of a city begins with the recognition that there are three broad types of "mass terrain." For military purposes, cities can be classed as hierarchical, multicultural, or tribal. This imperfect system of classification does not offer a basis for command decisions—only a starting point for understanding the operational environment into which the force will be thrust. It can, however, provide early warning of the intractable nature of the problems that may await even an initially welcome peacekeeping force.

HIERARCHICAL CITIES

Hierarchical cities are those we Americans know. Chains-of-command operate within a broadly accepted rule of law. The citizens assume at least minimal responsibilities, from the payment of taxes to patterns of public behavior. In return, they expect that they will not be routinely cheated by government or merchants, that the light switch will turn on the light, that water will come from the tap, and that the police will provide a reasonable degree of protection without unreasonable intrusions into personal lives.

Apart from the technological aspects and the unusual degree of freedom enjoyed by Americans, the hierarchical city is a traditional form, stretching back to the dawn of history. Cities of the past were more repressive, of course, but chain-of-command cities, governed by a generalized consent or acquiescence and with popular respect for the rules of interaction, are mankind's great success story (the herding of cats on a mammoth scale). From Athens, Greece, to Athens, Georgia, such cities have provided men and women with the highest degree of well-being available in their ages. Sometimes repressive, elsewhere delightfully liberal—when not libertine—the common denominator of successful cities is a sense of unified popular identity, which is far more important than legal specifics. (A common Western fallacy is to imagine that liberal laws are an end unto themselves; in fact, most populations have preferred restrictive laws impartially administered to exemplary constitutions corruptly applied. A law's consistent observation is generally more important than its inherent quality, and the first purpose of law is certainty.)

Militarily, hierarchical cities, with their united citizenries, can provide bitter, prolonged resistance to an attacker. Paradoxically, they can be the easiest to govern once occupied—if the population recognizes its interests lie in collaboration. At the close of World War II, the cities of Germany and Japan contained populations recently committed to total war, yet they proved docile and easy to govern by constabulary forces. The citizenry must see the advantage in cooperation; once convinced, its homogeneity eases successful reconstruction, both physical and behavioral. It has always been easier to govern Paris than to take it.

MULTICULTURAL CITIES

Multicultural cities, which have little to do with the fantasies of Liberal Arts faculties, are those in which contending systems of custom and belief, often aggravated by ethnic divisions, struggle for dominance. They are, by their nature, cockpits of struggle. Chains-of-command in government offices draw willing obedience only from their partisans, while groups that do not identify with those in power must be coerced into desired behaviors and will act subversively until a reaction defines the limits of what is tolerable. To those ignorant of local affairs, the multicultural city may resemble the hierarchical city, with its mayor or other administrator and its formal institutions. But real power is diffused beyond legal agencies into ethnic networks, religious and resistance organizations, and crime syndicates whose leaders usurp much of the authority and some of the functions of the "legitimate" government.

Multicultural cities, even in the best of economic times, squander creative energies and human capital on social struggles aimed at revising the balance of power. True multiculturalism of this sort is centrifugal, intolerant, and ultimately destructive. North American cities, even the most ethnically diverse, remain hierarchical—multiethnic, but not multicultural—while those that most closely approach the multicultural "ideal" described here tend to be the least safe and least prosperous. Successful cities require a community of values; multicultural cities may produce successful individual neighborhoods, but the sum is always less than the parts. Where cultural confrontation pits alternative value systems against each other, the city declines—no matter the relative merit of the contending values. Cities are, above all, cooperative ventures (with laws to protect the dull against the anarchic impulses of the creative), and require general agreement as to the social blueprint to be followed. Diversity may thrive within the cooperative, as it does in so much of North America, and may gradually reshape the society from the inside (although the opening of a Chinese restaurant does not presuppose the public's acceptance of Confucian values). But when cultural differences create a sense of assault on group values from the outside, the city is headed for riots at best and, at worst, genocide.

Perhaps the preeminent example of a multicultural city today is Jerusalem, with its irreconcilable differences between Jews and Arabs, whose beliefs, values, and ambitions are profoundly at odds. In this classic model, order is maintained only by the forcefulness of the more powerful faction, buttressing the hatreds of the group excluded from authority (and, by extension, from prosperity and social mobility). When a numerically inferior group holds a larger group or groups in thrall, the situation is especially volatile. The Israelis, with their settlement policies, attacked this problem long ago. Another recent example comes from East Timor, where a minority of Islamic Indonesian occupiers had oppressed and deprived the Catholic Timorese. The values of the two communities were bluntly incompatible (especially when overlaid with Indonesian fantasies of imperial grandeur).

Multicultural cities tend to develop along what Samuel Huntington has called the "fault lines" between civilizations—those marches and frontiers where dominance shifts between groups over centuries (and sometimes more swiftly). South Africa's harsh growing pains center largely on its multicultural cities, where British, Afrikaner, and native African cultural systems collided. When the restraining British hand lifted from the Indian subcontinent, the massacres inflicted on one another by Hindus and Muslims covered their cities with gore and disfigured their nascent states. Now cities such as Lahore and Delhi have returned, limping, to hierarchical status, but continue to suffer under the multicultural legacy of corruption and factionalism, aggravated by value systems ill-suited to modernity. Other urban areas, from Istanbul to its old polar opposite, Vienna, have devolved back into hierarchical cities more successfully, as empires collapsed, civilizational fault lines shifted, and "foreign" elements were expelled or moved on. Even in the best cases, however, the transition periods from multicultural flowering back to monocultural roots are unstable, often bloody, and disquieting to foreign observers.

The continual, generally peaceful cultural evolution in the United States suggests that healthy, prosperous societies can change by elective accretion, but that cultural amalgamation bluntly does not work. Secure in their sense of identity, the populations of hierarchical cities can learn from new arrivals, while multicultural cities barricade themselves—sometimes literally—against intercommunal exchanges. Even in the United States, the immigrant groups that excited the most resistance and proved slowest to assimilate were those who arrived quickly, in large numbers, creating a perception of threat to the established order and its values. Numbers matter, perhaps even more than do racial differences, as the long struggle of Irish-Americans toward equality compared to the comparatively easy acceptance of Korean-Americans suggests. And overt conformity to societal norms may be even more important than religious conformity in gaining acceptance, except in the most demagogic and primitive cultures. The group established as social hegemon wants, above all, obeisance to its values and cherished behaviors.

Statistically, there are surprisingly few multicultural cities at any given time, since they are inherently unstable. Reversion to monocultural hierarchy—or destruction—is the norm: Turkish Izmir or vanished Troy (a close reading of *The Iliad* suggests that the Trojans drew their support from inherently unstable intercultural alliances, while the Greeks arrived in a state of dynamic cultural coalescence). Unless the city falls to an external power, its less powerful population groups inevitably are massacred, expelled, or forcibly assimilated, whether in the cities of Silesia, Andalusia, or India at the hour of independence from British rule. The ugly fact of the devolution of multicultural cities back into ethnically or confessionally harmonious ones is that the population transfers usually bring stability and peace.

From the military standpoint, multicultural cities can be easy to conquer—with the aid of oppressed minorities as a fifth column—but difficult to administer after peace has been established. If you have made allies of one group, they will expect to dominate after the victory or intervention. Western notions of equitable treatment and the rule of law strike the population as risible, if not as an outright betrayal. Peace can be imposed, but not even a generation of occupation will convince the opposing groups to behave "like us." In cultures where compromise is, literally, unthinkable, the peacekeeping adventure will see a constant jockeying for favor and usually a hardening of physical divisions between groups. The citizens of all factions will be looking beyond the presence of the peacekeepers to the renewed struggle, violent or otherwise, for hegemony. Often, the nominal government imposed by the occupier or peacekeeper will have less real power than ethnic leaders, militia commanders in mufti, religious leaders, or mafiosi. The primary interests of each faction will be to exploit the power of the constabulary force for partisan purposes, to exploit gaps in the force's knowledge of the local situation for advantage, to shield illicit activities from the force's awareness, to consolidate power within the group, and, finally, to corrupt key elements of the force to facilitate prohibited behaviors and to undermine competitors. The primary challenge for a Western military operating in a multicultural city is to get at the facts—and the facts never hold still.

There are also plentiful exceptions to the proposition that multicultural cities are easy to conquer. If the population group with which you are allied is powerless or unwilling to fight, you may face absolutely furious resistance from the enraged majority or urban hegemon. The first battle of Grozny, in Chechnya, was a striking example of this. If the divisions cut so deep that the antagonist is willing to fight a scorched-earth (or leveled-building) war—including the massacre of the minority or weaker group that has bound its fate to you—the intervention force faces extreme combat challenges that will be resolved as much by a question of will as by objective military capabilities. In general, a declared or perceived partisanship on the part of peacemaking or peacekeeping forces prior to deployment creates a window of slaughter, during which the threatened group accelerates ethnic cleansing operations, as in Dili, Pristina, or Freetown. Peace operations resemble other military operations in that, so often, speed saves lives—but swift intervention is one of the rarest acts of the international community. The world reacts to horror, but refuses to anticipate it.

Regarding other multicultural cities of the collapsed Soviet empire, most in Central Asia are losing ethnic European populations, although the situation varies from state to state, but Europeans have not been the objects of violent outbreaks; rather, outside of Tajikistan, the ugliest instances of violence have erupted between indigenous nationalities in Central Asia's Fergana Valley. In Afghanistan, a war of liberation degenerated into an ethnic civil war, and the dominant Taliban movement is willing to lay waste cities in order to "purify" them ethnically and religiously, rendering them monocultural with a vengeance. The number of unresolved issues and artificial states between the Black Sea and China's western provinces make this area the least predictable in the world. No one can foresee whether it will drowse or erupt—but Russia's greatest challenges in the coming decades are likely to arise on its frontiers, not on the financial spreadsheets of Western banks. The

Russian Federation is the new "sick man of Europe," and, just as the collapse of the Ottoman Empire was triggered by events in Sarajevo, a dusty former city of that empire, so Moscow may face crises sparked in cities it once occupied, from Kiev through Baku to Tashkent. Indeed, Russia's large, creaking military, its loan-gobbling financial squalor, and its inability to control its remaining territories make it resemble the Ottoman Empire, but with rotting nukes. At a minimum, Russia's future military efforts will offer the West a laboratory in which to study the problems of urban operations, from the festering ulcer of Chechnya to terrorism in Moscow itself.

For the peacekeeping or constabulary force, the most promising environment is a formerly multicultural city that has been, regrettably, ethnically "cleansed." Problems will be directly proportionate to the extent to which status quo ante-bellum differences remain unresolved: Sadly, the more thorough the ethnic cleansing, the better the chances for the city's recuperation. The best hope for recovery in Dili, East Timor—difficult in any case, because of the ravages of violence and long-standing poverty—will be the complete departure of Indonesians who arrived after 1975. Although it remains to be seen, the hideous ethnic cleansing in the Caucasian cities of Baku, Sumgait, and Stepanakert—multicultural for generations, when not centuries—eventually may result in regional pacification. The deprivation of the object of hatred is a powerful force for peace. This is an unattractive concept for Westerners. It is also true.

TRIBAL CITIES

Tribal cities, the most difficult urban environments for peacekeeping operations, are growing in size and number around the world. Based upon differences in blood, but not in race or, necessarily, in religion, ethnic conflicts in this environment can be the most intractable and merciless. One of the many paradoxes of our time is that the greatest expression of human sophistication, the city, increasingly draws in those with primitive, blood-based allegiances. As traditional rural societies grow overpopulated and impoverished, the lure of the city disproportionately draws young males—society's most volatile population slice—seeking opportunity, adventure, and reinvigorated identity.

Whether in Mogadishu, Kigali, Dushanbe, or Karachi, violence between those of the same race and similar or identical religion has ruptured governments even where its remoteness has kept it off the television screen. While Tutsis and Hutus in Rwanda might differ in appearance to the tutored eye, they are not civilizationally different. In Mogadishu, peacekeepers could not tell the difference between clans without obvious cues. In Tajikistan, you have to know the *individual* with whom you are dealing. And in Pakistan, where the city of Karachi veers between ungovernable and barely governable phases, the city's explosive growth in the Independence period was based upon the relocation of religiously identical and ethnically indistinguishable "brothers" from the rest of the subcontinent. Now the brothers have turned fratricidal. Around much of the world, the tribe, once banished from the liberal vocabulary, has returned with a vengeance. It is mankind's basic killing organization.

Perhaps the most startling "tribal" conflict of our time has been the series of wars in the former Yugoslavia. While some might declare this a multicultural conflict based in religious and civilization differences, that is to subscribe to the rhetoric of Milosevic and Tudjman. The region's multicultural phase climaxed a century ago; since then, the local populations have blurred into a gray similarity. The day-to-day cultures of Orthodox Serbs, Croatian Catholics, and Bosnian or Kosovar-Albanian Muslims had converged to the degree that the urban Serb and urban Muslim, in Sarajevo or Pristina, had more in common with one another than either did with his rural counterpart. Religion was discounted, a dusty relic, until revived by demagogues. Ethnicity was an old scar, not a present sore.

Although couched in terms of civilizational conflict, the battles and atrocities in the Balkans have had more in common with those in Somalia or Rwanda than with the epoch-making struggles between Ottomans and Byzantines, or czar and sultan. At the same time, we are seeing a phenomenon the West had assumed to be impossible in our "enlightened" age: These Balkan tribes that had largely lost their primitive identities are re-creating them, and doing so with bloody exuberance. We know more about the atmosphere of Mars than we do of the ties for which men kill.

Tribal cities, from Sarajevo to Freetown, pose difficulties for intervention forces or peacekeepers on multiple levels. On the most basic level, it often takes long experience for outsiders to tell members of the contending factions apart when they fail to proclaim—or try to disguise—their identities. It is especially hard to crack tribal and clan cultures for intelligence purposes, and combatants vanish easily into the "sea of the people." But perhaps the greatest difficulty lies in the peculiar depth of hatred clan fighting and tribal traditions bring to bear on a conflict. Interracial pogroms erupt and quickly subside, but tribal hatreds are robust and enduring. There is no will to compromise, no sense of shared advantage through cooperation—except perhaps briefly against outsiders, such as peacekeeping forces. The pattern appears to be that the more similar contending factions appear to foreign observers, the more savagely they will oppose each other.

We seem to be moving from an age of imperialist genocide—European against African or Native American, Japanese against Chinese or Korean, Arab against African (the oldest enduring genocidal tradition, lingering in Sudan)—to a period of genocide against familiars, shifting from slaughter between civilizations to the slaughter of neighbors. The Germans lit the fire, with their massacre of the Jews who had immeasurably enriched German society over the centuries and who regarded themselves as every bit as German as any *Kanzler.* Now we see the new model of massacre from East Central Africa, to the Caucasus, to the Balkans. Except in the Arab and Persian Islamic world, where the style of hatred lags behind, hatred of the family next door has replaced the fear of the distant, different devil.

Our knowledge of ourselves is too primitive to allow us to understand why this change in humanity's choice of victims is taking place at this time, and we cannot know if it is a psychological response to history or a biological reaction to proximity or something else entirely, but the focal point of ever more contemporary violence—and the likeliest scene of future violence—is the city.

COMPREHENDING CITYSCAPES

Cities are far more complex organisms than any text can suggest. Suffice to say that the greatest illustration of the human ability to self-organize shows in the daily functioning of cities. The myriad actions required to make Manhattan go are no more subject to complete regulation than they are to thorough quantification. Law is the foundation from which human activity is elaborated, but even the most voluminous codes have failed to foresee the inventiveness of human behavior. The countless individual actions that sum to urban life defy logic in their ability to interact constructively. Anarchy should follow; instead we get Florence, Sydney, and Boston.

Yet, for all the marvels in even a poorly functioning city, there are worrisome trends. Obviously, the increasing size and number of cities pose practical challenges for urban operations.

Even in the smoothest operation, cities consume troops; in combat, they devour armies. We look back on a century in which a rural world became an urban one, and the practical and psychological changes are not yet fully apparent. The urbanization of the world's masses will require centuries of adjustment.

Whether or not civilizations are in crisis, they are certainly under pressure to evolve. Some are better-suited to change than are others. The problems for Western militaries will overwhelmingly arise in traditional societies that cannot or will not adapt. In our desire to please all and offend none, we fail to recognize that the civilizational difference between the antagonists in Desert Storm was greater than that between Spaniards and Aztecs, or between the British military and the Mahdi's horde.

The world is not becoming an even, equitable place, but a sphere of deepening fissures, some of which may prove unbridgeable. At a time when even the rich states of Europe are falling two generations behind the United States militarily, and when global economic competition is far fiercer than at the height of the Industrial Revolution, fragile states will not be able to support their unwieldy cities with hope, or jobs, or infrastructure. Look to those cities for conflicts.

This essay offers a crude framework for thinking about the military nature of cities. Doubtless, there are more insightful ways to frame the problem; the model here proposed should spark debate, not pass as a prescription. In an age of urban operations, with many more to come, we must think more deeply and clearly about this environment than we have done. A cold appreciation of the environment and firm resolve often will be of greater help than any technologies or even numbers. Above all, this brief discussion seeks to drive home the point that the center of gravity in urban operations is never a presidential palace or a television studio or a bridge or a barracks. It is always human.

Huhsters in Uniform

The Washington Monthly, May 1999

In the year of our Lord 2020, the young pilots of America's armed forces will fly aircraft designed in a previous century for that earlier century's wars. The Army's ground troops will be weighed down by leviathan systems unsuited to the knife-fight conflicts of the coming decades. And the Navy will be splendidly prepared for the Second World War. Along the way, the United States may pay a trillion dollars for weapons that constrain rather than enable, that bankrupt the services, and that preserve cherished traditions at the expense of practical capabilities.

The world has changed even more profoundly than we have noticed. 1989 marked not only the end of the Cold War, but the end of half a millennium of history dominated by the rise and fall of European empires. For the American people, a 250-year tradition of fighting empires came to a close—our major wars engaged empires and only empires, first those of kings, then those of demagogues. Even our Civil War was fought to cast off the vestiges of imperial inheritance from human bondage to a loathsome aristocracy of landholders. The American purpose, unspoken but accomplished, was to destroy empires and their patterns of human organization. Now a quarter-millennium's mission has been fulfilled, and we are victorious but without compass.

Our military does not know what to do, so it does what it long has done: It organizes for grand wars against conventional militaries. No matter that the few such establishments still in existence do not, cannot, and will not threaten our nation and, at most, are positioned to annoy their neighbors—the portion of our wealth spent on arms will purchase systems to fight a reflection of ourselves. To exploit the weapons we are buying, we would have to share them with our enemies, or divide into teams and fight each other. Meanwhile, underfunded soldiers and Marines will do our nation's dirty work abroad, while in the skies and at sea we display a shining, irrelevant legacy. We have entered the age of the impassioned butcher, with a crude weapon in one hand, a cell phone in the other, and hatred in his soul. As of this writing, we see him in Kosovo, and we shall often meet his like again.

In this age of brilliance and dissolution, individuals and organizations long for verities. This manifests itself in religious fundamentalism, ethnic separatism, rejectionist terrorism, and Pentagon stubbornness. Our military hides behind technologies that give an illusion of progress, while preserving the old ways of thinking, organizing, and fighting. But our military thinking, such as it is, looks backward, our organizations are ponderous and grotesquely inefficient, and, when allowed to fight by our political leadership, combat commanders must improvise their way to victory.

We are a land of fabulous, but not unlimited, wealth. As weapons costs increase—even as their versatility and dependability decrease—we must make sensible choices. Almost without exception, the services are determined to make disastrous ones. Our country will be ready for the war that will not come, but unprepared for the urbanizing, chaotic, and morbid conflicts whose coming is already upon us.

Consider a few purchases in progress:

At a time when no power can match our control of the skies and none intends to confront us with dueling aircraft, we are buying three new fighters at a cost of 340 billion dollars, according to the Congressional Budget Office's accounting. The CBO's figure is that of an apologist, and does not include the metastasizing costs of fitting these systems to the force and keeping them there. Further, the General Accounting Office— our government's unpopular honest broker—states that "cost increases of 20 to 40 per cent have been common for major weapon programs" and that "numerous programs experienced increases much greater than that." The trend-line for cost over-runs rises sharply.

Of those three "indispensable" aircraft, the most promising is the Navy's F/A 18E/F, based upon a proven airframe and fulfilling at least some legitimate needs. The Navy insists the program is within budget, but maintains its numbers only by deferring problems. The F-22 Raptor, a supremely unnecessary air-superiority fighter, is over budget 667 million dollars years before the first plane has been produced for combat. The contractor, in a wonderful blackmail effort, has warned that costs will shoot higher if the Air Force does not continue to buy an unwanted aircraft, the C-130J, to keep assembly lines open. The final aircraft, the Joint Strike Fighter, is lagging in development, but being rushed forward. Its purchase will force an annual doubling of the aircraft procurement budget, even if costs do not increase one dollar beyond current projections. Yet, in an air campaign such as those in Yugoslavia or Iraq, it offers little more than planes we have.

Ultimately, we can fund these three evolutionary systems that slightly improve current capabilities (if, unlike the B-1 and B-2 bombers, they work as advertised). But, consequently, we will not be able to afford the truly revolutionary technologies that will become available early in the next century. We will be imprisoned by these lavish purchases of past designs. Worse still, the trend in military technologies is toward cheap kills of expensive systems. We may spend well over half a trillion dollars to buy aircraft that will be defeated easily by innovative technologies available at a discount. While the generals, admirals, and the defense contractors who hire them upon their retirement will argue that threat-testing shows that these new aircraft are virtually invulnerable, the word in the Pentagon corridors is that tests that might expose weaknesses in the survivability of the aircraft are being watered down or simply avoided. Increasingly, our national defense is a business, and its business is not defense.

The Army, lumbering and unimaginative, cannot match the Air Force or Navy in the size of its expenditures, but exceeds them in its enthusiasm for yesteryear's solutions to tomorrow's problems. The centerpieces of its procurement program are the RAH-66 attack helicopter, an improved but far from revolutionary system little better than the currently fielded AH-64 Apache, and the Crusader, a leviathan artillery system that will be difficult to deploy, hard to resupply, and irrelevant to the most frequent threats the Army will face. Obsessed with building the perfect division at Fort Hood, Texas, the Army refuses to accept that the number one requirement for the future is the ability to get out of Texas on short notice. The Army is so overweight it cannot get to a crisis promptly. In an age when global mobility based upon advanced concepts of organization and lethality is the core military requirement, the Army's combat systems grow ever heavier, ever more costly, and ever more dependent upon a sprawling maintenance infrastructure. Instead of investing in research and development to design weapons for the future, the Army is determined to perfect the past.

Bewildered by the utter disappearance of enemy fleets, the Navy cruises toward the iceberg of irrelevance, still buying congressionally beloved submarines and surface combatants that have little combat power but enjoy tremendous political patronage. The Air Force and Army at least face genuine threats, if not those they crave. The best our Navy can do is to provide expensive, marginal firepower from inefficient ships and diplomatically useful but low-combat-power aircraft carriers.

Beyond their dreary hurrah rhetoric, not one of these services has developed a doctrine for our changed world.

And what about the Marine Corps? Breaking ranks, the Marines have taken an honest look at the likely future of conflict and have begun to prepare for it—mind you, this praise comes from a retired Army officer and traditional rival of the Corps. Accustomed to doing things on the cheap, the Marines have developed innovative doctrine and training to prepare for everything from sorting refugees to fighting in the hell of urban warfare. The Marine Corps is the only defense bargain the taxpayer gets among the services.

Given the traditional image of the Marines as straight of back, straight of mind, and straight into the wall, it's startling to encounter more freedom of thought, impassioned internal debate, and plain honesty in the Corps than anywhere else in our defense establishment. Even the Marine Corps' primary acquisition program, the V-22 tilt-rotor aircraft (an ugly hybrid of helicopter and propeller transport) fits actual strategic and tactical requirements—it moves forces into combat quickly, with ten times the survival rate of the best transport helicopter. It isn't glamorous, only useful.

The generals and admirals who recommend or acquiesce in the purchase of most of the systems we are buying resemble the middle-aged man who buys a Porsche he cannot afford instead of the family van he needs. Our military is short of spare parts, training funds, trucks, and infantrymen. We are buying the future force the generals and admirals, congressmen and contractors want, not the one we will need. This is waste just short of treason.

Why, in the face of daily evidence of the changed nature of conflict, do we insist on buying systems of marginal or no relevance? Tradition is sometimes the reason, often the excuse. Congressional pork chopping is a major factor—President Eisenhower got it only two-thirds right: We face a defense-industrial-congressional complex. Defense contractors contribute mightily to political campaigns, as well as providing the world's most expensive jobs in voting districts. In the defense community, corporate welfare is an art form. All this is clearly wrong. So why do the generals or admirals, whose patriotism is ever on their lips, fail to take a stand even against a rival service's goldplated mistakes?

The reason is greed. Anyone who has served in the Pentagon has slipped on the slime trails that retired generals and admirals leave in their wake as they navigate the hallways bearing a defense contractor's business card with their name on it. The employment of retired senior officers by the nation's largest, increasingly monopolisitic defense contractors is a scandal costing the taxpayer hundreds of billions of dollars, and it may cost our troops their lives. These men wear flags upon their lapels, but their minds are on the money. Their actions are not illegal because we have legalized corruption.

When, in the mid-1980s, a few voices on Capitol Hill called for closing this particular revolving door, representatives from the defense industry and the threatened officers themselves put on their red-white-and-blue war paint and chanted that the defense industry needed the expertise of senior officers. But colonels and captains, warrant officers and sergeants are the ones who have current expertise. Generals and admirals have connections.

We have seen the Babbitization of the officer corps, the rise of the huckster and shill with stars on his shoulders, and we will pay dearly for it. Like the small-minded, grasping anti-hero of Sinclair Lewis's novel, our senior leaders spout moralistic and patriotic slogans, but go for the bucks. Certainly, some retired four stars—men like Generals Colin Powell, John Galvin, Barry McCaffrey, and many a Marine flag officer—have continued to serve their country in other fields. But most insiders take the money. Often, if a general or admiral is not employed by a defense contractor, it tells you he was not a member of the club.

In our time, not one senior officer has resigned over waste. And none will.

Who is to blame? In the end, not the generals and admirals themselves so much. They are only living up to the values of their lower-middle-class backgrounds: speak piously and grasp vigorously. They are not all without genuine patriotism, but they have been accorded privilege for so long by the system they served that they have come to confuse the national interest with their self-interest. We cannot expect today's military to think, because the thinking men have left the military. Neither rigorous reflection nor self-criticism are common virtues among senior officers. Only a few of these men are willfully venal or consciously corrupt. Most simply rationalize their behavior, convincing themselves that the armed forces truly need the systems for which their service has acquired an appetite or their employer a contract.

The real blame for the practical and moral shambles in which our military finds itself lies with our nation's elite, whose privileged members turned their back on military service when our Indochina wars gave them an excuse.

Here I must inject a personal note—I never shed blood upon the field of Sidwell Friends, nor did I fight the battles of Yale Law. I am a miner's son, and my father was a self-made man who unmade himself during my youth. Education was not a family legacy, and my kin belonged to the United Mine Workers of America, not to Skull and Bones. My forebears fought this country's wars from the bottom ranks, and I began my own military career as a private. I have felt the full arrogance of those to whom much was given and, personally, wish that I might come to bury the elite, not to praise them. Yet, those who would rise need examples to emulate. It grates on me to write it, but our military needs the return of the nation's elite to the officer corps, to the extent that a traditional elite, with its spotty but essential ideals of service, still exists.

Certainly, our nation's elite never provided a majority, or even a large minority, of the officer corps even in wartime. When they served, the Navy was preferred by the bluebloods, the Army by the new-bloods. Plenty of the well-to-do did well by avoiding service, paying a three-hundred-dollar bounty to avoid service in our Civil War, or finding placement in an "essential" government job in World War II, or donning a Brooks Brothers uniform to serve Father's friend in Washington or London for the duration. But enough served to make a difference. It takes only a bit of seasoning to make the stew.

The elite, too, produced its cowards and incompetents. But it also produced officers such as George Washington and

George Patton, Robert E. Lee and George Marshall (the latter sprung of small-town gentry—even slight privilege once inspired obligation). Those officers had been imbued with social rules of integrity, both moral and financial, that set a tone for others to study and attain. Imagine but one of the men named above accepting a retirement job flogging metal for Lockheed Martin or Northrop Grumman. Such men knew when to take a stand, and would have turned in their stars before they acquiesced in looting the public.

Of course, many of our finest officers rose from humble origins. But Dwight Eisenhower served under and looked up to Marshall; in Mexico, Grant admired the golden Lee. Moral quality is infectious. The military knows this and speaks nobly of leadership by example. But the men who mouth those words now speak of ghosts.

Vietnam harmed our nation less than commentators imagine, but struck our military a savage, lasting blow. In each war until then, the sons of Harvard and Princeton served. Their names are etched on memorials to the dead. But something happened in our Indochina years. We fought worse wars, but thought them better. Somehow, in a manner Sociology does not explain, those who benefited most from America arrived at a new assumption that privilege no longer carried a burden of responsibility. Perhaps it only marks the decrepitude of the old elite—surely, they are not the social factor they once were. Yet the best of them are missed. Today, the military's uniforms do not even fit properly (except for the Marines again), and the sense of self-sacrifice, despite a torrent of self-congratulatory rhetoric, barely finds a place in the upper ranks. Young officers still believe in our country, middle rankers serve it with increasing cynicism, and the generals sell it. We have come a long way down.

I do not believe there was ever a perfect world or a perfect military. Upper-crust cadets mocked Tom Jackson the bumpkin, who was as stolid and dreary as a stone wall, and Grant won brief approval only because he could outride them all— but when he led victorious armies the officers from privileged backgrounds lost no chance to brand the hero a drunk. McClellan was closer to the elite than Sherman, and the South's highest sons brought the Confederacy low with their love of Walter Scott and slaughter. But enough men served who had been bred to take a stand—and who could afford to walk away from a career.

As I write, we are waging a thoughtless demi-war in the Balkans. In a curious manner, it illustrates our loss of moral example. The shared drabness of service no longer informs president or senator, and ignorance of military matters rules. When the Kennedys no longer serve, the Clintons will not. Today's aspiring politicians regard military service as a blue-collar detour unworthy of their time. As a result, an administration unparalleled in its arrogance has blundered into a disaster that has swiftly cost a people its homeland, that threatens America's last shreds of strategic credibility, and that may gut the NATO alliance. While weeks lie between this electronic dash of ink and the printed page, even a miraculous turnabout in the Balkans will not erase the incompetence with which the adventure was begun. At the heart of our nation's government, not one person has worn a uniform. We have seen the Babbitization of the presidency, too.

The past is a dangerous trap. Our military is caught in it. Perhaps my longing to see our national elite return to military service is only another lapse into nostalgia. But we have an Army run by a "Board of Directors" that is a combination mafia conference and small-town business club, a Navy intent on fighting against the future rather than against our nation's likely enemies, and an Air Force whose only strategy is budgetary gluttony. Something must be done. We are about to spend that trillion dollars (perhaps less, but don't count on it) on an arsenal of mediocrity. If no one rises to lead our military by example, our next significant expenditure may be in lives.

The Future of War

Maclean's, April 26, 1999

In much of this troubled world, only blood persuades. War and conflict have an enduringly human face. For all of the technological wonders available to Western militaries, we cannot defeat the man with the knife unless we are willing to take a knife—or gun—into our own hands. The basic human dilemmas, of which the urge to violence is one, still require a human response. That is the lesson of our Kosovo misadventure, and it is the fundamental principle of warfare that will endure throughout our lifetimes.

The air campaign against Slobodan Milosevic's Yugoslavia offers a better paradigm for Western folly than a novelist could invent. NATO and its first-among-equals, the United States, imagined that the military instrument could be used successfully without shedding blood, and that technological superiority would define the terms of a brief conflict. Homegrown myths live a long time in the Balkans, but foreign myths perish rapidly.

A new generation of Western political leaders, their views shaped by the blithe idealism of the 1960s and the increasing comfort of subsequent decades, long imagined that mankind

323

might settle its differences peacefully. Confronted with the reality of hatred and bloodlust in this uncooperative decade, they next convinced themselves that war could be waged on the cheap, at least in terms of human lives—not only the lives of their own soldiers, but enemy lives as well. Canada turned its military into global babysitters, and the United States sought to turn war into a computer game. Now, the myths of the peaceable kingdom and of bloodless techno-war are dead, murdered in the Balkans.

Military technologies are important. But they only matter if they are appropriate and properly used. In Kosovo, NATO chose not the instruments that might do the job, but the instrument of least risk. But war is risk. A month into the first yuppie war, the Kosovar Albanians are homeless and shattered, a discount Hitler has defied the world, and the NATO states wring their hands and look for absolution. That is the price of wishful thinking.

We have, indeed, entered a new age of conflict. It will not be an age of dueling computers, however, but of fundamental brutality: ethnic cleansing, religious pogroms, genocide, terrorism, and international crime on a grand scale.

In a sense, we are going backward. The enemies who will confront our soldiers appear between the pages of the Bible and the *Iliad,* in Thucydides and Herodotus, Tacitus, Caesar, and Gibbon. The model of war cherished by general staffs, with well-ordered army pitted against well-ordered army, is largely gone. Conventional war remains a threat, but a diminishing one. Today's—and tomorrow's—enemies are half-trained killers in uniform, tribesmen, mercenaries, criminals, children with rusty Kalashnikovs, shabby despots, and gory men of faith. The most dangerous enemy will be the warrior who ignores, or who does not know, the rules by which our soldiers fight, and who has a gun in one hand, a cell phone in the other, and hatred scorching his heart.

The paradox of the next century is that it will be one of fabulous wealth for us, but of bitter poverty for billions of others. The world will not "come together," but has already begun to divide anew between open and tradition-bound societies, between rule-of-law states and lawless territories with flags, and between brilliant postmodern economies and cultures utterly unequipped for global competition. We will be envied and hated by those without a formula to win. In the twentieth century, we had to worry about successful industrial states and the militaries they produced. In the next century, the threats will arise from the realms of failure.

Apart from terrorism involving weapons of mass destruction, none of the broad violence of the coming decades will threaten the existence of Canada or the United States. Rather, it is our economic interests and, even more often, our humanitarian instincts that will be challenged, and our soldiers who will pay the bills of blood. At the end of a century of slaughter, from Vimy Ridge and the Somme to Auschwitz and Cambodia, we in the West have taken refuge in the utterly irrational conclusion that mankind is fundamentally good and lacks only opportunity to demonstrate that goodness. In the next century, we will learn otherwise.

To behave effectively in tomorrow's conflicts, we need to back away from the daily tumult and dig deep into root causes. As with Kosovo, we cannot wish away horror. At least a minority of human beings—primarily male—thrive on violence, both psychologically and practically. Some men acquire a taste for killing. We ache to believe otherwise, but the cultural genocide and brutalities of Kosovo are not being committed by reluctant hands. Love withers, but hatred endures and inspires. Where is the tribe that loves its neighbour selflessly?

The slaughters in Rwanda, Sierra Leone, and elsewhere in Africa were not laborious chores, but descents into intoxication and even ecstasy. The atrocities and dispossessions of Chechnya, Nagorno-Karabakh, Abkhazia, Bosnia and Croatia, southern Iraq, and the Kurdistan that does not exist (except in flesh and blood), of Afghanistan and fractured Indonesia, of Algeria and Northern Ireland were not executed by men steeled to a despised task, but by enthusiastic hands. Until we face Man as he is, we will have no end of Kosovos and Rwandas, of well-intentioned failures, refugees and bones. Man remains a killer, and we cannot wish the killer away.

In broken states and territories beyond state control, from the African bush to American slums, violence is empowering. Privileged and insular with our college degrees and good prospects, we of the reading class hope to solve crises of blood and hatred with diplomatic niceties, failing to recognize the addictive nature of violence (genocidal murderers and spouse abusers don't do it just once). Worse, we reconstruct our opponents in our own image, imagining that all men want peace. But for the hard-boy gunman of Ulster or the Balkan bully, peace is the least desirable state of affairs—unless he can dictate the terms of the peace. We thrive on order, but our enemies prosper from disorder. The end of the violence means the end of the good times for the local warlord or black-market king.

Most human beings do not thrive on violence, nor do they wish it, despite the resentments they may feel towards their neighbors. But it takes only a fraction of one per cent of a population, armed and determined, to destroy a fragile society. That is another lesson of the collapse of Yugoslavia, where even now, after years of organized brutality, under five per cent of the population has a hand in the business of death and ethnic cleansing.

The object of our interventions cannot be treaties alone. Ours is a strategy of self-satisfaction, not of meaningful change. If we wish to rescue or help reconstruct troubled societies, our first military action upon intervention must be to disarm the violent actors—and to fight those who resist. The worst offenders must be captured (or killed) and tried for their crimes before they slip into the criminality that has paralyzed many a "peace." We failed to do so in Bosnia, and the peace endures only because of the presence of foreign troops. Advocates of disarmament have pitched their programs too high. It isn't the decaying nuclear arsenals that threaten the world, but the pistol in the pocket of the killer.

Back in the 1960s, one of the original alternative-rock groups, The Fugs, recorded a satirical song about the Vietnam War entitled "Kill for Peace." That is exactly what we must be prepared to do.

What kind of militaries will we need in the next century? Not those which we have. Canada's military is unprepared to fight, and the U.S. armed forces are prepared to fight the wrong war. The first is underequipped, the latter improperly equipped. Ottawa has pinched pennies, relying on the American defense umbrella, while Washington continues to lavish money on systems and organizations designed to fight the forces of the vanished Soviet Union. For Canada, the question is whether or not it will pull its weight (peacekeeping efforts matter, but they don't matter as much as the willingness to use a rifle in a good cause). For the United States, the issue is whether it can fight in a lower weight class than it has trained for.

Consider the American military today. The inability of air power to win wars by itself is on display as I write. What we attempted to do in Yugoslavia is equivalent to telling a metropolitan police department they can control crime only from the air—we cannot even find the little bands of butchers at large in Kosovo, let alone strike them. Yet, air power remains the glutton of U.S. defense dollars, the promised miracle cure for conflict.

The U.S. Navy is structured to defeat foreign fleets that do not and will not exist, and the U.S. Army, while potent, is so ponderous it cannot get to crises promptly with sufficient hitting power. Despite deep cuts to its forces during the 1990s, the U.S. military could "do" Desert Storm again—if the enemy again allowed half a year for our preparations. But the U.S. Army cannot even get to Kosovo, let alone sustain itself there, without a lengthy buildup that would guarantee the leveling of the last ruins in Pristina. If America's goal is to avoid meaningful interventions, its armed forces are perfectly structured to that purpose.

And yet, there is an exception. The U.S. Marine Corps, long regarded as thick of muscle and thick of head, has grasped the future with both hands. In a sense, the Marines lucked out, since the dirty little non-wars of the future are the same sort of fights they faced throughout their history. The Corps felt the Cold War least, and has cast off its legacy with relative ease.

The centerpiece of innovation in the Marine Corps is a focus on urban warfare, the ugly fight that all want to avoid. Urban warfare is the growth area for Western militaries. Other services do not want to face it (despite some lip service), since fighting in cities and industrialized terrain threatens traditional organizations and weapons-buying habits. Worse, it is warfare at its most savagely human and dangerous.

No sensible soldier wants to fight in a city. But in a grossly urbanizing world, conflict inevitably becomes urbanized. The fight follows the population. Cities have long been the object of military campaigns—today, they are increasingly the battle-fields as well. It is not a matter of choice. Demographics, wealth concentration, sources of power, and even our military effec-tiveness in other environments drive our enemies into urban jungles. Mogadishu in Somalia was an elementary version of the problem—this is war in close and deadly without neat lines on the planning map, surrounded by noncombatants, and fought in three dimensions, from multistory buildings down into sewers. There is no more difficult form of combat. For a military in love with technology, urban warfare's demands for large numbers of well-trained infantry come first as a shock, then as a critical shortage. City fighting produces casualties.

Western militaries will continue to operate in other envi-ronments, from rainforests to oil-rich deserts. But the days of ordered battles on green fields are behind us. Even were we to dispatch ground troops to Yugoslavia, the ethnic Serb military would not come out to duel with tanks in a grand battle. We would face guerrilla tactics and snipers, terror attacks and local armored skirmishes—but, above all, we would have to go door-to-door in villages and half-burned cities, to root out the hardcore killers in uniform. What began as an exercise in tech-nological prowess and war waged at a sterile remove may end in a gunfight in a darkened cellar.

Another instructive feature of the current debacle in the Balkans is the matter of initiative. In any fight, high-tech or bare knuckles, whoever can seize and retain the initiative has a tremendous advantage. Despite NATO's air attacks against empty buildings, Milosevic has done a brilliant job of forcing NATO to react, instead of allowing NATO to set the rules. He pulls the strings and Brussels jumps (while Washington spins).

NATO bombed and tried not to shed blood. In response, Milosevic accelerated a stunning campaign of ethnic cleansing and cultural genocide without impediment. He manipulated the refugee issue savagely and brilliantly. NATO must spend time and energy maintaining a fractious alliance, while Milosevic works to pry the alliance apart—though unsuccessful at rupturing it thus far, his efforts have ensured that the bombing campaign remains a tentative, nervous affair. Prior to the Orthodox Easter holiday, Milosevic declared a unilateral cease-fire, knowing that, should NATO accept, Brussels would find it nearly impossible to resume the bombing. With NATO's refusal, he was able to portray himself to his people and to receptive audiences abroad as a willing peacemaker. Thus far, Milosevic has managed to reduce NATO to a frustrated, impotent giant, unable to protect those it pledged to defend. Even if he loses in the end, Milosevic has outmaneuvered NATO thus far. He made NATO's primary concern the care of refugees, not the military campaign, and cast himself as hero to his people. Kosovo is destroyed, the mission a failure, and any eventual NATO victory will be as hollow as it is belated.

This ability of our enemies to set the terms of the conflict already had cost the West dearly in this decade, in Somalia and in Iraq. The reasons are twofold. First, for a variety of reasons, the West has been unable to muster and sustain the determination, the strength of will, that is the basis of all effective military operations; second, we consistently underestimate our enemies.

Fighting on his own turf, the illiterate tribesman may prove wiser than the well-trained officer who does not speak the local language, know the local customs, or understand the layout of the streets. Pride and its handmaiden, ignorance, have crippled our efforts, from the Horn of Africa to the Balkan fringes of Europe.

No better example is needed than the American administration's conviction that they knew Milosevic, and that he would back down at the threat of force. The American leadership failed to understand the man, his people, or his goals. Then NATO and the United States each took pains to assure Milosevic that ground troops would not be deployed, should the air campaign fail. All he had to do was hunker down with his fingers in his ears. Bill Clinton and Javier Solana of NATO wrote the epitaph of the Kosovar Albanians in advance.

How do we prepare for the future of conflict? There are numerous practical measures that should be taken, from resisting the blandishments of defense contractors peddling weapons that are marvelous but irrelevant, to streamlining military units for swift deployment and buying the transport aircraft to carry them. But such steps do not address the core of the problem: We must decide what is worth fighting for.

Our militaries, despite structural problems and materiel deficiencies, can do the ugly jobs the world presents. But they cannot do it bloodlessly, or instantly, or without injury to each last noncombatant. Our problems lie with a generation of leaders who deemed themselves of too much worth to serve in uniform, and who arrived at the pinnacle of power ignorant of what militaries can and cannot do. It is a generation accustomed to easy success, and it cannot understand why bloody-minded foreigners behave so badly. For all its international studies and travels, it is a generation sheltered from much of the world's reality. It knows how to win elections, but not how to lead.

And leadership is crucial to the effective use of the military. Whether the squad leader at the lowest level of combat, or the president or prime minister, the leader is the most important factor in deciding between victory or defeat (witness the unequal contest between the namby-pamby Mr. Clinton and the ruthless Mr. Milosevic). This has not changed since the battle of Jericho, or the fall of Troy—the fundamentals of the military art are so timeless they haunt our myths. The best leaders, of course, are not shoot-from-the-hip sorts, but thoughtful and resolute, knowledgeable and inspiring. The best-trained, best-equipped soldiers in the world are parade-ground toys unless their nation's leaders possess the vision to use them wisely, and the determination to support them fully and enduringly.

Wars and military interventions cannot be waged according to opinion polls. While the public's views matter, the citizenry is fickle and sometimes wrong in the short term. The public speaks, in our privileged societies, through elections. Foreign and military policies managed by polling make a mockery of institutional democracy, reducing it to instant pudding.

Finally, we must decide whether or not we are our brother's keeper. The truth is that most of the world's atrocious conflicts will not threaten daily routines in Montreal or Milwaukee, let alone the survival of our nations. We do not feel the axe that falls a continent away.

Yet, we must watch that axe fall, on television. Perhaps the media is a fierce tool in the cause of justice, one that will not let us look away. Does it matter if distant populations slaughter each other? May we close our eyes and still believe in our own decency? Our dilemma is that we want to care a little, not a lot. Peacekeeping efforts in their present form put a bandage on the wound, when the situation calls for taking away the knife. We want our humanitarianism painless and cheap.

The great issues of conflict in the coming decades will be moral ones. The signs that we will solve them well are few. We choose the rights of governments over the rights of man, and the sanctity of borders over the sanctity of life. We want to stop the killing with reason and kindness, or with promises of a peace the butcher despises. We have lost our sense of perspective, and even our sense of reality.

If we want a better world, we shall have to fight for it. Until we rise to the task, the Kosovos will continue. The future of conflict is here.

Coda

Dogma and the Dead

A room filled with university professors makes me nostalgic for the Khmer Rouge. Since I value intellect, I dislike intellectuals—those men and women, freed from the necessity of labor, who prefer theory to reality and who footnote while others fight our nation's battles. The enormous increase in the number of minds shielded from mundane concerns—thanks to our expanding wealth—is far more dangerous than the proliferation of weapons of mass destruction: Absurd theories killed vastly more human beings in the twentieth century than did the most terrible weapons. Those powers of thought that so enrich the years of the man or woman unafraid of life are employed by the intellectual to reduce life to a colorless, explicable sketch. The intellectual, whether a dean on a Cambridge campus or a scholar in a Cairo madrassah, perverts the power of the mind in order to force reality to conform to a simplified, strict, and inhuman vision of the way the world should be. With intellectuals in charge, of course.

No one hates creative thought or human freedom so much as the intellectual does; he always seeks to prescribe a way of life that is "good for us," whether we like it or not. The intellectual may speak loftily of liberty, but he loves the sound of a cell door slamming shut on his enemies, be they real or imagined. The man who thinks too much lives far too little. The intellectual lives in terror of experience. He hates talent and all things instinctive, the capacity for joy and the generous spirit. Far from hungry for understanding, the intellectual gorges on dry texts as a substitute for the far richer diet of knowledge consumed by the man of deeds. Throughout history, the great book-burners and the most determined censors have always been intellectuals. A fundamentalist dullard may castigate innocent children's books to hilarious effect, but it takes an intellectual to attack Shakespeare as an agent of Western hegemony, or to declare Jane Austen an imperialist, or to instigate a bonfire of "Jewish" books in a German street.

Intellectuals resent beauty, and pleasures available to others are always suspect to them. "Truth" is what they declare it to be, no matter that reality defies them. And their truth is always cold, and bitter, and cruel. But they reserve their deepest hatred for common happiness, insisting that the rest of us are miserable, too, that our joys are but an illusion, and that the society we find so rewarding is nothing but a wasteland (consider the past hundred years of dire predictions, by intellectuals, that the West was in decline and about to fail—despite overwhelming evidence to the contrary). Galileo was a man of intellect—but the men who tormented him, who forced him to recant his theories, who burned his works, and who would have liked to burn the man himself, were intellectuals. The Ayatollah Khomeini, too, was an intellectual. For the intellectual, heaven is an earth upon which all others are as deprived of joy as he is.

During the wildly misnamed "Enlightenment," intellectuals stumbling about in the Humanities decided that methods applicable to physical science also must be good for human societies, inaugurating, in 1789, the age of the human guinea pig for grand schemes of reform. The subsequent centuries have seen a horrifically violent struggle between theories of social organization constructed by intellectuals—which swelled into ideologies and then hardened into dogma—and the popular desire for a daily life that was slightly more decent, a bit more comfortable, and a little more free. Over millennia, humanity adapted well to incremental change and learned to fear the sudden, but intellectuals insisted that all things must change immediately. There are few, if any, quicker ways to excite human savagery than to tell men and women that everything they believe in, cherish, and to which they are accustomed must go—yet that is the consistent message of the intellectual. Whether decrying the capitalist system that was slowly, but inexorably, enriching the working and middle classes, or attacking the "inhumanity" of the American suburb (which provides the most comfortable, healthiest, safest, and most desirable lifestyle in history, despite the long insistence of sociologists, novelists, and filmmakers that the 'burbs are destructive of all civic virtue and cultural worth), the intellectual's *Sendung* has always been that "Everything must go!"

The intellectual demands change but hates change when it comes, since no alteration in the social order could satisfy his inner discontents. He is a chronically disappointed, petty, angry creature; fortunately, the average intellectual is too weak to have an enduring effect on other lives. The rare, brave intellectual may become a terrorist, but the vast majority prefer to live on hand-outs, whether in the form of tenure, grants, or stipends.

Consistently, those who "knew what was best" for the "workers and peasants" were those who had not worked themselves, who had no interest in the realities of daily life, and for whom real peasants were a conservative obstacle to be removed—if necessary, by annihilation. In the beginning, there was Jean-Jacques Rousseau, an irresponsible fantasist who exploited the preexisting myth of the "noble savage" to create an image of Man that was determinedly at odds with human nature. Even for those who dismissed Rousseau's mangled attempts at constructing a philosophy, the power of his abstract image of Man as inherently ideal—but deformed by the existing order—proved irresistible. It is an old adage that revolutionaries "love Mankind, but hate people." Marx, who avoided the mills of Manchester and their all-too-human workers, built his theories on industrial capitalism from research done in the British Library. He remains the quintessential intellectual—a man who let his children die of hunger rather than go to work, who lived on charity (and declined to pay his debts to those who had to labor for a living), who trusted dusty books over observable reality, yet who knew what was best for all the world.

While Marx is always viewed as descended in spirit from Hegel, his real heritage harks back to Rousseau, who rejected the human reality around him in favor of a fantasyland constructed in his own mind (in its most benign form, this impulse is exemplified by the German novelist Hermann Hesse, who imagined an ideal, virtuous India in his books, only to have a nervous breakdown when he belatedly encountered the real thing—a pattern many another discontented Westerner would follow in subsequent decades). And without Marx, there is no Lenin or Stalin, no Mao or Pol Pot. The difference between Hitler and a Liberal Arts faculty commissar on an American campus is only a matter of energy, power, opportunity, and courage, but certainly not of morality. Intellectuals on the left are as subject to fascist impulses as any on the right—the differences between them are merely rhetorical—and the rage directed toward Samuel Huntington's brilliant, scrupulously honest essay, "The Clash of Civilizations," in the last decade was reminiscent of Hitler's reluctance to accept the Olympic victories of Jesse Owens. One suspects that Judas was the most adept theologian among the Disciples—only an intellectual could feel such intense jealousy toward the goodness and gifts of another. Perhaps the only redeeming quality of most intellectuals is their cowardice—when the purge comes, they are always quick to betray one another, which makes their elimination easier.

The greatest inheritance the mighty dictators of the last century had from the intellectuals was not theory itself, but their utter disregard for the worth of the individual. And the greatest, enabling gift the United States received from England, our mother country, was the Anglo-Saxon distrust of intellectuals. Easy to caricature, the anti-intellectual strain in American life may be every bit as great a guarantor of our freedom as the Constitution. Nor is it as the intellectual would have it, that only the stupid and cloddish despise the "pure life of the mind." Shakespeare, who understood passion and admired soldiers, skewers the intellectuals in his plays (and bookish Hamlet makes a bloody mess), while putting wisdom in the commoner's mouth or drawing it forth from the tongue of a fool or a tavern slut. There is no greater cry of self-realization anywhere in literature than the terrified last words of Dr. Faustus, Marlowe's incomparable personification of intellectual vanity, as the devils his deeds have summoned drag him down to Hell: "I'll burn my books!"

This is no argument for illiteracy. On the contrary, great literature can only be fully appreciated by those who have lived with courage and loved selflessly, who have embraced risk and felt the savagery of nature firsthand. Only a soldier can fully "get" *War and Peace,* and only one who has loved past folly can identify with *Anna Karenina* (a basic reason critics prefer theories about literature to literature itself is that they simply cannot relate to the basic human emotions and dilemmas brought to life for the rest of us by literature's masters). The intellectual always prefers the critic to the creator. An active mind and curiosity about the world seem to me indispensable for a worthwhile life, but I see no difference in merit between the man or woman who only reads and the man or woman who does nothing but watch television. They are all hiding.

As an Army officer, one of my greatest advantages was that I was well-read. But reading informed my practical experience, it did not replace it. The value of reading soars with experience of the world. In military parlance, experience and study are mutually reinforcing. But experience without critical examination is almost as bad as study without experience. The best military officers are those who embrace the world beyond the military, who yearn for knowledge about the world around them, just as the best teachers are those who realize that the library steps are not the edge of the universe. Intellectuals always remind me of virgins determined to write sex manuals. They would be laughable, were they not so dangerous.

The twentieth century was nearly done to death by intellectuals and their theories, and hundreds of millions of human beings *did* die as monsters on two legs sought to enforce their notions of how mankind ought to be. One thinks, of course, of Hitler, Stalin, and Mao, then of the lesser demons who followed them. But the titanic struggle between the theoretical ideal and the humanely practical was not only a matter of great wars, purges, and concentration camps. The tyranny of the intellectuals reached much farther, and it haunts us still. (It is no accident that intellectuals around the world were the greatest apologists for and supporters of tyrants, since freedom for the average citizen—the freedom to laugh and thrive—is the one thing the intellectual cannot bear.)

Although theories of art and architecture have existed for thousands of years, they always were grounded in experience, necessity, and, last but not least, a sense of beauty. But the intellectual rejects any beauty that pleases the "common" man or woman. Thus, in the twentieth century, architecture and design were forced to conform to all sorts of intellectual nonsense and to theories that dismissed human individuality and even comfort. From backbreaking *Bauhaus* chairs to le Corbusier's monstrous housing projects, the average man and woman was expected to sit the way the intellectuals told them to sit and to live in uniform cages intended to eliminate human disparities. The massive, monstrous, soul-killing public housing complexes, from Cabrini Green in Chicago to the high-rises of Glasgow, were little more than concentration camps for the poor. But they conformed wonderfully to the theories about how men and women should be housed, and they were allowed to destroy generations. The same social critics who damned the suburbs—which drew and delighted the average citizen—applauded the housing projects that delivered the poor into despair. And even as I write this in December 2001, a major article has just appeared "explaining" that the theory behind those merciless barracks of poverty was actually correct, but that human failures were to blame for all that went wrong (which is, of course, the argument used by diehard Communists). That is just the point: Humans *do* fail. But in the theory-crippled world of the intellectual, there is no room for failure. Or for humanity. Schemes for human perfection always end in suffering or slaughter.

In the arts, theory decreed that beauty was beneath contempt. Formal music was subjected to rules as rigid as any

Stalinist decrees (in fact, musical composition was allowed more practical freedom in the Soviet Union than in Western Europe, where the intellectuals were in charge). From the twelve-tone scale to atonalism to anti-tonalism, music was deemed "better" the less it pleased the senses. Unhappy audiences were told that they were backward and that future generations would mock them for their ignorance (but it's still hard to round up an enthusiastic audience for the "great" works of the mid-twentieth century). The audience was viewed as an assembly of fools who could not grasp the high import of the intellectual's coded messages.

Likewise, in painting, representations of the world were judged unacceptable, and beauty was exiled. Theory, not joy or transcendence or a record of a single brilliant moment, ruled the galleries. Again, the "philistines" were mocked because they failed to "get it." But it is a long way downhill from Vermeer or J. M. W. Turner to Jackson Pollock, no matter how great a genius the latter is proclaimed to be by critics, and it already appears likelier that future generations, far from laughing at the ignorance of the audience, will howl at the absurdity of the last century's cultural dictators. Andy Warhol was a brilliant social commentator, but he was no Picasso (nor even a Daumier).

The question no one ever asked was the essential one: "What's wrong with beauty?" Of course, beauty pleases and comforts, and the intellectual's self-appointed role is to shock mediocre souls such as our own out of our complacency. No matter the cost, we must not be allowed to be happy or to enjoy anything—except, perhaps, the latest work of criticism from a subsidized university press.

Desperate to excite a reaction, the arts became ever more excessive and childishly offensive; yet, nothing is duller than relentless excess. The uncompromising self-examination of a

Rembrandt self-portrait remains, almost four centuries on, far more "shocking" than a museum installation of cow carcasses. Again, though, America came through: There remained an anti-intellectual strain in the American arts so obstinate that its most fervent creators finally gained recognition by sheer talent, from Edward Hopper to Duke Ellington. In a phenomenal about-face, the art establishment has even made room for the popular works of Norman Rockwell and Maxfield Parrish of late, though not without a good bit of qualification and condescension. As the superficiality and outright stupidity of the last century's art preferences grow more evident with time, the critics are hedging their bets. And when the critics turn on the intellectuals, there's going to be blood on the powder room floor.

Of note, the only field where "modernism" never fully caught on was in literature. The unreadable *nouveau roman* is already forgotten except by scholars, and although unreadable novels continue to be published as "prestige" ventures, the public refuses to reward them with sales. Another reason why literature always remained better-grounded was that, unlike formal music or painting, it relied on actual sales, rather than on conning socially ambitious patrons out of large checks—and the medium of film, which relies upon immediate box-office receipts, adhered to basic storytelling from its beginnings. The deep human craving to be told stories simply would not surrender to intellectual fiat, and the battle to inflict incomprehensible (but theoretically deserving) novels and poems upon the public has already been lost. As the last of the unreadable old guard dies off, even the most pretentious young writers recognize that they really must tell a story of some sort.

The German word *Kulturkampf,* or cultural struggle, was used most frequently to describe the tensions between Prussian Protestantism and Rhineland Catholicism, but it is, in fact, a perfect word to describe what we've all undergone in the last few centuries. In every field where intellectuals have been empowered, from social theory to musical composition, there have been furious attempts to deny the average citizen freedom of choice. Disappointed and discontented by nature, the intellectual tastes the happiness of others through a mouth full of venom. Despite the failed nature of his or her own life, the intellectual knows what is best for all, and the prescription always includes suffering. Incapable of valor or of deep, self-denying love, the intellectual is a very good hater.

The times are such that common sense is prevailing. Reality ultimately insists on having its due. Just as the practical power of freedom defeated the great political ideologies in the last century, so, too, has architecture returned, tentatively, to an acceptance of beauty and comfort, and formal music has become sonorous again. (Curiously, it was East European composers, who had had their fill of all sorts of dictatorships, who led the way back to beauty; intellectual critics tried to dismiss them, but a tide of tonal, gorgeous music is sweeping the world, penned by the geniuses of the Baltic lands, by the likes of John Tavener and James MacMillan in Britain and by Tan Dun in China.) The arts are coming back to those who love them, fleeing the embrace of their abusers.

But there is one important sphere in which theory still dominates and does tremendous harm. That is why I close a book on strategy with a digression into seemingly unrelated realms. Dogmatic theories of international relations, of conflict, and of development continue to cripple our foreign policy, blind us to necessity, and impede essential global changes. We remain the prisoners of a twentieth-century strategic intellectualism, which already was threadbare as the old century waned and which does not fit a new century's realities. Unlike those mighty dictators who ultimately turned on the intellectuals ready to justify any terror—until the jackboots running up the stairs stopped before their own doors—we need not kill the theorists. But we had damned well better kill their theories.

Nor would I offer any theories to replace those we must destroy. The great age of theory is over. Certainly, I do not speak of the sciences, where practical observation proves or disproves theory and experiments need not be carried out upon hundreds of millions of human victims. Nature does have laws, and those laws can be tested. Some of nature's laws apply to human biology or to elementary behavior. But attempts to construct a system of "natural" laws to predetermine the course of human societies have failed, and good riddance. Science—at least as we know it—stops where the human heart and soul begin. We are not even rational creatures, let alone subject to mathematical rules. Now we must choose what works, even when that which works in country X is contradicted in region Y. All theories of human relations try to make the world smaller and more manageable than it is. But the world refuses to cooperate. Philosophy is little more than an excuse to massacre; we must embrace the practical, despite its lack of glamour, and judge all purported wisdom by results.

In place of theory, which prescribes, we must content ourselves with simpler concepts and frameworks that might help us to see without forcing us to see only what conforms to predetermined dogma. This book of essays offers no overarching theories of how to fix the world. It is only about seeing. If I am convinced of any single thing, it is that no theory can encompass human inventiveness, diversity, and plain orneri-ness. We must think about things, but not within guidelines laid down by others. Clichés such as "thinking outside the box" won't do. We must throw the box away, since it only obstructs our view. Above all, we need to open our eyes to the obvious. And good instincts are worth a library full of books.

When I speak of frameworks, rather than theories, it is the difference between opening a window to view what already exists and determining that everything must be rearranged because the view does not look as theory says it should. My goal is to see what is; the intellectual's goal is to force us to see what he insists we must see. Perhaps my vision is flawed, or it may be that I do not understand what I see, but at least I am looking at the world as openly as I can. I hope the reader will, too. If I may presume to offer any message, it is simply this: When that which you experience does not conform to the theory you have been taught, believe the experience.

Why make such an issue of the pernicious effects of theory in the fields of strategy, foreign policy, and military affairs? Because even when the theories are dreadfully, transparently inept, their name is Legion and, as Stalin observed, quantity has a quality all its own. At the end of the Second World War, the men who designed (remarkably well, too) a new Europe and a reborn Japan were blessed. They did not have the "help" of a parasitic industry of university faculties and think tanks, whose forces number in the tens of thousands, to confuse, obstruct, bewilder, bullshit, and clutter the media of the day with nonsense. I do not believe George Marshall (or Jean Mon-net or Konrad Adenauer) or Douglas MacArthur could have done what they did in the postwar years had they been besieged by hordes of professional "experts" who compensate for their lack of experience by the self-righteousness of their indignation when their advice is not accepted.

Foreign policy, international relations, and military affairs have become a sort of last bastion of socialist mediocrity, where producing to institutional norms is better than creativity and where nonthreatening mediocrity is always preferred to originality. If the Sierra Club really wants to preserve our forests, it should begin by declaring war on policy think tanks, whose publications kill more trees to no good end than the most savage, greedy logging company. But these think tanks are headed by those awaiting another turn at executive positions in government and staffed by those hopeful of a lesser opening in some next administration, and massed together they compose a modern cancer that will not be rooted out easily. They deal in influence, not ideas, and the universities, operating at a still-greater remove from reality, are worse. If there is anything remarkable about think tanks, it is how little original thought they produce, and if there is any saving grace in policy-related departments on campus, it is that their combination of arrogance and mediocrity ultimately alienates those they intend to persuade. Above all, these institutions cling to a gray blandness. Averse to the risks essential to success, they make the avoidance of failure their priority. In Washington, policy professionals would much rather escape embarrassment than inspire positive change. Perhaps our greatest enemy as we try to respond to a swiftly changing, tumultuous world is the comfortable dullness that passes for strategic thought.

Several weeks into the aftermath of the attacks of September 11, 2001, I found myself performing as one more monkey in the media circus. Having said what I had to say about events, I had begun to repeat myself—and none of us has anything to say worth saying twice on television or radio or in print. I was also unspeakably frustrated by the near-worthless role of talking head, while my friends still in uniform were serving our country practically and meaningfully. I had caught the retired soldier's disease of yearning to be part of that to which he once belonged, of wishing to be a player again and not merely a weak voice high up in the bleachers. I was jealous. For the first time since taking off my uniform, I regretted it—as doubtless the great majority of retired officers and NCOs did. The uniform might be banished to a back closet, the skills atrophied, and the knowledge dated, but even the oldest soldier longs to run to the sound of the guns when his country's flag is raised in time of war. Tennyson, an enduring poet hated enduringly by intellectuals, put it more nobly when he wrote of the aging Ulysses and his frustration at finding himself condemned "To rust unburnish'd, not to shine in use." Well, the only shine on my snout was from the glare of the lights in television studios. When I found myself sharing a panel with a bloated creature who had never served in the military or been to the region where the conflict raged, who knew absolutely nothing of relevance, but who felt perfectly qualified to declare our military effort a failure when it had barely begun, I had had enough. I did what that truest of all American characters, Huck Finn, did—I lit out for the West.

My wife and I hiked down into the Grand Canyon, climbed the Red Rock hills above Sedona, and rode horses into Monument Valley with a Navajo guide. Of course, news of the war followed us. But the great divide between our intellectuals and the American people, between the prison of theory and the freedom, vigor, and courage of our day-to-day reality, followed us, too.

I have long been fascinated by semi-known cultures, by mystical belief (from Swedenborg to the Sufis), and by the surprising constancy of human nature. The Anasazi people of the bygone Southwest meet all three charges and I took a casual interest in them over the years. Now, as a former intelligence officer who has looked at troubled societies and the wreckage of other men's wars, the existing evidence about the rise and swift collapse of Anasazi culture a millennium ago seems strikingly clear: What remains strongly suggests that the Anasazi culture centered in Chaco Canyon was a severe, cruelly hierarchical theocracy the Taliban would have found hard-hearted. While periods of drought are blamed for its decline, they seem rather to have been accelerators and enablers of dissident internal violence and intervention by external forces. We may never know all the details of the Anasazi "Golden Age," but we may be assured it was not at all golden for the suffering, brutally regimented masses, who served a priestly caste obsessed with its own grandeur. But evidence hardly counts. The recent suggestion, based upon very hard evidence (bones, in fact), that cannibalism occurred at some point in the Anasazi decline—if not before—met with howls of outrage.

The campus experts and their gullible adherents have decreed that early native populations were peace-loving and gentle, respectful of nature and freely devout from overflowing hearts—obviously better than contemporary Americans and their consumer culture. The intellectuals project a sort of dryland Atlantis onto the ancient desert Southwest, implying that only the arrival of vicious Europeans spoiled it all (no matter that the Spaniards didn't show up until four centuries after the catastrophic collapse of Chaco Canyon culture). Facts be damned and common sense discarded, the professors have decreed that human nature did not exist in pre-Columbian America. And that, ladies and gentlemen, is that.

Go and look at the ruins yourself. You may still smell the fear of those whose oppression ended only when they were slaughtered or driven off in terror that came by night.

Yet, there was another, far more inspiring America on display as well. In the months after September 11, I visited small-town New York and Pennsylvania, Virginia and Indiana. In Arizona, I found the same forces at work as I found elsewhere—patriotism, cold anger, resolve, and the willingness to sacrifice to do what needed to be done. Flags flew everywhere and the common sense of the American people, the willingness to tackle the tough, necessary work of defeating terrorism, was a given. It was an America refreshingly unlike that of the cynical, selfish, inbred classes that populate the upper reaches of our federal government. And one area stood out from all the others. It was the poorest, least privileged part of America I visited that autumn, the vast Navajo reservation. I saw none of the resentment upon which sociologists insist. The Navajo flew more flags than any other Americans. On the walls of small-town diners, framed portraits of military veterans looked down proudly at the customers, and soldiers were respected almost lavishly. Services, ceremonies, and memorials honored those who had worn their country's uniform. There was none of the disaffection one meets among the spoiled brats of Bethesda or Georgetown. Only pride in our country. Given the endlessly shabby treatment of American Indians by our government, their example literally brings tears to the eyes of any decent citizen.

The message, I suppose, is that we need not worry too much. When Washington and Cambridge fail us, the kids from upstate New York and the worn-down Pennsylvania coal towns, from the farms of Indiana and the high-mountain deserts of Arizona will pull us through. As they are doing now, on this seventeenth day of December, in the year of our Lord 2001.